International Law

International Law

Isaac Alden
Editor

KOROS PRESS LIMITED
London, UK

International Law

Edition 2015

Published by
Koros Press Limited
3 The Pines, Rubery B45 9FF, Rednal,
Birmingham, United Kingdom

Tel.: +44-7826-930152
Email: info@korospress.com
www.korospress.com

Originally Published in US by Nyx Academics LLC

ISBN: 978-1-78163-663-3

Editor: Isaac Alden

10 9 8 7 6 5 4 3 2 1

Contents

Preface

At the beginning of the twenty-first century, the era when the United States and European states imposed capitulations on non-European countries seems light years away. Most of today's international lawyers and international relations scholars were reared in their expertise during the era of decolonisation, or in Hedley Bull's phrase, the developing world's "revolt against the West." It is all too easy to forget, or as is the case with many students today, not even to know how basic and systematic the capitulatory regime was in the nineteenth and early twentieth centuries. An example drawn from international legal literature illustrates this point. One of the best known general treatises on international law, Ian Brownlie's Principles of Public International Law, deals with the system of capitulations in less than two sentences.' Compare this modem-day mention of capitulations with nineteenth century and early twentieth century international legal treatises, which deal extensively with the system of capitulations. In this brief comparison, we sense a transformation in international law and politics from the end of the nineteenth to the end of the twentieth century.

The origins of the capitulatory arrangements of the nineteenth century can be found as early as the late twelfth century. In 1193 the Sultan of the Ottoman Empire "extended extraterritorial jurisdiction to European `infidels' who could not be expected to understand the religious codes which regulated the daily lives of the Sublime Porte's other subjects." The first extraterritorial rights granted to Westerners in China likewise represented "special concessions unilaterally bestowed by a benevolent emperor upon a limited number of `barbarian' traders, who otherwise would have been unable to function in an unfamiliar Chinese society." In this situation, capitulations originated in a non-Western ruler's sense of superiority and power over Westerners living within his jurisdiction. This origin would become ironic given how the system of capitulations developed between the late twelfth century and the end of the nineteenth century.

While various motivations can be attached to the capitulatory regimes established in the nineteenth century, the primary intention was to establish some fundamental conditions for commercial interaction between the United States and European states on one side and non-Western countries and regions on the other.' Exempting Americans and Europeans from the application of civil and criminal law in non-Western countries would facilitate trade and economic intercourse because legal uncertainty and risk were removed for American and European enterprises seeking to do business abroad.' Capitulations were a crude form of legal harmonisation to facilitate the conduct of international trade and transactions in the early era of global commerce. As experts on international business transactions today argue, legal uncertainty and risk created by the diversity of legal systems among countries cause friction and inefficiency in doing cross-border transactions. A common answer to these problems is harmonisation of domestic legal systems through international agreements.

The book contains legal systems of foreign countries and their constitutions and constitutional courts.

—Editor

Chapter 1

Treaties in Domestic Legal Systems

Direct Application and Self-Executing Nature of Treaties

The degree to which an international treaty is "directly applied" or "self-executing" in a national (municipal) legal system, i.e., to what extent the treaty norms are treated directly as norms of domestic law ("statutelike law") without a further "act of transformation," has been debated in an extensive literature for more than a century. This subject is now receiving increased recognition as part of a broader trend acknowledging that understanding an international legal system necessitates understanding the relationship of national legal and political systems to that international system. In connection with treaties, the basic concepts of "monism" and "dualism" have long been used to explain some of the relationships of treaty law to domestic law.

This chapter explores some of the policy considerations relating to the effect of an international treaty in domestic law. Many excellent works have endeavoured to explain the complex and often-confusing legal effects of this relationship. Often these works have taken the legal status of those effects, in one national system or another, as relatively given, perhaps by a constitutional rule. Sometimes, however, their legal status has been hotly disputed, or even deemed to change over time within the same country. Some commentators have extensively debated the theoretical underpinnings of a rule on the domestic legal effects of treaties, relating them to views about the nature of law and the basis of international law. (In practice, in certain nations that do have such a rule, the courts and other institutions have seemed to find ways to evade applying it.) Rarely has a systematic attempt been made to explore the policy grounds for the contending positions, on the basis of empirical and pragmatic considerations.

Currently, a great deal of "constitution making" is taking place in the world, as nations in East and Central Europe reconstitute their governments, the actual and potential member states of the European Community continue the demanding, but exciting, process of developing a European constitution, and other regional groupings of nation-states explore closer trade and treaty relations. Some of this activity entails consideration of rules regarding the making of treaties and their status in domestic law. In addition, since within some existing constitutional systems the legal status of international treaties is not entirely clear, courts and other bodies still have room to influence this status in differing directions. Thus, the *policies* concerning choices among different types of status for international treaties in domestic law are very important. These policies may relate to the pros and cons of the direct application of treaties. They may also suggest intermediate positions: only certain treaties or certain parts of treaties would have direct application, or treaties might have certain direct effects but not others, or such issues might be influenced or determined by the way certain clauses in the treaty itself or its preparatory work are drafted.

Furthermore, a crucial issue raised by the direct application of treaties involves the hierarchical status of the treaty norms in the domestic legal system. In some jurisdictions, when there is a clash between a directly applied treaty norm and another norm (such as a statute, even a later-enacted statute), the treaty norm may prevail. This "trumping" effect obviously can affect the desirability of direct application, and also relates to (or derives from) the constitutional processes of treaty making (such as the parliamentary or other democratic contribution to the process).

One of the basic conclusions of this chapter is that there are sound policy reasons for a national legal system with typical democratic institutions to avoid the combination of direct domestic law application of treaties and higher status for those treaty norms than later-enacted statutory law. This conclusion depends greatly on the relative degree to which constitution drafters trust international institutions and treaty-making processes compared with national institutions and legislative processes. But, in any event, the premise here is that these relationships and policies are too little understood and that gaining an understanding of them can have vital consequences both within national systems and beyond. It should be quickly noted that even if a treaty norm does not prevail as a matter of domestic law, it will likely still be "in force" as a matter of international legal obligation. Furthermore, as we shall note below, it can have certain "internal effects" other than "statutelike direct application." Thus, this chapter treats two questions: the status of treaties in national legal systems, that is, the question of "direct application"; and the hierarchical status in national legal systems when directly applied treaty norms clash with other norms of the same system. Although these two questions most often are visible in the action of courts, they can also be manifested in the working of other institutions.

It may not always please some readers' sense of style, but it is convenient and sometimes promotes precision to use acronyms for key concepts. Consequently, "direct application" of a treaty in response to Question 1 is sometimes abbreviated below as DA, and the according of higher status as HS. When both direct application and higher status are provided, the abbreviations may be merged to DAHS. Obviously, alternatives to DAHS include the lack of direct application (requiring an act of transformation, as discussed below) and, in cases where direct application has occurred, a status for the treaty that is not higher than that of other norms such as subsequent legislation.

It should be noted that the analogous and important issue of the status of *customary* international law in national legal systems is not treated in this chapter. Some (but not all) of the policy issues are similar, but that subject is left for other works.

The Legal Setting: Understanding the Alternatives

Monism and Dualism

For those who have not had contact with the literature and practice on treaty effects in domestic law, let us first examine the broad outlines of the existing international situation with respect to the direct applicability of a treaty, using a simple paradigmatic hypothetical to illustrate it. Suppose nations *M* and *D* have entered into a treaty that includes the following obligation:

> *With respect to the right to own property within the territory of either contracting party [nation* M *or* D*], the citizens of the other contracting party shall have equal and nondiscriminatory treatment as compared to treatment received the citizens of that contracting party within which the property is located.*

The intent of this language is to equalize the property ownership rights of both countries' citizens within the territory of each contracting party, a traditional expression of "national treatment" obligations found in many bilateral and multilateral treaties, although the subject of the obligation may differ widely. In traditional explanations of the effect of treaties (going back a century or more), a distinction is made between "monist" and "dualist" states. This terminology has been criticized, and clearly it is too "dichotomous" in flavour, since there are various degrees of direct application of treaties, to say nothing of the considerable confusion about it. Nevertheless, even though not precise, these terms are used and may help to demonstrate the major alternative approaches.

Let us assume that state *M* is considered "monist" and state *D* is considered "dualist," and in each state a citizen of the other has been refused rights to own property by the national government even though that state's citizens possess those rights. What is the *national* legal situation?

Traditionally, the "monist" state's legal system is considered to include international treaties to which *M* is obligated. Thus, a citizen of *D* can sue as an individual in the courts of *M* to require that he be treated in accordance with the treaty standard.

On the other hand, the term "dualist" has been used to describe the contrary result in state *D*. In a dualist state, international treaties are part of a separate legal system from that of the domestic law (hence a "dual" system). Therefore, a treaty is not part of the domestic law, at least not directly. Without further facts, a citizen of *M* who is refused the property ownership privilege in *D* that *D*'s citizen has there, has no way to sue in the courts of *D* because those courts apply the law of *D*, which does not include the rule expressed in the treaty (at least not yet). The citizen of *M*'s only recourse is to persuade his own government to use diplomatic means to encourage D to honour its obligation and assure him equal property ownership rights.

It is generally said that for the treaty rule to operate in the domestic legal system of a dualist state, there must be an "act of transformation," that is, a government action by that state incorporating the treaty norm into its domestic law. This may be a statute duly enacted by the parliament that uses all or part of the treaty language and incorporates it as a statutory matter into domestic law. Sometimes such a statute may paraphrase the treaty language, or "clarify" or elaborate on the treaty language. In all these cases, the domestic law is that of the act of transformation, but the treaty language usually has "relevance" in interpreting the statutory language, under various theories of domestic jurisprudence. Other legal instruments can also serve as an act of transformation, including a regulation of an administrative body (if its authority so permits), and possibly even an action or decision of a court or tribunal (again, depending on the authority of the tribunal). Like other concepts discussed here, "act of transformation" is not uniformly defined, and there are several other terms that compete with, or may (in the view of some) be subsumed within, this phrase, such as "incorporation," "adoption," "reception," and similar terms. Likewise, the term "implementation" of treaties must be contrasted with, and in some cases embraces, the "act of transformation," as well as "direct applicability."

Issues of Treaty Application

The direct application of treaties is only one of a series of legal/constitutional issues relating to treaties and national legal systems. In this chapter we do not deal with all these issues, but an appreciation of the existence and relationships of some of them — in other words, the "landscape" or setting of the subject — may enhance understanding of direct application. Indeed, the issue of treaty making, that is, how treaty-making powers are allocated among national government institutions and the procedures required for entering into a treaty, is closely related to policies concerning direct application.

For instance, if a constitutional treaty-making procedure does not provide for "democratic participation" such as parliamentary approval, it would not be surprising to find reluctance to have the treaty affect domestic law until a parliament has acted. The parliamentary act can be the act of transformation, and its requirement as part of the domestic lawmaking system can substitute in part for the direct participation in treaty making of parliaments in other constitutional systems. This "landscape" of legal/constitutional issues regarding treaties in domestic law certainly includes the following (and perhaps more):

1. the power to negotiate;
2. the power to "sign" (usually ad referendum, only to certify the text);
3. the power to "accept" the treaty as a binding international law obligation;
4. the "validity" of the treaty under national constitutional law (closely related to (3));
5. the power to implement the treaty obligations;
6. direct applicability of the treaty in domestic law;

7. invocability in municipal law (contrasted with direct applicability);
8. a hierarchy of norms in domestic law when treaty norms conflict with norms of that law; and
9. the power to administer the, treaty, which includes a series of issues, such as the procedure for formal "ratification"; the power to interpret the treaty for domestic application and as a matter of international law; the power to represent the country in institutional procedures relating to the treaty (e.g., bilateral or multilateral meetings); the power to "vote" in such procedures; the power to amend the treaty; and the power to terminate the treaty various grounds, including the exercise of a termination clause).

A complete description of each of these powers is not feasible here, but a brief comment on a few selected issues will illustrate the broader setting of the subject of this chapter. The first and second issues need not detain us, although they can be problems in certain circumstances. The third issue, the power to "accept" the treaty, is more significant. Whether a nation is bound by a treaty, as a matter of international law, by virtue of having accepted it has substantial bearing on the *international* law determination of whether the treaty is "valid," in contrast to the *domestic* law question of validity.

Fourth, whether the treaty is "valid" under domestic law (usually constitutional law) can be a very difficult question in some constitutional systems (including that of the United States). A treaty that is valid and binding under international law may nevertheless be *invalid* under the constitutional law of one of the participants, perhaps because that nation's representatives acted *ultra vires,* or (similarly) because the treaty is inconsistent with a provision of the domestic constitution. Generally speaking, domestic invalidity does not itself preclude the validity of a treaty under international law. This issue may relate to the prior issues listed; for example, *ultra vires* actions of officials in undertaking negotiations could in some systems taint the subsequent domestic validity of the treaty thus "concluded."

Fifth, even though a treaty may be validly entered into by a nation's representatives, there may be a question of the power to fulfill or carry out the resulting obligations. In some cases, this capability may require (under a national constitution) an act of the parliamentary body (e.g., to appropriate money). Sometimes other constitutional bodies must act. Indeed, an "act of transformation" may achieve partial or full implementation.

Sixth, we have one of the questions posed by this chapter, whether the treaty is "directly applicable" or, more generally, what role the treaty plays in the domestic legal system of a state party. Obviously, if a treaty is "invalid" under either international law or national law, this issue would usually never be reached. In some circumstances, direct application of a treaty might be one form of "implementation" of certain types of treaties. Here again, we refer to "statutelike" application, and note that there may be other types of internal effects of treaties that are not directly applicable.

Seventh, comes the important, but often misunderstood, question that can be called "invocability." This term can refer to a group of concepts, one of which is similar, but not necessarily identical, to "standing"; even though a treaty is directly applicable in the domestic legal system, in a specific case a determination may need to be made as to *who* is entitled to invoke or rely on the treaty norms. In some jurisdictions this concept may be expressed as "partial direct application" or may be governed by the idea that a treaty is directly applicable for some purposes but not others. For example, a treaty might be directly applicable in disputes between different units or levels of government, or between the government and a private person ("vertically"), but not between private citizens or enterprises ("horizontally"). One way to analyse this is to conclude that the treaty as such is directly applicable, that is, becomes part of the domestic jurisprudence. Then the applying institution (e.g., the courts) must determine which parties/entities are entitled to "invoke" or rely on the treaty norms. Alternatively, it may be determined that only portions of a treaty are directly applicable (sometimes depending on the precision and other attributes of the language of specific portions), while the rest of the treaty is not.

In some cases courts or governments have confused (or fused) these two questions (Nos. 6 and 7), judging "direct application" or "self-executing" partly by reference to whether a party may invoke the treaty. This author believes that it is analytically preferable (to avoid confusion and potential error) to separate these concepts, particularly since the policies that relate to each one differ considerably. For example, direct application may primarily be a question of intent of one or more of the treaty parties, while invocability may depend on the precision of the language, definitions of categories of persons (e.g., "citizen," "adult male"), or concepts of justiciability or "political question."

The eighth issue, hierarchy of norms, relates closely to the two previous questions, and it is therefore these three issues (Nos. 6, 7 and 8) that are central to this chapter. Hierarchy of norms refers to the questions that arise when a directly applicable and invocable treaty norm is unavoidably inconsistent with other norms in the national legal system. Those other norms may include the constitution, prior national-level statutes, subsequent national-level statutes, various regulatory acts, and laws of subordinate governmental units (states in a federal system) and, among other things, may be either prior or subsequent to the treaty. In fact, a fairly elaborate matrix of possible clashes can be worked out, and the answers for each "cell" can differ in different legal systems. With only one or two exceptions, constitutions generally are deemed superior to treaties, but a key question is usually the status of a treaty norm that clashes with a later national legislative enactment. In the United States, the later in time prevails. In some other countries, the treaty will prevail even over such later enactments, and this is the crux of the most important policy issue (in the view of this author) concerning direct application.

It should be noted that for this issue (No. 8) to arise, a few other issues must be determined. That is, the treaty must be valid both internationally and domestically, it must be applied directly, and it must be invocable. Unless all these conditions are met, hierarchy of norms does not arise as a matter of domestic law. Of course, issues remain under both international law and internal law. For example, a treaty may be internationally and domestically valid but not directly applied, and thus a domestic system may perform a legal act or make a legal determination that violates the treaty. In that case the acting nation is still "liable," as a matter of *international law,* to the contracting parties of the treaty. However, international processes would have to be invoked to "enforce" the treaty obligation. Furthermore, the treaty (even though not directly applicable) may still have a variety of internal law effects, such as influencing the interpretation of municipal statutes and laws, operating through a statutory provision that makes reference to "international law" or a treaty standard, or influencing an appraisal of "public policy."

Finally, the ninth issue subsumes several matters relating to the administration of treaties, which this chapter cannot practically discuss. Among the more important administrative topics is interpretation of the treaty. Both who within a country has the authority to interpret a treaty and which techniques of interpretation will apply can be serious issues, and are sometimes heavily contested (as in the United States in the controversy over the Anti-Ballistic Missile Treaty). As suggested above, an important internal effect of a treaty may be its bearing on interpretation of a municipal law, and in such a case it may also be necessary to interpret the treaty.

Approach of Various Countries

This chapter does not propose to describe the various national systems of treaty application. Many important works, published both recently — the 1987 volume edited by Francis Jacobs and Shelley Roberts is an outstanding example — and earlier, deal with the subject, as well as with topics affected by it, such as ILO Conventions and the European Convention on Human Rights. Nevertheless, a few brief descriptions may provide background for some of the policy issues to be discussed.

The United Kingdom is generally considered the prime example of a dualist system. Treaties never have direct "statutelike" application in the United Kingdom, but of course may have other internal effects. Many national systems derived from that of the United Kingdom, such as the Canadian and Australian systems, follow similar approaches. The legislature may enact laws that incorporate ("transform") treaties or treaty norms into domestic law, but, interestingly, the UK Parliament does not have a formal role in treaty making. Treaties are entered into by the "Crown" (today, obviously with the counsel of ministers). Sometimes (such as with the UK European Communities Act of 1972) a parliament can make provision for the "transformation" in advance. Variations on this approach are found in many other countries, for example, Germany and Italy.

At the other extreme, perhaps, is the Constitution of the Netherlands, which could generally be called "monist" since it expressly provides that certain treaties are directly applied and that in such cases these treaties are deemed superior to all laws, including constitutional norms! The 1958 Constitution of France also calls for direct application and a higher status for treaties than later legislation. With a variety of nuances, such provisions are found in the Constitutions of Belgium, Switzerland, Japan and other nations. The United States stands somewhere in between. Under U.S. jurisprudence, some treaties can be found to be self-executing, in which case they will be directly applied. To determine "self-execution," U.S. courts look at a series of factors, but (it seems) primarily at the intent of the drafters, including intent implied or expressed in the treaty itself. When that language is sufficiently precise and indicates that no further government action is needed to apply the treaty norms, a U.S. court will be willing to conclude that the treaty is self-executing. However, under a long string of precedents over a hundred years, U.S. courts have ruled that a directly applied treaty has the same status as federal laws (statutes, etc.) and that the latest in time therefore prevails. Thus, for internal law purposes, a later U.S. statute will prevail over the international agreement (which sometimes causes the United States to violate its international obligations).

The situation in the European Community is more difficult to describe, and is apparently still evolving. The details and arguments must be left to other authors, but broadly it can be said that the Community has struggled with these problems in two contexts: application of EC *law* (the basic treaties, regulations, directives, etc.) within the member states, and the application of external treaties between the Community (sometimes with member state participation) and "third countries" (i.e., non-EC nations) in EC jurisprudence, including the national legal systems of the member states.

Although there is some tendency in the opinions and literature to equate these two categories of problems, the policies relating to them can substantially differ. Regarding the application of EC law in the member states, it can be argued that direct application (and trumping) is essential to developing the internal cohesion and coherence that will achieve the goals of a true customs union and (perhaps) federal system. Regarding the application of external treaties, those with third countries, direct application may be much less significant (although arguments can be made both ways). In any event, this chapter relates primarily to the latter category of problems: the effect of EC-third-country treaties on the internal law of the Community (including that of member states). With these brief, but complex, descriptions of the setting of our problems, we now turn to the policies relating to the two questions: (1) the direct application of treaties, and (2) their hierarchical status when so applied.

Policies Relating to Direct Application of Treaties

What does it mean in practice to "directly apply" a treaty in a domestic legal system? The concept was outlined in the paradigmatic hypothetical discussed in the previous section. Although the answer to this question may vary, depending on the legal system involved, "direct application of a treaty" generally seems to mean that courts in the system (as well as all other government bodies) will look to the treaty language itself as a source of law, analogously to the way they look at constitutions, statutes or certain other instruments of domestic law. The language of the treaty (for example, by constituting "judicial notice" and thus obviating the necessity of "proof") will be a required source for the court to examine so as to determine the legal rules applicable to particular cases. It therefore seems convenient to refer to the result of direct application as statutelike status, even though considerations of the hierarchy of norms (Question 2) may suggest in some cases that the treaty enjoys higher status than statutes. We now turn to the various policies that favour or oppose direct application of treaties.

Policies Favouring Direct Application

Why should treaties ever be given this statutelike status in domestic law? Some writers respond by taking a theoretical approach, suggesting that all laws are part of one system (monism), so that international law is automatically part of all national systems; indeed, many of these writers see international law as a higher form of the world legal system and thus as having, a priori, a higher status than domestic law. The latter point, in touching on the hierarchy question (Question 2), illustrates the close relationship between these two questions.

Apart from this theoretical approach, which has not been accepted by many important nations and evokes skepticism in many quarters, including theorists and scholars, we can ask further if there are any significant practical reasons advanced for the direct application of treaties.

One such argument stresses enhancing the effectiveness of international law; giving direct application to treaties (and maybe also to customary international law) increases their importance and weight and decreases the likelihood that national authorities will refuse or neglect to provide for transforming the treaty norms into domestic law. Direct reliance on treaties by citizens may also add to treaty effectiveness (although it can be countered that acts of transformation are much more likely to be found and utilised by the domestic legal institutions).

Another related argument suggests that direct application better assures the other parties that all parties will carry out their obligations under the treaty. It has even been suggested that customary international law should impose a good faith obligation to give treaties direct application. However, this proposition is hard to sustain, since state practice is so contrary. Not only do many states not give direct effect to treaties, but many important states (as noted above) *cannot* do so under their constitutions. Nevertheless, this inability does not prevent parties from *expressly* obligating themselves in a treaty to its direct application (some states would obviously avoid making such impossible commitments).

Yet another argument for direct application is that it better assures the rights of individuals in the legal system when a treaty contains norms designed to apply to those individuals. The individuals can thus base claims on the treaty norm without the need for government intervention or an act of transformation. An act of transformation, it can be argued, gives too much temptation to governments to depart from the precise wording of the treaty and therefore to "transform" a norm that does not accord with the treaty norm itself.

These various arguments for the utility of direct application also reinforce another, more general contention — that disrespect for international law is increased when international norms are not effective. Since, it is argued, direct applicability will enhance the effectiveness of international norms, it will also generally enhance the respect for and general prestige of international law, to the benefit of world order.

Some arguments for direct applicability depend on the coexistence of a principle of higher status (Question 2) for the directly effective treaty norms. This point is easily illustrated by internal laws of a federal system (such as that of the United States and the developing EC structure, which some view as "federal"). When governments desire a federal system to be closer knit, more responsive to the federal level of authority, it makes sense for federal law to be both directly effective and trumping, as is made explicit in the U.S. Constitution, and is evolving by judicial treaty interpretation in the European Community. Moving from this sphere to the international level, however, does not automatically imply that the same principles should prevail, as we will see below.

Policies Opposing Direct Application

Still putting aside Question 2 ("higher status"?), we find that various arguments are made against the direct applicability of treaties. On the theoretical side, commentators have argued for a century that international law is a separate legal system from national legal systems (dualism) and that, consequently, there is no a priori reason that an international treaty norm should automatically be part of national legal systems. Perhaps closely related to this argument is a notion that builds on concepts of national "sovereignty": that when a nation undertakes an international obligation, that nation is entitled to determine for itself its method of implementing or fulfilling that obligation, so long as it does so in good faith. Indeed, it is sometimes argued that urging the direct application of treaties is tantamount to "interference in the internal affairs" of a sovereign state.

Perhaps more significant, however, are the functional arguments that can be advanced to oppose direct applicability. One of these concerns the procedures for treaty making. Some constitutions provide for very little democratic participation in the treaty-making process; for example, by giving no formal role to parliaments or structuring the government so that control over foreign relations is held by certain elites. In such cases, it is argued, the need to obtain parliamentary approval (or approval by some other democratic lawmaking process) of the act of transformation serves as an important democratic check on the treaty-making process. The importance of this safeguard can be multiplied many times if (Question 2 again) the directly applied treaty would have a higher status than many other types of law.

Another consideration militating against direct application is that legislatures may wish to tailor the act of transformation in certain ways, perhaps by rewording the treaty to match domestic circumstances. The most obvious example would be those agreements (usually multilateral treaties) whose official language is not the (legal) language of the implementing nation. But even when the language is the same, certain nuances of usage may differ and legislatures may wish to express the norms in accordance with local usage. The legislators may also wish to elaborate on the treaty provisions, which they may view as ambiguous. (In the United States, for example, the ambiguity of some treaty language has caused concern that its direct application to individuals might violate constitutional standards of due process.) Language in the act of transformation may clarify some ambigui ties (for use by domestic courts and other applications), or specify policy choices left open (implicitly or expressly) under the terms of the treaty. All of these eventualities may occur in the context of a good faith effort fully to apply the treaty norms.

Legislatures may also have other policies in mind. They may desire to place their interpretation of the treaty norm on record. Perhaps the treaty is ambiguous or leaves room for interpretation.

The act of transformation can be used to impose an interpretation for domestic law. Such an act (and the domestic action under it) will constitute "practice" of a treaty party and may then become relevant to later international interpretation of the treaty. In some cases, however, the domestic interpretation may concern domestic law only, such as by indicating the allocation within a country of authority to make certain decisions or to take certain actions in connection with the implementation of the treaty. Indeed, the act of transformation sometimes becomes part of a purely *internal* power struggle, and may be used by certain governmental institutions to enhance their powers vis-à-vis other governmental entities. (*Per contra,* advocates of direct application may have similar motives, viewing it as a way to forestall the adoption of alternative policies or allocations of power, or as a way to have them determined in accordance with their preferences.) Some constitutions may require a form of lawmaking that is circumvented by direct application of a treaty. In these circumstances, one might conclude that this should be a matter for national decision and that direct application should generally be avoided.

Legislatures may have still other motives in opposing direct application. For example, they may wish to limit direct application to portions of the treaty, or to apply it in ways that may not fully conform to the international obligation. Or a legislature may find it politic to delay application to allow internal consensus and acceptance to develop (or to wait out an imminent election!). Some of these examples suggest less than full "good faith application" — and even, perhaps, that the legislature desires to preserve the *option to breach* the treaty in its method of application. Is this approach to policy making desirable or valid? Certainly, traditional internationalists will frown on it. Yet national sovereigns often have prerogatives enabling them to breach treaties; why (say some) take away one particular mode? Moreover, some breaches may be "minor" and therefore preferable to the alternative of refusing to join the treaty altogether.

These considerations move the discourse further into the general jurisprudence of international law and the question of treaty compliance. Is the international system better off if it relies on general democratic acceptance of treaty norms as the major technique of promoting effectiveness, rather than on sanction or legal constructs such as direct application? These questions are not easily answered. For individuals, including statesmen and scholars, the response may depend somewhat on their degree of faith in the international system as compared to their national system. It has been maintained in the literature that some breaches of international norms may be desirable. The relative status of directly applied treaties (Question 2) accentuates some of these arguments.

A related consideration is that national officials may fear that direct application will result in court determinations that their government is acting in violation of the treaty. Such findings could embarrass that government and undercut its effectiveness if it should participate in an international proceeding where it is charged with breach of the treaty obligation. For this reason, it has been said that some domestic courts tend to avoid determining that their government has breached an international treaty.

Another argument is based on the diversity of national constitutional systems regarding treaty application. The fact that some nations never permit direct application may make governments or citizens of nations that require it feel that the asymmetry of the system is unfair. Where direct application is constitutionally permissible, this asymmetry may argue in favour of avoiding its implementation. Sometimes direct application may expressly be conditioned on reciprocity. (Counter to this is the view that what other governments do is not relevant; what matters is how the acting nation best lives up to its obligations.)

Still another argument for avoiding direct application is much stronger if higher status (Question 2) is given to the applied norm, and therefore will be discussed below. In those circumstances, direct application may inhibit national authorities from entering into international agreements that would otherwise be desirable.

Direct application also prompts an interesting question about interpretation. If a treaty is directly applicable, it can be argued that an international body's inter pretation of a question of international law is definitive in domestic law as well. According to this view, since the domestic law consists of the international treaty applied directly, the international interpretations are binding on the domestic legal institutions, including the courts. In contrast, an act of transformation is an act of the domestic legal system, and thus can be interpreted by that system's institutions, including the courts, just as the courts would interpret other legislation or domestic legal acts. However, even in the case of a directly applicable treaty norm, domestic courts may believe that they have the power of interpretation. They certainly have that power preliminarily until a definitive interpretation under international law is set forth. The interesting question is: What happens when an international interpretation of the treaty norm clashes with an interpretation by a domestic legal institution, in a case where the treaty norm is directly applicable? There is at least a 'suspicion, or hint, that the domestic legal institutions will "strain" to apply their own interpretation, through one or another legal technique.

These considerations also suggest that the attitude of national policy makers toward direct application of treaties could be influenced by their view on the relative merit of national judges as compared to international judges. Since application of the law requires its interpretation, a key question will always be which institutions should hold the power to interpret the municipal law being applied. Should a nation rely primarily on its own courts? Or does it believe that the international tribunals will do a superior job?

In legal systems with some form of direct application (including the U.S. self-executing mode), there are a variety of possible approaches to the question of which domestic institution decides whether a treaty norm will be directly applied. Moreover, in actuality, a variety of countries seem to utilise virtually every approach. One policy would be to adopt a seemingly simple and firm rule providing for direct application of all treaties, leaving flexibility to the concept of "invocability," discussed earlier. However, even the so-called monist countries probably do not take this approach. For example, the Netherlands directly applies a certain category of treaties, but not necessarily all treaties. Other countries may distinguish between treaties that are approved by a parliamentary body and other treaties (sometimes called "executive agreements").

Even when the rule of direct application covers most, or theoretically all, treaties or certain broad categories of treaties, courts will find ways to avoid applying the treaty norm in particular cases, perhaps by relying on one or another concept that can be lumped under the rubric of invocability (e.g., standing), or by holding that the treaty norm is designed to constrain or assist certain government agencies and not private litigants. Or the court may refuse to apply a treaty directly because it is not "specific and precise" enough for that purpose, a concept akin to "justiciability." Other disqualifying concepts may also be employed.

In other systems, domestic legal institutions may be given greater latitude in determining whether a treaty is directly applicable. In the United States, for example, the courts have said that whether treaties are self-executing depends heavily on the intent of the treaty makers.

Direct and precise language in the treaty enters into the evaluation of this intent. In addition, a treaty may call for implementing action by the state, which will lead a U.S. court to conclude that the treaty was not intended to be directly applicable.

Two important questions will give some leeway to the system making this type of analysis. The first is, Who decides? Often that is a court because the issue may come up in the context of litigation. The second question is, What are the criteria this decision maker or court uses? As noted, the U.S. courts speak of intent that the treaty be directly applicable, but it is not entirely clear whose intent is key. Although some courts speak of "mutual intent" manifested in the treaty, or possibly also in the preparatory work, or negotiating history, of the treaty, the argument can be made that the controlling intent in some systems, such as that of the United States, is the unilateral intent of the treaty-making officials or government entities in the state applying the treaty.

This approach is supported by the fact that under some national constitutions, direct application *cannot* occur. Thus, the unilateral approach of those constitutions has determined the domestic courts' approach to direct application. Likewise, in nations such as the United States where the matter is not predetermined, the issue arguably is one of domestic constitutional, or legislative policy, law and need not involve (as a matter of domestic law) the intent of other parties to the treaty. Of course, the other parties could express their desire or view, and the treaty could even include an *international obligation* of direct applicability-but that would not necessarily control whether, as a matter of *domestic* law, the treaty should be directly applied.

At this point, the arguments become more complex. A general concept of international law holds that an international obligation binds all of a nation's govern mental institutions, so that departure from the norm by any governmental unit (court, legislature, executive, subordinate units such as states and localities, etc.) engages the international responsibility of the state. Thus, in a national system that allows some leeway on the issue, a court that is determining whether to apply an international treaty directly, when the treaty itself so mandates, might find itself bound to uphold the international obligation so that it will not cause the nation to breach that obligation. This rationale, however, is analytically distinguishable from a determination that the national constitution requires direct application. Indeed, the propriety of such reasoning depends on the power of the domestic court. If the court is entitled to carry out the international obligation of direct application, it arguably should do so in these circumstances to avoid the breach of the international norm. In some circumstances, however, this power would not vest in the local court (for instance, in the dualist nations, such as the United Kingdom).

During the last several decades, the United States has seen an exercise of congressional authority regarding direct applicability. Congress (sometimes as a whole, and sometimes the Senate acting to give its advice and consent) participates in most of the treaty making of the United States Government. Congress in some important cases has expressed the intent, either in its statutory approval of a treaty or in the legislative history of that statute, that the treaty should not be directly applied. Thus, the domestic U.S. law implementing the treaty is the law of the statute as passed by the Congress, i.e.,

the act of transformation. To the knowledge of this author, there has been no indication that the courts, or other institutions of the U.S. Government, would try to contravene this expression of congressional intent. It seems safe to conclude that the U.S. constitutional practice and status is that the treaty-making officials, as a unilateral matter, will control the determination of "self-executing" in the domestic legal system. This is probably, on balance, a wise constitutional solution. It enables the democratic parliament to control some of the problems posed by direct applicability that were discussed in previous subsections of this chapter.

Overall, what can be said about the policy advisability of direct application of treaties? It is probably not feasible or accurate to overgeneralise and say "never" or "always." Clearly, the situations and the criteria for direct applicability differ from country to country, as do the circumstances. Likewise, who makes the final decision about direct applicability differs from country to country. However, there are enough negative policy considerations to suggest considerable caution in embracing direct application. Perhaps if various circumstances are favourable (e.g., democratic input in treaty making, a preference for international over national institutions), a presumption of direct application (controllable by the legislature) could be adopted. On the other hand, more serious problems stemming from "higher status" are revealed in the next section. Rather than a presumption of direct application, a national system might prefer a standard "act of transformation" as an expression of both parliamentary approval and incorporation/implementation in domestic law.

The Policies Relating to Higher Status of Directly Applied Norms

When we move to Question 2, that is, whether a directly applied treaty norm has a higher hierarchical status than most other laws, many of the above policy considerations are not only implicated but accentuated. To use a paradigmatic hypothetical, suppose the legal system of nation M requires direct application of treaty norms and its constitution provides that such norms will trump all other laws except the constitution, even laws enacted later at the highest legislative level. Suppose further that M is party to a treaty that imposes the type of "national treatment" obligation hypothesized in part I above. Ten years after M's accession to the treaty, its legislature, citizenry and government leaders wish to enact a special rule giving M's poor citizens preferential property ownership rights (but they argue that to give these rights to noncitizens would attract an influx of poor persons from other countries who would exploit the rule and make it unacceptably expensive). The envisioned rule may accord purchasing preference to poor citizens when the government disposes of property it owns or has validly seized or repossessed. Yet the treaty norm (sometimes unexpectedly) may seem to preclude this act or be determined internationally to prevent it. Since the domestic application of the norm trumps later legislation, the government's hands are tied. It must either renegotiate the treaty (or terminate it) or refrain from enacting the desired legislation.

For the purposes of our discussion, we will assume that at least some treaty norms are directly applied, since it makes no sense to be concerned about higher status in domestic law unless the norm is part of domestic law. We now consider whether it is wise policy for treaty norms to be both directly applied and given higher status in domestic legal systems than most other laws.

Higher Status as "Constitutionalisation"

In essence, DAHS (the acronym for "directly applicable with higher status," described in the introduction) means that the treaty norm has been "constitutionalised," or given a sort of "constitutional status" almost equivalent to the nation's own constitution. It occurs through a procedure that often falls short of the rigor or democracy of constitutional amending procedures, which may surprise certain interest groups that did not focus on the treaty issues years ago. In these circumstances, what are some of the policy considerations?

One is immediately struck by how many of the arguments in part II are accentuated by higher status. In the absence of higher status, a later statute or other law might correct some of the problems raised in part II (e.g., a legislative desire to "interpret" the treaty or to reallocate internal decisionmaking power), albeit perhaps with some additional trouble and shifting of the political burden of taking the necessary initiative. When higher status is added, however, the problems become much more difficult. For example, the asymmetrical situation noted above, in which some nations do not directly apply treaty norms while others do, is even more anomalous when some that do, do so with a higher status. Those nations find themselves more locked into the norms than the other parties.

Once again, the issue of the "democratic deficit" arises, but more acutely. If the procedures for treaty making do not permit adequate democratic participation, the DAHS treaty norm can be criticized as imposing an elite's vision of control on a society (or worse, that of a special interest group). Indeed, it can be seriously doubted whether such a norm would be truly effective; governmental units, including courts, would struggle to attenuate the norm or avoid it altogether.

Usually, this is not an either-or question, for the degree of democratic input varies and in many cases may be said to be sufficient, even for a "constitutionalised" norm like a DAHS. Yet a series of other concerns can be raised that should at least be understood by policy makers who wish to oppose or to accept the DAHS idea. The most significant of these was noted in the hypothetical above, that the DAHS norm imposes considerable rigidity (almost equal to a constitutional rule) on future government action. Arguably, a constitution should generally contain norms deemed so essential to government that they need to impose rigidity: norms that preserve human rights, allocate power among governmental branches or entities, specify the rules for democratic governance (elections, terms of office), and the like. To constitutionalise the whole body of potential treaty relations is quite another matter. A government with DAHS would need to be very restrained in accepting treaty obligations, or it could find itself hamstrung at many turns by thousands or tens of thousands of treaty norms (especially on economic subjects).

Treaty making, incidentally, can also mean the development of "secondary" treaty rules, i.e., regulations or decisions by international bodies pursuant to treaty authorisation. Thus, a nation with DAHS could find its legal system bound both by rules that only a few of its own diplomats (maybe instructed by an elite or small group within the executive part of their government) participated in drafting, and by the majoritarian or other (sometimes defective) voting procedures of multilateral bodies. A nation in that position could refuse to accept such treaties, or it might work toward building international institutions that avoid secondary norm making, but this approach could substantially inhibit the progress of the world legal system.

International Institutions and Rules

A serious problem is the weakness or inadequacy of international institutions (especially multilateral ones) that engage in treaty making. Even if we assume that international institutions can adequately (and democratically) create new rules, many find it difficult to change, amend or improve treaty or secondary rules. Sometimes nations have the unenviable choice of living with rigid and/or out-of date rules, terminating (withdrawing from) their treaty obligation entirely, or breaching it. If it were easier to change treaty norms, a DAHS nation might more easily tolerate them, obtaining modification at the international level when needed, but that very difficulty adds to the risk of DAHS.

Thus, a DAHS approach can lead governments to be wary of accepting international norms. That may be good (some argue that many international norms are not carefully drafted or wisely adopted), but it also may not be so good. As the world becomes "smaller" and more interdependent, accelerated international coordination is needed to prevent disputes and misunderstandings, and to allow enterprises to make plans and maximise economic welfare and development. This activity could be greatly inhibited by DAHS.

The amount of confidence that policy makers have in international institutions relative to their national institutions has important influence on their thinking about these issues. Government officials and citizens who look upon their national institutions as having endured for a long time and as seeming to protect citizens' rights, sound economic policy and democratic procedures will be inclined to trust those institutions. If at the same time they doubt the wisdom or durability of international institutions, they may reject a DAHS approach.

On the other hand, if government officials and citizens have a higher degree of trust in the international institutions and treaties than they do in their own governmental structure, they will probably prefer DAHS as a conscious or implicit check on their government. Thus, it is entirely understandable that some persons in recently autocratic countries might favour an international regime to protect human rights. The European Convention on Human Rights can be a convenient reference point, as well as a *constitutional check on Participating national governments,* and this role will be enhanced by DAHS — the direct application of the treaty and even higher status for its norms than for subsequent legislation. In other countries, persons who have seen a recent shift from socialism or state planning toward market-oriented economic principles might feel more secure about the permanence of that shift if their nation accepted international treaty norms (such as in a customs union or free trade area agreement) that would directly apply with higher status — again, as a *check on their own government and any subsequent decisions* (even by democratic elections) that might alter the new market orientation. Indeed, the DAHS principles might effectively introduce 'judicial review and protection" of either human rights or economic structures in situations where they would never be assured by the national constitution.

Implications of Differing Constitutions

The ease with which the national constitution can be amended will also influence the choice of protection by international norms rather than national norms, or possibly even constitutional norms. An easily amended constitution will facilitate the rectification of DAHS problems (as long as the higher status does not trump the constitution) through constitutional changes. Although in this case the difficulties of DAHS are less worrisome, the DAHS principle is less effective in protecting against or restraining national government actions contrary to treaties.

As with direct application, higher status also presents the question of what domestic legal institution will decide which clashing norm prevails. If the treaty norm has higher hierarchical status, however, the domestic court is likely to have less discretion or leeway; that is, the question facing the court is much more likely to be a "constitutional" one.

Of course, such an issue may be left to the court to determine on the basis of, say, the drafters' intent, or other criteria. Nevertheless, as surveys of constitutional practice suggest, the issue is more often deemed to turn on a constitutional rule. For example, United States courts for many decades have accepted the rule that the "later in time prevails," basing it on early court opinions interpreting the Constitution itself. The rule has been criticized, and in at least one odd recent case it may have been somewhat softened, but it generally seems to be accepted as a constitutional requirement. Still, in some constitutional systems the issue has not been completely resolved, and some opportunity may remain for the courts to make that determination on the basis of various considerations, including some of those expressed in this chapter.

Several Cases

Various specific cases and practices suggest that courts will often strive to seek a "way out" from the rigidities and other policy problems they face when a DAHS rule exists in a legal system. An example is the jurisprudence of the European Court of Justice; the Court early refused to grant direct application to the GATT treaty (General Agreement on Tariffs and Trade), for reasons that have been criticized. On the other hand, if the EC Court at that time was worried that a directly applicable norm might also have a higher status (i.e., the potential for a DAHS system), one can readily see why a court and all other policy makers in the Community would have been nervous about directly applying the GATT. Thus, if the court has some leeway regarding direct applicability, but worries that it may not have such leeway regarding higher status, it would be highly tempted to discover an appropriate way to refuse direct application.

A 1990 Japanese Supreme Court case had some similar characteristics. Once again the GATT was invoked. The case was brought by Japanese necktie producers, who argued that their Government's restraints on the importation of silk for neckties (to protect domestic silk producers) violated rules of the GATT. The complainants claimed that the GATT was directly applicable and that, under the Japanese Constitution (Article 98), directly applicable norms were endowed with a higher status than legislation or other legal norms. The lower courts (in 1984 and 1987) concluded that the GATT did not apply to the situation, but their reasoning (or lack thereof) has been criticized, and on appeal the Supreme Court of Japan merely affirmed with very little analysis. It can again be surmised that a court would find great difficulty in directly applying the GATT, with its many elaborate constraints on national government actions in international trade, in circumstances where those GATT norms would also have a higher status than even later-in-time legislation or other acts. Thus, it comes as no surprise when a court somehow manages to evade this consequence.

The Netherlands, in the view of some, may be the most monist legal system in the world, but even there, according to eminent commentators, courts have ways to avoid the direct application of treaty norms that would take, precedence not only over later legislation, but also over the Constitution itself. The empirical observation that national courts in systems with DAHS try to avoid its logical consequences suggests that legal systems that have not yet fully decided the question should exercise great caution before embracing DAHS.

A DAHS system can also significantly inhibit a national government's willingness to enter into international treaties. A recent example occurred in the European Communities. Although there may be an argument that Community-level law has not yet been fully determined to be a DAHS system, the apprehension that it would be apparently influenced the negotiations between the Community and the Government of Switzerland concerning a treaty on international trade in insurance services. The Community side feared that if it entered into such a treaty, and it became both directly applicable (as many desire) and superior to even later EC legislation, the Community would be greatly hampered in its ability to develop harmonisation of national law and other regulatory principles on insurance in the future. The solution chosen by the negotiators was a fairly elaborate clause in the draft treaty permitting a contracting party to opt out of some provisions in certain circumstances.

Applications and Policy Implementation

Some national legal systems have largely determined the internal rules about direct application of treaties and the hierarchical status of such norms, but in other systems the issues may still be evolving or completely open (e.g., if a constitution has yet to be completed). In the latter cases, the policies discussed in the previous sections should be carefully considered by the constitutional drafters, officials or judges responsible for the further development of the question. Even when the issues are ostensibly "settled," we have seen that judicial and other institutions have ways to evade the full logical consequences of a DAHS system. In this section we discuss some variations on implementation, and the techniques of applying the rules so as to realise the policies selected from those discussed previously.

In broad brush strokes, we can consider three different circumstances: (1) the constitution is still being written; (2) the constitution is still evolving through practice or court decisions; and (3) the treaty or its implementing language can play an important or even decisive role in how a national legal system handles treaty norms internally.

In the first case, when the constitution is still being written, close attention to the questions of direct applicability and higher status seem merited. Of course, failure to spell out the pertinent constitutional principles may leave the issues open for later elaboration by the national legal system, which may be precisely what the constitution makers wish (perhaps as a compromise to a standoff). However, the various policies discussed suggest the value of normally avoiding a full DAHS system. Direct application combined with a later-in-time principle at least affords the national government some relief from the rigidities of a full DAHS system, and is less likely to inhibit that nation's willingness to enter into international treaties. Rejection of direct application altogether would go even further in this regard.

In certain circumstances, however, the constitution makers and their democratic constituencies may strongly desire to constrain their government. As mentioned above, two subjects in particular have been noted in this connection: the protection of human rights and the preservation of a market-oriented economic system. Discussions in newly forming democracies such as those in Eastern Europe, as well as in countries in other parts of the world, demonstrate that their officials and citizens sometimes trust an *international treaty* to protect human rights more than their own governments. This consideration would have to be weighed against the policies that do not favour DAHS. The extent and specificity of the international treaties that are candidates for DAHS treatment must also be weighed. A treaty that is not overly broad in its reach and is reasonably precise and unambiguous would seem a better candidate for DAHS treatment than treaties with contrary characteristics.

Similarly, in the flurry of privatisation and evolving market-oriented economies that the world is currently witnessing, some national leaders and citizens see an advantage in international obligations that would restrain later domestic political attempts to overturn or erode the market mechanisms put in place. Membership in a treaty system such as the European Communities, or similar regional groupings elsewhere, may be understood as playing an important constitutional role in this regard. This constitutional role will be stronger in a DAHS system.

Often these policy considerations are only dimly perceived and not articulated (at least with candor). They obviously suggest that the participants place a relatively *higher* trust in the international institutions than in their national constitutional institutions, and historical observation sometimes indicates that they have good reason to do so. In that case, is there any way to avoid some of the negative policy implications of a DAHS system? Several possibilities can be suggested.

First, a new constitutional provision could treat different treaty subjects differently. It is certainly possible for a constitutional clause to give DAHS treatment only to "human rights" treaties, although the definitional problems would require great care. Similarly, a constitutional provision may give DAHS treatment only to specifically named treaties (allowing future constitutional amendments to add to the list). It is even conceivable for a DAHS provision in a constitution to be limited in time, e.g., to operate for x years and then cease (perhaps in the questionable optimistic belief that national institutions will develop sufficient strength and credibility that overriding international protection will no longer be needed).

DAHS treatment might also be given to membership in an international (regional?) economic treaty organisation. In some cases, a constitutional amendment could provide for this treatment (or otherwise secure the treaty norms). Some constitutions may now require this approach. A new constitution might refer to this possibility and leave it to be implemented in the future by an amendment. It could even provide for a special amending procedure (perhaps one that is easier to execute than that for ordinary amendments) to incorporate international norms for the human rights or market-structure cases.

The second situation, where the constitution is still evolving, may require different approaches. Of course, if the evolution is achieved by amendment or changes in the constituent "treaty," the choices may be varied and considerations mentioned above could come into play. However, if the evolution is produced by judicial decision (or other practice of national legal institutions), the choices may be more limited. For example, if higher status for directly applied treaty norms already seems to be embedded in the legal system, the court or officials may wish to stress ways to avoid direct application, arguing that it requires either an overwhelming expression of intent or the framing of the norm in precise and direct language, or both. To rule against direct application would enable national officials to implement the treaty by means of an act of transformation. Even with direct application, courts could employ various judicial doctrines used to "duck" issues, such as nonjusticiability, lack of definiteness, mootness, political question, standing and ripeness.

Alternatively, the question of higher status may not have been finally and firmly determined. In that case, national judicial or other officials might still have the option to avoid conferring such status on treaty norms, which would make it easier to accept direct applicability (and to enter into treaties in the first place). In the third case, where the treaty or implementing language can play a major role, it is assumed that this constitutional process gives great or decisive weight to the intent expressed in the treaty, in its preparatory work, or by national negotiators. For example, a treaty could incorporate a clause, "It is intended that this treaty shall not have direct application in either or one listed party." Would the national judiciary or officials act accordingly? In many countries (including the United States), they probably would. One could envisage a sort of boilerplate clause that a nation's officials would *always* include in treaties, with some carefully considered exceptions, so as to clarify this question and avoid the policy pitfalls of either direct application or higher status.

Although strong evidence of this type of intent might be stated (or discovered by a court) in the preparatory work of a treaty, such an expression might be considered more ambiguous and could give greater leeway to the inclinations of the national legal system's courts or officials. Finally, somewhat more removed and raising certain other issues would be a unilateral statement precluding direct application by the officials of one of the parties, during the negotiation of the treaty or the national constitutional process of its approval. The prime examples are probably found in the United States when the Senate gives advice to the President allowing him to ratify a treaty, but only if it is not self-executing, and when Congress authorises the President to ratify a treaty but specifies in the enabling statute or the legislative history that the treaty shall not be self-executing. The President alone may even issue such a statement, and it is likely to be followed by the U.S. courts.

Expressions of intent are less likely to be used to govern the question of higher status when treaty norms are directly applicable. Although it is theoretically possible, this author knows of no such cases. Moreover, higher status is more likely to be considered a type of "constitutional" or judicial issue that only the courts can decide in a particular society. Of course, a constitution could determine who decides, perhaps by relegating it to an executive or to parliamentary vote.

The questions of direct application of treaties into national legal systems and the hierarchical status of the norms so applied are extraordinarily complex and vary from country to country, depending on constitutional and other municipal rules. The various answers to these questions can have enormous impact — as great as that of some constitutional norms. Although these answers are supported by assorted theoretical and functional arguments, many of the policies (some deriving from empirical observation of national practices) are often overlooked or not explored when decisions about these matters are made. In this chapter we have attempted, by referring to a variety of country practices, to explore the policy pros and cons of direct application, or higher status, or both. Obviously, "theory" has been relatively ignored, and we have not assumed that international law is always better than national law.

In general, it can reasonably be said that both direct application and higher status of treaty norms involve enough policy difficulties to suggest caution in introducing them into a national legal system. When a system includes both rules, even more significant policy difficulties are presented, such as rigid treaty constraints on future government action, the possible avoidance of democratic procedures for rule making, and inhibition of further treaty making. Sometimes these difficulties are offset by policy preferences, as when national officials and citizens feel that international constraints to protect human rights or market economic mechanisms may be more effective than national constitutional constraints. In addition, some of these difficulties may be ameliorated by certain approaches of the courts or officials in national systems, or by the language in treaties or their preparatory work.

In sum, however, it behooves national officials to understand the various policy arguments and difficulties before making some of the policy choices that may be available to them. Where constitutions call for approval of a legislature to accept a treaty, the best approach may often be for the enactment of approval to provide as well (in a dual role) for an "act of transformation" of the treaty itself by incorporating it into the statute. This procedure usually affords domestic lawyers easy and noticeable access to the treaty text, while preserving certain legislative checks against some of the drawbacks of direct application and/or higher status. (The procedure is apparently common in the German system, and is sometimes used in the U.S. and other systems. It is obviously available to the dualist systems, where direct effect is not possible.)

Sometimes the relatively abstract concepts expressed in this chapter are more easily grasped when a concrete case or circumstance illustrates the application or policy problems of the subject. Several such cases have been mentioned in the text and footnotes above, but many more could be inventoried. Let me suggest the following, by way of summarising and integrating some of the considerations discussed here.

It is this author's opinion and observation (shared by others) that treaty rule making already has an important bearing on economic activity in a shrinking world and interdependent global economy and is very likely to become even more important — furnishing by far the largest number of international norms with which national societies will have to contend. Competition policy (antitrust), regulation of banks, insurance, the sale of securities, investment flows, the mobility of labour and professional services, protection of the environment and consumer protection are only a few of the many subjects the global economy must deal with. Many subjects involve difficult compromises and trade-offs between the desire for greater economic efficiency and legitimate social goals, such as protection of consumers, workers, the poor and the environment, as well as numerous other legitimate governmental objectives, including prudential policies for banks, insurance companies and brokerages, among others.

Some national societies have much more experience with such regulation than many others, and certainly more than any international institutions. The regulations are often the result of tortured compromises among many different interests, and are also evolving in the light of experience with the regulations. Moreover, different societies adopt different approaches, some using a legalistic or punitive approach, while others prefer the less formal avenues of societal pressure or moral admonitions. Societies also take different governmental approaches to rule making, democracy, elites, religion and special interests. Thus, it can be very difficult to obtain an international consensus on treaty rules that are precise or "permanent." Yet the option of drafting treaties to deal with problems of cooperation and coordination across societies must be available and reasonably effective. The teachings of economists and game theorists (e.g., the analysis of the prisoner's dilemma) reinforce this conclusion.

Now let us examine one particular subject, a prominent feature of recent news accounts, regulation of the sale of corporate securities to the public. There are huge differences among the regulatory practices of similar societies (e.g., the major industrial societies), to say nothing of those among disparate societies (e.g., developing countries, state-trading countries, raw materials producers). As the market for corporate securities (and investment funds) rushes to become global, multilateral regulation (through treaty rules) will obviously increase in importance. Yet it is also obvious that agreement of the various countries to many details of the rules will be hard to achieve.

Several implications of these facts can be noticed. Nations with some confidence in their own regulatory systems will be much more reluctant to enter into the relatively unknown territory of international treaty obligations if those obligations will suddenly be directly applicable, superseding (where conflict exists) their domestic regulation. This reluctance will be heightened if the treaty rules not only are directly applied, but prevail over domestic later-in-time rules. Of course, treaties can be drafted to permit national flexibility and allow for other problems of direct application and higher status. But like all human endeavour, and perhaps all national legislation, many treaty rules will not be perfect. Indeed, chances are that treaties will be more ambiguous than national laws (because of the difficulty of reaching consensus), and that vague treaty norms will therefore be used to challenge national regulations. Also, vague treaty norms may later be interpreted by international institutions in ways that undermine municipal regulations. In addition, multilateral treaties generally are much more difficult to change so as to evolve in tandem with economic and societal circumstances. And democratic nations that have achieved a (possibly uneasy) compromise of interests to construct a regulatory system will be interested in minimising actions that might upset those compromises.

In these circumstances, in my view, prudent national political officials or statesmen would be reluctant to embrace a DAHS system for treaties, and if already constrained by a DAHS system, or even a DA system, they would be well advised to avoid the treaty process altogether for many endeavours. Without the rigidity of, DAHS, nations might well find the treaty process useful and effective (if not perfect, of course) in furthering vitally needed international cooperation for handling the problems of a shrinking world. If this flexibility results in an occasional misfit between treaty obligations and national legal norms, is that not a worthwhile price? Would it not be better to devote efforts and attention to making treaty norms more effective, by devising processes for dispute settlement and for ensuring the democratic participation of each party's citizens in accepting the treaty norms, than to rely too heavily on the notions of direct applicability and higher status?

Chapter 2

French System: Convergence of French and English Law

Commonly Believed Causes of the Differences

Many in England take it for granted not only that French and English law are different from each other but also that in most respects the French and German legal structures and reasoning are closer to each other than either is to the English. At the political level, the French/German elective affinity is exemplified-at least in the minds of ordinary citizens-by the imaginative post-War close political links forged between the two countries by General De Gaulle and Chancellor Adenhauer. For lawyers in general, this belief is reinforced by René David's classification of the legal systems into distinct legal families. Finally, legal specialists have also pin pointed the causes of the legal differences between England and France to a number of specific factors (or events) of which the following five seem to be the most oft cited. Geography, inchoate cultural beliefs, and specialist thinking have thus combined to shape the conviction that France and Germany are closer to each other than either has been (or can ever be?) with Britain.

That the differences between English and French (and, indeed, continental European) law are both important and obvious is beyond doubt. Yet this chapter will attempt to suggest that these relationships, affinities, or differences are not as simple and, above all, as clear cut as many would have us believe. The true differentia specified between these two systems may thus lie elsewhere. My suggestion is that the role played by practitioners in the two systems accounts for some of the most interesting, perhaps also important, differences. I also suggest that in their history the two systems often converged only to diverge again later. It is a sub-thesis of this chapter then that the convergences occurred when practitioners took the lead in the law-shaping process of both countries and was weakened whenever "theoreticians" obtained the upper hand. This is the thesis of a comparative lawyer, not a legal historian; and it is put forward tentatively for the sake of further consideration. Before elaborating this thesis let us turn first to the traditional reasons given for the separation of the two cultures.

Praetorian Law Versus Statutory Law

Praetorian law is the term used in France (but never in England) to indicate the case law nature of English law and contrast it to the statutory character of French law. The point, if valid once, seems an over-simplification now. For not only are important parts of French law largely created by judicial decisions-administrative law is the obvious example-but existing, statute-based law has also been substantially enriched, and even transformed, by judicial decisions. The French law of tort offers an excellent illustration for this last assertion; but the same goes also for other parts of the French Civil Code (CC).

The contrary proposition is also not correct. For anyone who thinks that modern English law is found only (or even mainly) in case law may be surprised with the reality. Thus, vast swathes of English law stem from statute, which is often-but not always-fleshed out by decisions. What is even more significant-to French lawyers, perhaps even surprising-is the fact that, confronted with new social and economic problems, our highest courts have often been tempted to invoke the aid of the legislature. The French lawyer who believes that English case law is more flexible than his own (because it is "praetorian") may well be wrong!

Codification

This is a variant of the first point but particularly appropriate for a country like France, which has just celebrated with pride (and some trepidation) the 200th anniversary of the Code. Yet is the rich case law surrounding Article 1384 CC really based on the opaque (and, in its inception, deliberately meaningless) words of that Article? Or is la protection de la vie privée founded on anything other than a "praetorian" construction of Article 1382 (even though the basis of the case law acquired in the 1970s a statutory expression (Article 9 CC))? Was the French Code, particularly the wording of Article 1121 CC, the real source of the rich development surrounding the notion of stipulation pour autrui or was its vagueness the opportunity exploited by the court of cassation to approve a legal institution (the life insurance contract), which in Portalis' days was considered immoral? And was not the Code in many cases so clearly unable to adapt itself to seriously changed circumstances that in the end it had to be replaced by special legislation? Even more paradoxically, given the amount of time spent on these issues, have the Code's family provisions withstood the test of time?

The correct answer to these questions will surely reveal an image different to that supported by traditional doctrine. The Code's real importance is, as I and others said recently, that it is a sui generis symbol. Perhaps, the above could also be used as an example of the proposition that in the European legal tradition, all judicial decisions must, ultimately, be pegged on one of the Code's provisions. But I do not think this feature can any longer be used to set French and English law apart in a rigid manner. It most certainly cannot be quoted, as it once was by an eminent English judge, to support the idea long dead that the Code contains a clear and complete statement of private law. At best, arguments distinguishing English from French law and based on Codes must be seriously qualified.

Influence of Roman Law

Here is another shibboleth. To the extent that it suggests that Roman law gave French legal language and the arrangement of French legal material a helping (and distinct) hand, this is true (just as it is true to maintain that Latin provided the basis for the French language). Also, to the extent that many specific ideas or institutions can be traced to Roman law, the argument is surely powerful. Likewise, Roman law can be credited to have furnished continental European legal systems as a whole with a common set of terms and notions, many of which are not easily matched by the common law. But these points are not decisive.

For first, modern scholarship has shown that Roman law has penetrated more areas of English law that is commonly believed in France. Secondly, one must stress, especially as far as French law is concerned, that Roman law penetrated it not directly but largely through the work of French jurists who worked on it and, at times, adapted it substantially (or even changed it) to meet French requirements. Roman law in the French Code Civil also never had the purity (nor the influence) that it had in the German Civil Code (BGB) in its 1896 version (a result much criticised by the Germanists such as Otto von Gierke) even though Roman law was, at times, seen by some French jurists as the true embodiment of reason. The assimilation of France and Germany must, once again, be attempted with great caution. Conversely, the distance from English law must be qualified.

Yet there is yet another reason why this reverence toward Roman law must cease to be invoked. Quite simply, the significance of Roman law for contemporary law, be it French or a fortiori English, is decreasing by the day. Important areas of the law such as media law, commercial law, financial law, technology-related law, intellectual property law, welfare law, and labour law, and even traditional areas of private law, such as family law, show how the distance from Roman ideas is both growing and unstoppable.

The diminishing number of teachers of Roman law are the only persons who pretend otherwise. If anything, new thinking-even for the French-is nowadays coming from the AngloSaxon world-America and the major countries of the Commonwealth such as Australia and Canada. Whether this is liked or resented is another matter; but the innovations taking place in those systems cannot be ignored with impunity.

University Law

Another feature separating common and (modern) civil law is the role universities played in the formation of legal reasoning and teaching in the systems under comparison. Valid to a great extent this point is, I think, likely to be over stressed if we focus on France and England instead of England and the continent of Europe as a whole. Nuances are again needed. For though our universities-and anyway in England we only had two until the beginning of the nineteenth century-taught only canon law and Roman law, the same is true of France until the edict of 1679 created the first chairs of French law.

And in many parts of France, even these chairs were not really established until the middle/end of the eighteenth century, only to be mothballed (along with the law faculties) by the early revolutionaries! I would lay a bet with odds often to one that very few English lawyers know this fact and have drawn from it an inference that actually helps bring closer together the approach both these systems (originally) had toward academic law.

I would also be willing to bet that most English lawyers would ascribe to the French university education of the Middle Ages and pre-revolutionary years a more important role in equipping lawyers with legal education than it really had. For, as French legal historians have pointed out, the bulk of the legal learning was often acquired outside the walls of the university class room.

Language

Since the time the story of the tower of Babel was invented even the most ordinary people are aware of the problems of communication that language can pose. Professor Legrand thus warns his readers in his original book in the Que sais-je? series that contract is not contrat or vertrag and so on. Perhaps this is a necessary warning for the wider kind of readership that consults the books included in these series. Yet his presentation could also be seen as a misrepresentation insofar as it downplays the fact that comparativists have tried hard to devise ways to overcome the obstacles that form such a large part of his argument.

Thus, Rabel's work and school has for decades now developed the "functional" way of looking at foreign law that minimises differences that stem from words or untranslatable national legal concepts. Professor Rodolfo Sacco's theory of "legal formants" is, likewise, very sensitive to the problems of language. On the very example Legrand quotes-contract-Zweigert and Kötz and I, in my German Law of Torts, now in its fourth edition-spend literally pages elaborating this point and making it clear (with specific reference to decided cases) how various German variations of the contractual notion-including the judge-made notion of vertrag mit schutzwirkung für dritte-are really addressing tort problems that the rigid drafting of the German Code has forced German lawyers to push into the law of contract. The language problem, undoubtedly acute when drafting multinational legislation, can thus be magnified beyond all proportion.

The Search for the Real Differences

Before launching into the main part of the chapter, an interim conclusion is called for. Quite simply, it is that challenging long-held beliefs cannot be done decisively in a few paragraphs. The preceding observations, however, should make readers pause and think. I am referring to those who have seen in these five factors the reasons for the great differences between English and French legal approach. In my view, if once they could be invoked as being decisive, they no longer can. Our attention for the differentia specifica must thus focus elsewhere, though we must also guard against mono-causal explanations of historical events. This caveat applies, of course, to what I say as much as to what others have written before me.

In my view, the main reason for the differences between the leading European legal systems (English, French, and German) is to be found in the legal professions, the role each was assigned to play in their respective country and the way they chose to employ their talents and energies. In looking at these different facets of my main proposition, one can detect times when, in the legal evolutionary process, the French (i) and English (ii) minds converged, displaying considerable similarities of thought and attitude. Other factors, however, intervened to interrupt the progress of convergence.

The Slow Path to the Unification of France

As an outside observer, I regard this as an important turning point not only in the evolution of French law but also in its comparison with English law. For present purposes, three topics, among many, deserve our attention. The first points at things to come namely, administrative but not legal centralisation. The second is the idea that the king is the source of justice and he grants it as a favour. I think this came to mean that judges, dispensing justice in his name, did not have to give reasons; and when later they had to do so, they had a good head start in being economic about them. In fairness, however, other reasons can be added to this historical one and explain the opaqueness of the decisions of the highest French courts. Finally one must look at the interacting role played by French academics.

The Consolidation of the Monarchy

With the English and religious wars over, the French kings were able to move, from about the end of the sixteenth century onwards, toward the political unification of their kingdom and the consolidation of the absolutist nature of their power, a target firmly set by the two cardinal ministers of the seventeenth century and taken to new heights during the reign of the Sun King. By the eve of the Revolution, both these aims had been achieved at the expense of alienating both their aristocracy and their bourgeoisie. Thus, the first was left isolated, powerless, (except for a brief partial revival in its political influence during the regency of the eighteenth century and then the reign of Louis XV), impoverished but privileged (and in this respect an object of envy), whereas the latter, while not sufficiently privileged, had become both pampered, ever-more ambitious, and yet also frustrated. The poor, in the countryside or the cities, remained marginalised and, literally, vulnerable to recurring crop failures due to bad weather conditions.

On the legal front, the French kings did not use the political unification to suppress the legal diversity that had established itself in their kingdom while it remained divided and he weak. On the contrary, they were quick (at least from the Ordonnance of 1254 of

Saint Louis) to hold themselves out as the guarantors of the local customs, something which the Parlements of the eighteenth century would even use against them. French kings thus proved restrained and pragmatic, resisting attempts to impose their will on the regions, at least when it came to matters of private law. Thus, as Professor Halpérin has summarised the situation, "l'unité, telle qu'elle est conçue autour de la personne du roi à la fin de l'Ancien Régime, est faite de diversité; c'est l'unité organique et pragmatique qui respecte les privilèges tout en les limitant"-in effect the exact opposite of what would turn out to be the case in England!

For these two reasons, the French monarchy, increasingly aided and abetted by prevarication and bad advice, allowed itself to enter into and traverse the intellectual turbulence of the eighteenth century without having achieved the political compromise with the other classes that their English counterparts had been forced to accept after two revolutions one hundred years earlier. The restraint of the French kings over the matter of legal unification, echoed by the output of their reforming ministers of the seventeenth and eighteenth centuries, such as Colbert and D'Aguesseau, thus went unnoticed by the most corrosive forces of the eighteenth century: the intellectuals (or, "les philosophes" as they were known at the time) who often made legal diversity the butt of their mockery.

Justification of Judgments

With the king unable and/or unwilling to press for wholesale unification of the law of their progressively unified kingdom, his lawyers were left with the task of picking up the pieces of the resulting fragmentation. For as physical movement and trade within (and outside) France increased, especially as a result of an improvement in the road system in the late seventeenth and eighteenth centuries, this state of affairs began to pose serious problems both to traders and those demanding advice on matters that required the most delicate balance between competing and diverging authorities (Roman law, customary rules, canon law, royal ordinances and administrative regulation, etc.). The requirement to create a workable whole out of such multiplicity of sources became so complex that only the most specialised practitioners could undertake it properly. The need to attempt a reconciliation and simplification thus gained new momentum from the time that Lamoignon-First President of the Parlement of Paris-began advocating the standardisation of customs. This move followed by efforts to create a truly French law (rather than just a reconciliation of the customs) out of all these mixed sources. Most of those who attempted this synthesis (Lamoignon, Colbert, Daguesseau) were practitioners or Royal officials-many with a very broad culture-while others (such Domat and, later, Pothier) with a more theoretical bend of mind (though not totally separated from the world of practice either, especially the latter) tried to find in reason and logic the tools to achieve the desired synthesis. For present purposes, it will suffice to note that the former group outnumbered the latter; and that overall, both, even when searching for maxims or broad principles, remained pragmatic and incremental in their work.

Such a background, with practitioners in key positions, created similarities to the legal approach in England that I do not think have been noted adequately. But the similarities could only go so far and no further. To a large extent, I think this is because of the form taken by the pronouncements of the Parlements and the way these were used by practitioners.

For decision making was seen as something delegated to the Parlements but done in the name of the king. Since the king did not have any obligation to give reasons for his decisions, neither did his judges. The position gained surprisingly wide acceptance, especially if one is to judge from the very scanty calls to change the status quo evidenced in the thousand cahiers des doléances submitted to Third Estate 1789 onwards. With the passage of time, other reasons would be added to this original one to ensure that the justification process of a judgment remained skeletal and often opaque. This would slowly mark an important difference between French and common law judgments, which, certainly by the eighteenth century, had become much fuller in content. It would also have consequences for teaching and the kind of qualities prospective lawyers were expected to acquire in order to practice their profession. Indeed, there are some who believe that even the Yearbooks had predominantly a teaching function.

The skeletal structure of the French decision was not made any easier to follow by the fact that French practitioners did not seem to work on the decisions of the Parlements as their English brothers did with their Yearbooks and, later, the named reports of the seventeenth century. Indeed, they could not do so even if they wanted to. For, as stated, the decisions of the Parlements, unlike those reproduced in varying degrees of fullness in the Yearbooks, (and, later, in the "named" reports, often drafted by practitioners for their own use) would contain only the decision and no reference to either the facts of the case, the arguments of the advocates, or the reasons of the judges. To practitioners, the material was, it would seem, in most cases little short of useless.

The French practitioners do not appear to have cared too much about this state of affairs.35 For either they tried to work out the solution to the problem through their own synthesis and interpretation of the diverse sources of law potentially applicable to their case in total disregard of any existing case law or, when not working for a client, indulged their spare time in the effort of working out their own synthesis of the divergent customary laws (for the sake of the eventual unification of French law). Indeed, to this day it is a matter of some surprise to me to be told by many of my French colleagues with a strong interest in legal history that they have rarely felt the need to consult decisions of Parlement since they were so devoid of any real information!

Two consequences from what I have sketched above deserve to be singled out for comment. The first is that French lawyers, though mostly practitioners, ended up undertaking, essentially, a different task than that of their English brother. In the course of time, this meant developing different techniques, an interest in different sources and, more importantly, a different frame of mind in order to accomplish it. Certainly, the English practitioner never had to expend effort in trying to find ways to solve the problem of geographical fragmentation to the extent that the French did. Likewise, except where canon law had to be consulted, the reconciliation of diverse legal sources was never the major headache that it could be for his French counterpart.

Secondly, judicial styles came to differ substantially from those we find in common law jurisdictions. I shall return to this point later on but, for now, and in my capacity as a comparative lawyer, I declare my prejudice in favour of the Anglo-Saxon type of judgement, which I find richer and clearer than the modern French parade of "whereas" clauses!

The Role of Academics

An interesting side effect of the points discussed above is that the incremental and pragmatic approach adopted toward legal unification was shared by legal writers. Indeed, though great names can be found from at least the seventeenth and eighteenth century advocating greater harmonisation, their efforts tended to be focused largely in trying to reduce the customary diversity or, later, to construct a French law out of logic. In most if not all cases, the aims are practical, i.e., to help courts, practitioners, and citizens avoid the extreme complexity that flowed from the different sources of law. Indeed, even those who attempted to synthesise the different customary laws were anxious to avoid extending their conclusions or proposals to the countries of the "written law" of the South. Pragmatism, it would seem, underlay most of these efforts more than the ideal to give law a geometrical expression!

Incidentally, I refer to the above as legal writers rather than academics since it strikes me that, leaving aside the sixteenth-century humanists who were academics of the purist kind, the vast majority of French legal writers writing for practitioners were practitioners themselves (or judges or legal officers), and were primarily addressing practical needs. Few, in other words, were writing for educational purposes alone or at all; and even fewer shared the love of abstraction, generalisation, and theory that became the hallmarks of their German counterparts in the seventeenth and, again, the nineteenth century. In that sense they are thus not "system builders" (as the German counterparts are) but, like their English brothers, "problem solvers."

In my view, Domat is, notwithstanding some unusual features, no exception to the wider point I am making. For, even though he attempted (under the influence of the rigorous mind of Blaize Pascal) to describe the law within a very logical (indeed, even, religious) framework, thus coming closer to his German contemporaries than any other Frenchman, his work did not seem to have any effect on the practice of the contemporary courts and may even have had a limited impact on legal education. His profoundest influence may thus have been on Pothier (a judge and counsellor turned holder of one of the early chairs of French law). Yet even this observation needs some further reflection.

For, it can be argued, both of these important authors made their major contribution to French legal thought by facilitating through their treatises the codification process that culminated with the enactment of the Code in 1804. Moreover, this "facilitation" process may, in no small measure, have consisted in the adaptation, rational ordering, or out-right abandonment of Roman law material in order to make the "inherited" (imperial) Roman law fit in with "contemporary" French needs. This end product is invaluable; and seeing their work in this light is not meant to devalue it. But it is meant to suggest that, essentially, it is different to that pursued by the German and Dutch seventeenth- and eighteenth-century scholars in whose work geometrical and mathematical thinking seems to play a dominant role. Pothier's own work, if anything less dogmatic, distinctly less religious than his mentor's, and in intellectual terms, arguably, less original, is in style and aims not that far removed from English tastes of his time and, even more so, of the next century. Indeed, to me it is noteworthy that, unlike Domat, he maintained his interest in practice for the whole of his life; and it is his real life illustrations and hypotheses that have often survived in the classrooms and courtrooms of many professors and judges, English as well as American!

This must lend some support to the wider thesis of this chapter that the dogmatic, abstract, systematising features of French law are not, necessarily, autochthonous in their origin, nor do they represent that system's most original and exportable features. My preceding thoughts, some advanced more tentatively than others, acquire additional significance by the observation of Professors Jestaz and Jamin. For these learned colleagues observe that in France, from the mid-seventeenth century onwards, those aspiring to a senior judicial career had to pursue a practical apprenticeship rather than an academic training, a point also confirmed by Professor Arnaud in his discussion of the careers of the major protagonists of the Code Civil. I, for one, was not, until recently, aware of this important but spontaneous similarity between the two ways of thinking-the French and the English; and I still believe that it has not received the attention it deserves from legal historians.

The English Focus on the Administration of Justice—The Writ System Versus the Generalisation and Abstraction of the Glossatores

The development of early English law displays all the procedural hallmarks of Roman law and it is surprising to note how few have discussed its similarities with early Roman law. More importantly, as scholars such as the late Harry Lawson and Jack Dawson (among others) have shown, the divergence between common and modern civil law began with the rediscovery of Roman law in the West and the gradual move toward generalisation and abstraction that this generated. Perfected by the jusnaturalistes, some of these generalisations eventually found their way into the Code Civil.

This marks another difference with English law that continued to carry the scars of the forms of action well after they were formally abolished in the middle of the nineteenth century. But in France (unlike Germany) this tendency to think in terms of principles and wider-almost manifesto-like propositions-is not due to academic (in the sense of logic or mathematics-based) system building but, in my view, traceable to other factors some of which I mentioned already. And it should not obscure the fact that the call for law reform came mainly from (or was achieved by) practitioners, often conservative in temperament, incremental in their approach, practically motivated in their aims, and anything but revolutionary. I stress these features because I think they can help minimise the differences between the frame of mind of the lawyers of the two systems under comparison during this period of their legal histories.

The Dominance of Practice

If I may give to some the impression that I have overestimated the importance of practitioners in the shaping of modern French law, I can never be accused of the same sin when talking about English law. For though practitioners played a key role in the shaping of both systems, they performed it in a very different way.

One important difference flowed from numbers: the number of English judges was (and has always remained) a small fraction of the French. The difference in numbers is crucial not only because small numbers helped foster a closer esprit de corps but also because it encouraged the keeping of legal education, discipline, and promotion within this small group. Such a cohesive group was in a better position to resist outside influences, resist "outside" pressures to tell them how to ordain their affairs and, during most of the twentieth century, arguably, even developed something barely short of disdain for law taught in university cloisters.

Such a group would also develop its own ways of looking at law. System building was not its concern except insofar as it constantly tried to elaborate as efficiently as possible the inter-relationship between various judicial decisions. In England, the way of arguing a case thus became different, more detailed, more fact oriented, than it was in France; and given that the judges came to be drawn from the ranks of high ranking practitioners, the way of motivating their judgment was, likewise, adjusted to this different setting even if this did not appear in the early reports as fully as it does in the modern ones.

A small number of judges also meant developing a different attitude to the frequency with which one could attract their intervention, as well as a diminution of the workload that would be placed on their shoulders. The right of appeal (as we know it today) was thus not accepted for a long time, the Courts of Error initially being restricted to a consideration of errors on the face of the record.

The overall workload of the Roman-canonical procedure was also avoided by the adoption of jury trial that, in its early form, meant that the jury found out what happened and not the judge! Jury trial, overall, entailed huge consequences for substance, procedure, and evidence. The English trial thus had to adapt to the above requirements, which meant continuity rather than discontinuity in the judicial process, orality rather than written pleadings, while clarity of expression and presentation came at a premium given that so much of the process was being addressed to impressionable individuals and not learned scholars working in the solitude of the libraries.

The result of all this is that the Yearbooks (the earliest form of "reports" of English decisions) almost from the earlier times, had to give more facts, a fuller indication of the arguments put forward by the advocates, and (progressively) more of the reasons that allowed the judges to lead to their particular conclusion. The French ideas on the subject could thus not be more different; and the consequences this approach had for the kind of talents that the practitioners of each country had to acquire in order to practice his profession also came to differ. Once again, then, the possibility of enhanced or even accelerated convergence thus slowed down. Two other events were in the end to bring this convergence process to a screeching halt. They are discussed in the next subsection.

Missed Chance to Meet in the Middle

What has been said in the preceding paragraphs draws on existing knowledge but also tries to stress, more than has hitherto been done, the role-actual and potential-of practitioners in both English and French law. Given that in both countries the practising element was so strong in the law-shaping process, it would have been reasonable to expect a further convergence between the systems. Why did it not happen? Some reasons have already been suggested; and not all were legal in nature. Others must now be looked at more closely.

The Impact of Skewed Opinions by Foreign Observers

When Edmund Burke fired his famous broadside against the Revolution, he managed to colour thereafter in a hostile manner most English reaction toward it and its products. The fact that much of the seventeenth century was spent in a state of overt or dormant antagonism and even conflict between England and France obviously made the former fertile soil for anti-French propaganda. But much of Burke's success was also due to the fact that he timorously foresaw the worsening of the situation during the years of the Terror. For present purposes, just as important is his tirade against the lawyers who drafted the early revolutionary texts, especially the Declaration of Rights. In fact, few books have done more to project in a more unfavourable light the French penchant for wide principles instead of concrete remedies. Yet for the reasons already given, the search for maxims or general principles had started much earlier, indeed it can be traced back to the way some customs had been recorded in writing and thus has little to do with the Revolution.

Burke was no less charitable toward the qualifications of the legal protagonists; yet in the light of recent French historical research his sweeping condemnations also need qualifying, especially if seen as applicable also to the men and the material that eventually created the Code. Without referring to Burke, Savigny made just this extension when he criticised Portalis' and Maleville's knowledge of Roman texts and "damned" (with an unnecessarily broad brush) those in the Conseil d'Etat who reviewed the draft of the four "authors" as "dilettantes"! Yet Savigny's objections are different in their aim and their motives than Burke's.

For, as a scholar, Savigny is objecting to the French understanding of certain Roman texts, a point of view stressed by many (but not all) German lawyers of the nineteenth century. But Savigny's criticism is also influenced by the fact that he approached the end product as a German, critical of Napoleon's authoritarian and imperialistic tendencies from which Germany had much suffered. Both these optics, understandable though they are, prevented him, however, from appreciating the Code's sociological role and, in particular, its aim to put an end to the bitter divisions of the mid 1790s, to a large extent caused by the teaching of the philosophers. Thus, to the extent that the Code provided a framework within which the bourgeois society that emerged after the Revolution could operate, it must be judged as a total success, untarnished by any objections about the use it made of Roman law materials. In that sense, the drafting of the French Code is also a very different exercise from the making of the BGB almost 100 years later; and Karl Marx may have understood better than Savigny the measure of Napoleon's achievement much as he, too, disliked Bonaparte.

Justified or one sided, the fact remains that in England the hostility toward French lawyers and their Code, generated during the turn of the eighteenth century, was toned down once the political (and, one should add, commercial) threat from France subsided with

Napoleon's fall. Pothier, in particular, emerged with a substantial popularity both in England and the United States, something that, in the latter country, manifested itself strongly with a flurry of articles when the first centenary of the Code was celebrated. Yet, overall, in England the image of French law and, above all, its style of legislative drafting, remained negative. The Code's tendency toward generalisations and abstractions continued to be distrusted, as was the "mechanical"-or so it was seen-application of its provisions by the courts. It took over a century for even specialist English observers to begin to realise that, even if ever true, such an interpretation of the Code had changed spectacularly by the end of the nineteenth century as a result of some very bold "interpretations" of the Cour de Cassation. As for the idea that all this was due to "academic" influence, my view is that to this day it has not yet really been shaken off. I offer below some reasons why, in my view, such wrong impressions could have persisted for so long.

Different Influences on the French Legal Process and Mind

This theme, vast and undoubtedly important for comparative lawyers, can only detain us briefly here. It is thus with great interest that an English lawyer will note the impact that factors such as religion had on the thought of eminent jurists such as Gény, Saleilles, and Josserand and how it succeeded in transforming the German ideas which these authors were quick to espouse. In my view, common law lawyers must always feel perplexed by the fact that the law-changing process in France (be it through legislation or judicial decision) has attracted to such an unusual degree the attention of not only judges and lawyers but also philosophers and, in a more indirect manner, political theorists, writers, and artists.

One thus feels inclined to agree with Antoine Garapon when he writes that, "legal culture does not really allow itself to be fully revealed except in works apparently far removed from law, proper, such as cinema, theatre, literature and the Press." For instance, Balzac's entire Comédie Humaine is closely linked to a school of thought also found in contemporary legal scholarship according to which the complete equality in succession introduced by the Code led to the weakening of the "old families" (with adverse social effects according to many authors).

Though these groups and professions may not have acted in concert or, even, with any degree of coordination or, finally, succeeded in establishing a direct influence on French lawyers, they still, in my view, present an influential background factor that hardly has an equivalent in England.

For in England, matters pertaining to law and law changing were, as stated earlier on, for a long time dominated by a small group of specialist professionals, with politicians acquiring some input only much later when the statutory part of law acquired greater prominence in the legal system as a whole. And this "dominance" of the legal profession extended not only to the content of the law and its "teaching" but later, as statutory law grew in size, also to matters of legislative drafting. Indeed, even a lesser involvement in the law reform process by philosophers, taking the form of reform proposals, invariably came to grief, Bentham offering, for present purposes, the most apposite illustration. Bentham correctly believed that the legal profession was his greatest enemy, unwilling to accept any interference from "outsiders."

I will return in the next subsection to the particular role of one group of thinkers-the eighteenth-century French philosophers-in setting blue water between the French and English law. For, though singularly untrained in matters of law (with the exception of Montesquieu), they tried (and to some extent succeeded) in shaping French law. More unfortunately, they also helped obscure the similarities that existed between French and English law of the time given that this was par excellence the period of the cultured practitioner. But before doing this, a word or two must be said of the phenomenon of the "cultured" practitioner. Portalis is the best illustration, though the breadth of his interests may also make him rather exceptional.

A Broader Culture: The Revealing Example of Jean-Marie-Etienne Portalis

I have repeatedly stressed in this chapter how different the "way of writing" is in France, England, and Germany. In light of what has been said above, one can understand the difference with the last system dominated, in the eighteenth and, again, in the nineteenth century, by the academic mind. But the difference with England needs a word of explanation.

The highly specialised training received for generations by English barristers, coupled with the cloistered life in the Inns of Court, for a long time gave them, I believe, a reduced participation in the wider affairs of the country. As legislation increased in volume, others who were not lawyers were slowly drawn into the legislative process bringing along their own talents. But even here, the actual drafting was increasingly shifted onto the shoulders of specialists while the wider learning that followed the spreading of the printed word was not allowed to merge as freely and as regularly into the legal discourse as I think it did in France. Thus, a Benjamin Constant, not otherwise discussed in this chapter since it focuses on private not public law, would never find a role in the English legal scene as he did in France (on matters of private as well as public law). And it would be unthinkable in England for the discussion of a complex piece of legislation to be arrested midway so as to give "philosophers" the chance to review it! Nor can we, I think, find tangible evidence in England to show how the constant exposure of lawyers to political clubs, salons literaires, and the like not only enhanced their wider culture but also became reflected in their legal work. Yet in France, the life and work of Portalis show all of the above.

In 1797, Portalis wrote a monograph entitled De l'Usage et de l'Abus de l'Esprit Philosophique Durant le XVII Siècle. Its first chapter summarised the development of French language and culture from Carolingian times to its summit during the reign of Louis XIV. At the beginning of the second chapter, where the crisis brought by the eighteenth-century philosophers slowly begins to be sketched out, we find the following few lines:

> *Il existe entre la simple érudition et la véritable science la différence que l'on remarque entre le jugement et la mémoire. La simple érudition n'est qu'un dépôt de faits et de matériaux divers; la science suppose dépôt, mais elle le transforme en propriété et elle en règle l'usage. On est érudit par la multitude ou par la masse des choses acquises; on est savant par la manière de les choisir et de les employer. L'homme purement érudit possède; le vrai savant jouit. La science aide le génie; presque toujours la simple érudition le tue.*

I have chosen this example from Portalis' endless series of memorable phrases because it was written, as most of the work, while he was exiled in Holstein in the midst of different groups of philosophers, pietists, at the same time widening his reading to include the ideas of authors as varied as Burke, Herder, Locke, Montesquieu, and Adam Smith. Only a few years later he would, to his surprise, find himself submerged in drafting the Code Civil. This staccato style, pregnant with mature reflections of the kind we later find in writers such as Tocqueville, is admirable. More importantly, we will find it duplicated in his legislative work, especially his Discours Préliminaire.

It will thus colour the way he will phrase the maxims which, he will tell us, have dictated the rules he is putting in the Code. The link between a private work which, indeed, was not even published until after his death and his public work is there, clear for all to see.

Important though this observation is, the few lines cited above tell us more about how he thinks and writes. (To a large extent, this can be said of the work of the other draftsmen of the Code, since most left work of different kinds, though none equalled Portalis' breadth of reading.) For in the text above we see a man externalising his experience of life-in many respects a harsh one as was, indeed, the lot of almost all who lived through those difficult times. Learned he is, in law and other things as well. His book leaves no doubt as to the extent of his reading. But he is also a man of the world-not of the cloister. The few lines cited above make this obvious.

His thoughts also clearly distinguish him from a German or Englishman in his position. For how many German practitioners can we imagine writing an overtly jurisprudential book and so obviously pooh-poohing the amassing and display of knowledge? My readers could, I am sure, choose their own examples of German books-old and contemporary-that, weighed down by endless footnotes compiled by armies of assistants, show how, indeed, 'la science aide le génie; presque toujours, la simple érudition le tue." And can we, if we swing to the other end of the pendulum, imagine a common law practitioner-even a more contemporary academic-writing a book like that, emulating the poetry of Portalis? If the German scholar would be excessively abstract in his desire for completeness leaving nothing to the imagination, the English writer would be muscular but dry. To be sure, one can think of judges such as Holmes, Cardozo, Denning, Posner (and, occasionally, Lord Goff) who have to varying degrees introduced a literary element in their writings. But few lawyers would regard them as "typical" of the breed; and the younger ones, both in England and the United States, decry this flowery style.

Yet for Portalis-and for many later French scholars or judges-the externalisation of his views-even on legal matters-cannot be done in the drier manner that best suits the English temperament. The likes of Esmein, Planiol, Savatier, or Carbonnier would thus continue to write in a manner that drew into their legal arguments their wider participation in the cultural life of their country. Portalis, himself, thus wrote a few pages earlier what for him is a self-evident proposition: "la language est le tableau de la vie et de l'assamblage de toutes les idées d'un peuple, manifesté au-dehors par des sons."

If it appears strange if not alien to a contemporary English lawyer to see a specialist legislator display such a broad interest in wider philosophical matters and write about them, it may be because the English "tradition" of an education and career centred around the Inns of Court has left such an imprint on law, the way we write about it, teach it, and practice it. My wider conclusion is thus this: if language-mentioned in the first section of this chapter-is a hindrance in bringing the two systems-English and French-together it is in the sense just described rather than any other!

The Impact of the Eighteenth-Century Philosophers

I am now thinking of the French philosophers of the Enlightenment. Of the disparate groups of people who were active in France during the pre-Revolutionary period they, in my opinion, were the most influential in separating French and English legal thinking. Yet in France, the input of the philosophers to the internal harmonisation and development of private law, especially of the eighteenth-century lawyers, was, I think, indirect and, I would be tempted to add, destabilising.

By indirect I mean that their influence on private law was exerted mainly via the impact the philosophers had on the Declaration of Human Rights as well as the establishment of the new political order and, via them, on private law. By destabilising, I refer to such things as the effect that the conflicting eighteenth-century views on celibacy and equality had on various parts of private law, mainly family and successional law, during the darkest years of the Revolution, i.e., 1792-94. This, at any rate, is what I read French writers as suggesting; and I am intrigued to see that the two main protagonists of the Code-Napoleon and Portalis-likewise had a dim view about some of these philosophers (notably Rousseau and Voltaire). Indeed, even the few English philosophers who were to favour the idea of codification-Bentham is the best example-would balk at the idea of "natural" and "imprescriptible" rights.

Yet generations of English lawyers except, dare I say, the most specialist among them, have suspected the wide and often extreme formulations in the works of Rousseau or Voltaire that have coloured their opinion of the French Code, its content, and its draftsmen. Thus, while the legacy of the philosophers remained alive, the fact that the Code was a carefully crafted compromise between North and South, old and new, liberal and dirigiste, achieved mainly by practising lawyers seems to have gone unnoticed even by educated English lawyers. Also unnoticed has been the incremental approach of generations of French lawyers, the use of material that came out of practice, even if commented upon and in some cases systematised by a handful of writers alluded above.

Finally, unnoticed is the search for practical solutions, even when writing treatises, their detachment from dogmas and theories, as well as their determination to be flexible, brief, and clear as a way of allowing the law to respond to future fundamental changes in society. The French Code thus fully endorses the value of flexibility in contrast to the later German Code, which placed such emphasis on certainty. These must surely be the reasons why the text of the Code survived so many political and social changes during the nineteenth century with so few alterations. To put it differently: this was a document, prepared by people of the world not of the cloisters, that reflected the compromise political settlement finally reached by a long-divided society.

The Side Lining of Practitioners by the Emergence of the French Doctrine

All of the above qualities are, in my view, linked to the kind of world that practitioners, not academics, inhabit. I stress again, they set French law and lawyers apart from the German model and could have brought the English and French systems closer together. And yet, as I keep saying, this fact has not been mentioned let alone explored by lawyers thus far, probably because the factors herein explored frustrated in the end this rapprochement. Needless to say, my hypothesising finds even more support if and when we move from private to public law and trace not only the development of French administrative law but also the writings (dominated by judges and practitioners) about it during its formative years of the nineteenth century.

Yet the above (potential) conversion between the two systems (English and French), knocked on the head by the images, ideas, and language of the eighteenth-century philosophers, received a further blow when a second wave of what I am inclined to call "pure Germanomania" hit France from about the end of the nineteenth century. Arguably, this was to prove much more influential than the jusnaturaliste movement of the seventeenth and eighteenth century. This second wave, however, was to prove not only more influential but, in some respects, also more welcome. For in the excellent monograph of Professors Jestaz and Jamin on the emergence of the very French term of "doctrine" (described by them at the beginning of their book), the Germanic influence on the great figures of the turn of the nineteenth/twentieth century-Saleilles and Gény and Planiol-is seen as a great turning point for French academic culture as it gained confidence, homogeneity, and status.

The advantages of the new thinking that surrounded the creation of the BGB made this German influence understandable. So, too, is the influence it had in moulding a French professorial along similar though not identical lines to those found in Germany. It thus, or so it seems to me, brought to French legal culture a strong dogmatic flavour as well as strengthened the cursus honorum nature of the French academic career with its aggregation process strongly resembling that of the habilitation. That all this has strong points is not in doubt. The question that has not been fully explored, not even in the Jestaz/Jamin monograph, was its down side.

From a comparative/historical angle, it cannot be denied that this influx of ideas and habits brought the final blow in the approximation of French and English legal thinking that had occurred in the past whenever practitioners rather than academics had the upper hand in France. It was, undoubtedly, also accompanied by an indifference shown (deliberate or not is not the issue here) toward the slowly growing importance of the Anglo-Saxon legal world. In my view, these trends also helped nourish the idea alluded to at the beginning of this chapter that the continental legal systems are radically different to the English but very close to one another-an idea that has even led some English scholars to imagine the whole of European law as being Napoleonic in origin. Indeed, what a compliment to the French and what a lèse majesté to the Germans to treat, even implicitly, their masterpiece as a Napoleonic creation!

In my view, therefore, the clear diversion of English and French law, which had flowed and ebbed during the preceding centuries, was consolidated during this period. This is also the period that brings the greatest rapprochement between French to German legal cultures notwithstanding differences that French academic writers are always willing to remind us of. It will be interesting to see if the German legal mind succeeds in imposing itself on the French now that European efforts at codification seem to have fallen-again-under the spell of German (and to some extent Dutch) minds clamouring for a European Code. The first products that have surfaced from the laboratories make some of us hope that they do not; but the outcome is still uncertain.

Consequences

The above shifts in my view had some important consequences that are best looked at under two headings.

The Teaching and Writing of the Law

The above shifts in taste have affected the way the French teach and present through their writings their law. In brief, and compared with the English, the emphasis is increasingly on structure, theory, and logical presentation of the ever-growing case law within accepted structures. Professors Jestaz and Jamin could not be clearer in enunciating a proposition which would send shudders down English spines: "La tradition française s'attache à l'étude des textes (destinée à forger des principes, puis des constructions juridiques, selon un processus qui tend à toujours plus d'abstraction) et non à l'investigation des . . . ."

Just as importantly, judicial decisions, though increasingly accepted since the end of the nineteenth century as sources of law, will rarely be used as building blocks for further developments but as a secondary, amplifying application or illumination of a wider general principle. In a textbook or treatise, a judicial decision will thus appear more often than not in the footnote of a text rather than the text itself consisting, as an English treatise would do, of a serial discussion of decisions, incrementally leading the reader to the current state of affairs. This does not make the style and presentation of the English book intellectually or stylistically more attractive than the French; nor is, of course, the reverse any truer. But it does bring out a difference, enhanced by other (less important) presentational differences (such as the presentation of the material in short, numbered paragraphs or the constant subdivision of the text, undoubtedly for the sake of logic, in a manner that-an English reader at any rate-may even find distracting).

The utility of legal writing to the world of practitioners also seems-to an outsider at least-to be secondary in the minds of French academic writers even though the interplay between court decisions and academic reaction, mainly in the shape of extended notes or articles, is an enriching feature of the French legal scene. In England, a similar dialogue has only in recent times begun to be noticed by the courts, the overt taking into account of academic views still remaining something of an exception favoured by some judges only.

Though, as stated, some of these trends are beginning to be visible in England, overall I see the French interest in dogma, structure, abstraction as, once again, representing a swing back to a model that appears off putting to English eyes. What is more regrettable still is the fact that it tends to present the law separated from other disciplines that help bring it to life and often may explain its solutions. Law and economics or law related to policy values is lacking from French academic works as is the avoidance of any discussion of practical issues-what the common lawyers tend to call "law in action"-that might help put a doctrinal decision in a different perspective and reveal how much of the law in the books corresponds with reality. Though fashions have changed over the years, one cannot help the "impression" that some academics regard such approaches to law as being beneath their status and mission and thus to be avoided. But these are the impressions of an outsider and outsiders are notorious in getting false impressions about other people's lives and attitudes! So let me be more specific.

As a tort lawyer I, for one, have often asked French colleagues about the level of damages only to be told that is a matter for practitioners and of little concern to academics. Yet, could the theoretical generosity of French law, private or administrative law, for damages resulting from illegal acts be in part traceable to the fact that the availability of damages in theory is seriously watered down in practice by the stinginess of the awards? For comparative lawyers, such ways of approaching and even trying to explain differences, real or apparent, are essential. Asking these questions may reveal that the availability of a right of action often has more adverse effects in practice than its theoretical recognition may present benefits.

To my previous example, I add two more, this time from pure private law.

First, is the potential liability for pure omissions often invoked in practice in a civil context? If so, does this achieve any real purpose beyond asserting in the legal sphere the presence of a moral rule? Secondly, the availability of damages for what the common lawyers call pure psychiatric injury (i.e., emotional trauma without physical injuries). Does this really work in French law? Is a flood of actions avoided because the amounts are low or rarely claimed? Is it really convenient to leave the control of such actions to causation devices that can only be applied in trial? And are benefits of wide rules diminished by the cost of excessive litigation? I am prepared to accept that the more restrictive common law rules may be unfair insofar as they reflect administrative expedience rather than serve the notion of justice. But I would also like to know more about how French law copes with the kind of concerns that occupy-should I say preoccupy-common lawyers. Yet the accounts I find in books brush these points aside, at any rate to the extent that they do not raise philosophical or dogmatic questions but seem to reflect practical concerns.

The Way Decisions are Justified

The differences between the systems are even more notable in the style of judgments, especially of the highest courts. Here, French scholars cannot take the blame. On the contrary, the past seems to have retained its grip on the style of reasoning, strengthened by some new factors to which allusion was made. But how does the litigant know why he lost the case? How does the lawyer know what was the real reason the court decided it in a particular way? How does one address a wave of arguments, often vaguely presented by the national and even academic press about, for instance, the Americanisation of French law? The Perruch affair illustrated some of these points with the French discussions being-in my eyes at least-almost monotonously preoccupied with legalistic understandings of causation. The legislative reversal of the decisions of the French Supreme Court showed, at its worst, what lobby pressure and political weakness can do.

It is of little use for a foreign observer to complain about the style of a the judgment of a foreign supreme court and to the extent that I am doing it is because as a foreign lawyer, I feel it makes it difficult to teach French law to young foreign lawyers who ought to be made aware of the richness of your culture. But it is also interesting to find eminent French judges, academics, and practitioners sharing my concerns for more practical reasons than my own. In any event, the comparatist, by asking such questions and delving into such problems, can at least feel that he is getting close to what are the real differences between the legal systems; what are the results of accidents of history and what, by contrast, are core ideas of the foreign system. If such a scholar has an international rather than national disposition, if he believes that the world is shrinking and not closing in within national frontiers, if he sees economic globalisation as being here to stay, he may also try to find ways to diminish (both as a teacher and as a practitioner) these differences or at least try to explain them in a constructive way.

New Forces Favouring Convergence

This chapter has traced, through the eyes of an outside observer, the vacillation of French law between theory and practice and the results this has had in making it resemble to or differ from English law. Over the centuries, and due to developments internal or external to France, this trend has alternated in an intriguing way. This is not surprising since one notes similar vacillations in the political relations between the two countries, though the waxing and waning in the strength of similarities between French and English law cannot be linked to the changing state of the political relations between these two countries.

Since the last Great War, all countries, their cultures and economies and legal systems, have come to imitate one another and depend more and more on each other as well as on developments in the world legal order. In this concluding section we must allude briefly to this linking of national law with international legal and economic trends since in its extent (if not its nature as well) it is a new development (A) and, then, ask ourselves whether it could be possible that in these international developments the national systems may, finally, find the impetus that will bring them closer together. (B)

The Increasing Interaction of National Law with the International Scene

It is a truism to say that in the study of the past we find some explanations of the present. Nowadays, however, we must also stress how national developments are increasingly sensitive to international trends or events. This is an important point and, essentially, a new one since all European countries are challenged by the shape they must give to a new, more integrated, and more competitive Europe. In this battle over who may exercise the greatest influence over the new "product," could English (or Anglo-Saxon) ideas surface in a position that is disproportionately influential to the insular posturing that the country has traditionally adopted toward the continent? My enquiry is deliberately widened at this stage of this chapter. For what happens to law, its teaching, its financing, and its practice, is increasingly going to be affected by new factors: globalisation of finance, trade, and legal services; professionalisation of the law degree; and the role of private enterprise in the educational sector. The future of any legal system can no longer be seen in isolation from what is happening around it; and this new environment may provide a new impetus for the convergence between French and English law that came so close in the past and yet never happened. It is the "novelty" of the factors that is bringing this rapprochement closer that needs to be evaluated.

Growing Convergence Through New Factors

In this chapter, I tried to show how the style of legislation, legal writing, and judicial decisions can be seen as responses to certain historical developments. It is these twists and turns in history that have made our two legal systems different, in reality or sometimes only in appearance. But if the external stimulus is the same, years, often centuries, of difference may begin to yield to a transformation that leads to convergence. To avoid generalisations, one example will suffice; but others like it could be given.

Take the European products liability directive and see what it has done to French law. Let us look at it from the point of view of classification of the law, style, and result.

Classification (and dogma) of the law first. What used to be found in the law of contract is now the domain of the law of tort. The original, French, fictitious expansion of the contract of sale was replaced by the open admission of tort as the basis of liability. And the dogma that made English law and French law irreconcilable-the doctrine of consideration that made in English law the "action directe" impossible-has now been overcome by the European directive, effectively confirming a judge-made tort action. English and French law are, in classification terms, now ad idem whereas forty years ago, such rapprochement would have been founded on dogmatic discussions over the doctrine of consideration. This assimilation of classification was thus achieved not by assimilation of dogma but by external, political developments. The great German/English comparatist Otto Khan-Freund expressed the basic idea beautifully when he wrote nearly thirty years ago: "Taught law . . . is tough law, and what is taught are primarily the general doctrinal foundations to which in after life the lawyer will cling as he may cling to the religious beliefs he learned at his mother's knees. Practical details on the other hand, are negotiable. Fortunately for the future of Europe what matters are the practical details, and the diverse doctrinal foundations can look after themselves."

Style next. The new paragraph 1386 CC is, effectively, eighteen articles and thus long. To be sure, not as long as the English Consumer Protection Act, but then neither is it as terse as the preceding five articles of the Code given that it only deals with one type of tort liability. Pity some might say to alter the terseness of the old Code, once an admired feature of the original version. But, again, the common external influence has forced this change upon national law. In this instance, the way the desired result was achieved showed that radical change can be made without betraying too much national tradition. But this cannot be said of other (new) provisions of the Code, while other EU directives raise the problem of where they should be inserted or, indeed, to be left in a freestanding way. I would say that Article 1386 CC is a success. I would also argue that our German colleagues are wrong when they argue, as they have done in the past when considering the lapidary style of the Code, that conciseness and even generality is a sign of loose thinking. It can be; but it need not be.

Content finally. The directive has affected a considerable degree of harmonisation in this part of the law across European borders. In France, its coexistence with an arguably wider national law and the relevant infrequency of its use in litigation in England may raise other issues. But from the point of view of convergence, it shows not only how it is happening and how, also, it is prompted by causes that lie outside the boundaries of one country. Incidentally, it also shows how the fears expressed at the time the directive was passed (certainly in Britain by the Confederation of British Industry) about the dangers it would bring for British industry have proved unfounded. Scaremongering is a favourite argument used by all those who fear change even when it is desirable. My "directive" example shows more than how an external factor can provoke convergence. It also shows that this tends to work better when the change is partial, not unnecessarily broad in its ambit, and has been worked out in concert with all the varied interests that have a role to play in the shaping of the law.

This does not mean academics only; it also involves practitioners, politicians, industry, insurance, and maybe other sectors of society. The French understood this in 1804; and they were rewarded with a text that despite its inevitable aging remained alive for 200 years. The Germans on the other hand could never bring themselves to accept a reduced status for academics. One can wonder (but should not attempt to answer) the question, "what will the present debate in Germany about universities bring to that great legal tradition?"

Will We Take the Next Step?

The differences between French and English law do not lie in language, though language does more than separate: it makes proper comparisons difficult. Nor are the main differences due to the reception or not of Roman law, though that too had its impact on the content of legal rules and the minds of those who made them. The island status of England and its people may have given them an insular mentality, a sense of separateness, a suspicion toward change for anything that they did not, themselves, fashion. But, in addition, it gave them stability, enhanced their respect for tradition, and, in promoting a pragmatic approach to life, nourished a dislike for adjectives and generalities. But that argument, too, is nowadays losing its force as ideas, and tastes and habits become so much more internationalised than before. So where, really, are the differences?

This chapter has suggested that in the legal field, the most crucial difference may lie in the type of unification achieved in England after the Norman invasion of 1066. Unlike that of France, it came earlier and was not only political but also legal. The architects of this achievement were normal civil servants and an increasingly cohesive legal profession. Academic lawyers were not part of it; and remained in the margins of legal science until the middle/late-nineteenth century. Few would thus hesitate to admit that in England the senior partners in the law-shaping process were the judges and the practitioners.

The situation was different in France; and even more different in Germany. If one sentence had to be used to capture these differences, I would say "legal mentality." Legal mentality may differ from country to country. But transcending countries is the difference in mentality between academics and practitioners. Academics like theory, order, logic, and structure. Practitioners know life is untidy and unpredictable and learn how to live with such a state of affairs. They deal with real problems and are concerned with solutions-mostly remedies for wrongs-not structures and the formulation of wide principles. The law they generate is different because their mind is focused on specific issues, evaluating specific arguments, rather than formulating general principles. Both of these frames of mind have their advantages; neither on its own is perfect. But that is not the point I am making. Rather, what I have tried to say, albeit in different words, is that a practitioner understands a practitioner because they share common problems and are not bogged down by different concepts and notions.

Perhaps we are moving toward a compromise; once I referred to it as the gradual convergence. Though other jurists denied this phenomenon few can really deny that it is happening! Understanding what propels it might make it smoother and more workable. In England, our court procedure has thus acquired a stronger written element. At least half of our practicing lawyers now have a law degree (whereas when I started as a law teacher thirty-five years ago only a tiny minority had, indicating a growing awareness of the need to acquire an academic grounding in law). In public law, having decried the French Bill of Rights as "nonsense, upon stilts". We now have our own. Likewise, having decried through one of our greatest constitutional gurus "droit administratif" we now respect it much more having created a version of our own. And there is more. For we have moved toward a "federal or regionalist" model-we call it devolution-and are even toying with the idea of signing up to a European constitution. On the private law front we are even flirting with the desirability of enhanced "structure" as distinguished academics are advocating more of it to be imported in our private law and our teaching.

All these are moves in the French or, to be more comprehensive, the continental European direction for there is a very strong element in the German law of human rights that will, sooner or later, inspire through its richness French and English lawyers alike. To the extent that this travelling of ideas generates new thoughts and reflection it must be welcomed heartily. Indeed, in some areas we in England may even be ahead of the French (and the Germans) insofar as our supreme court is giving out some (faint but real) echoes of its broad mindedness by citing foreign law and even using it as persuasive authority.

Will there also be moves in our direction from the other side of the Channel? Many of the pressures forcing change upon the English are international. They may also usher changes into French law and society. French law may thus be forced to turn more of its attention toward the needs of practitioners. Unlike German law, it has, in its past, been well served by both sides of the profession so it should not fear such a shift. Moreover, when the practical world was in ascendancy in France, the differences between France and England were reduced. From a dogmatic point of view, it is regrettable that this observation has not received as much attention as 1 think it deserves and has instead been obscured by the principle-oriented, generalised, dogmatic features that academics always try to imprint on the law. The germanisation of French academic culture during the first quarter of the twentieth century may be understandable given its indisputable richness. But to the extent that it helped close further French minds toward the Anglo-Saxon legal worlds, it came with a high price.

But I also think that in the modern, finance-led world the importance of practice, finance, trade are things that the French will have to listen to more carefully than they have in the recent past. This is not only a matter of concern for politics and trade. It has, however, gone unnoticed by French academics or, at any rate, some have tried to pretend that the challenge is not there. For through funding research (as happens in applied sciences) the world of commerce, trade, and practice will have a growing impact on universities and their curriculum. By this I mean what they teach, who teaches it, how it is financed, and so on.

The spectrum that these ideas invokes must be frightening for most French lawyers accustomed to the supporting hand of the state even if it is accompanied by an asphyxiating regulatory regime and growing poverty in resources. But French law did not do badly in the past when practitioners where at the helm. They will do badly in the future if they do not see and respond to this challenge by adapting (not abandoning) some of their practices. It would be a shame if a great culture experienced a further decline in its international influence because it failed to adapt to the demands of a new world. Portalis is himself a living example of what happens with a man who, though attached to the world of yesterday, is also willing to be shaped by other worlds and thus gaze with confidence at the world of tomorrow. And the reason why some people are considered "classic" and most of the rest of us ephemeral is because the former can see ahead of their times and thus, through appropriate action, last longer. A comparative lawyer and even a legal historian must remain pure jurists; but they must also retain the common instinct for survival.

Chapter 3

Judicial Decision Making at the International Criminal Tribunal for Rwanda

Mations of the world are increasingly resorting to international law to adjudicate and resolve violent disputes and wars in places as diverse as the former Yugoslavia, Rwanda, Sierra Leone, East Timor, and Cambodia. The end of the Cold War, a heightened resolve to hold accountable brutal dictators who had acted with impunity because of an international reluctance to violate national sovereignty norms, and the success of the Rwandan and Yugoslav tribunals have led to greater demands for international justice and the enforcement of international humanitarian laws. This movement to provide international justice culminated in the establishment of the permanent International Criminal Court (ICC) to prosecute those suspected of violating international humanitarian laws. Whether one supports or opposes this increasing legalisation in international relations, it is an inescapable fact that international criminal and humanitarian law are becoming more codified and supplemented by a plethora of important judicial decisions coming from these international tribunals, and that the international machinery of justice is becoming increasingly institutionalised.

As the creation and utilisation of these international institutions continue, the demand for experienced international defence lawyers will also continue to grow. The international courts are developing a substantial base of expertise and personnel skilled in this fairly novel area of international law, and are supported by a significant commitment of resources from the international community. As reliance upon international law to adjudicate conflicts continues, this prosecutorial advantage in expertise and support can only grow as well.

But what of those charged with the defence of alleged war criminals? Are they equally as skilled and also provided with sufficient resources to defend their clients to ensure an equality of arms in the courtroom? Are some of these defence lawyers better prepared than others to defend their clients? Many critics charge that there is an inequality of arms between the relative experience of the prosecution and that of the defence. This preliminary analysis seeks a better understanding of this issue by exploring how defence experience and background might affect the outcome of international criminal trials.

The international criminal tribunals are unique hybrids of international law, common law practices, civil law practices, and their own rules of procedure and evidence that have often developed sut generis in response to the tribunals' own changing needs and circumstances. Therefore, we must wonder to what extent the background of defence attorneys influences their ability to argue successfully their clients' cases in these unique environments. Are lawyers skilled in the arts of courtroom argumentation belter able to defend their clients in the adversarial proceedings of the international tribunals? Are defence attorneys coming from nations whose judicial systems provide for greater judicial independence and fairer trials better able to adapt to the Western model of justice the tribunals rely upon? (an increasing the number of a defendant's attorneys help alleviate the advantages enjoyed by the prosecution in expertise, resources, and institutional memory?

This chapter focuses on the International Criminal Tribunal for Rwanda (ICTR), which despite the lack of attention accorded to it in comparison to the International Criminal Tribunal for the Former Yugoslavia (ICTY), has issued a number of important rulings and precedents in international law. The ICTR is also unique in the wide variety of defence attorneys who practice before it and hail from around the world. While defendants at the ICTY generally choose lawyers from the former Yugoslavia, defence attorneys at the ICTR have come from a variety of common law, civil law, customary law, and developed, developing, democratic, and non-democratic nations.

The chapter investigates what role defence attorney backgrounds play in the likelihood of obtaining a verdict or sentence favourable to their clients. It first discusses the procedures in place at the ICTR by which defendants select their counsel. It then analyses why the background of these lawyers and the number of lawyers a defendant retains might influence the verdicts and sentences handed down by the ICTR judges. Using data from the ICTR, the chapter then analyses these decisions and offers some preliminary assessments regarding the impact of the quantity and quality of defence attorneys on judicial decision making.

This is a preliminary inquiry. The ICTR continues to reach decisions that will need to be incorporated into future analyses. As well, this initial analysis relies principally on fairly simple statistical techniques. More rigorous conclusions must await the passage of time and more in-depth analyses through interviews with judges and attorneys on both sides.

Defence of the Accused

The ICTR, headquartered in Arusha, Tanzania, is authorised to prosecute persons accused of genocide, crimes against humanity, and violations of Article 3 common to the Geneva Conventions (on war crimes) and of Additional Protocol II. It can only hear cases relating to events that occurred in Rwanda during the calendar year 1994. Natural persons, including government officials, are liable for prosecution, even if they were acting under orders (Article 6.4 of the ICTR's charter). The ICTR has concurrent jurisdiction with national courts, but does have supremacy and so can request national courts to defer to its "competence" (Article 8.2).

The Tribunal is divided into three sections: the Registry, the Chambers, and the Prosecutor's Office. The Registry performs administrative duties for the Tribunals, such as language translation, witness protection, and public affairs. The Chambers comprise the judges who sit in three-judge panels and are elected by the UN General Assembly for four-year terms. The Prosecutor's Office manages the investigation of allegations of violations of international laws under the Tribunal's jurisdiction, develops indictments, and tries cases. Allegations of war crimes and other violations of international law are brought to the attention of the Office of the Prosecutor by staff, victims, the media, human rights organisations, and others.

The Prosecutor conducts investigations and, "shall assess the information received or obtained and decide whether there is sufficient basis to proceed" (Article 17.1). If so, an indictment is delivered to the Chambers where a judge evaluates whether the Prosecutor has established a prima facie case. If the accused is not able to afford counsel, the Tribunal will pay for the expense. The judgment of the Chambers is by majority vote, guilt must be proved beyond a reasonable doubt, and verdicts can be appealed. Life in prison is the maximum penalty; capital punishment is not permitted. According to the ICTR's

Charter, the judges shall consider in sentencing convicted war criminals, "the general practice regarding prison sentences in the courts of Rwanda . . . the gravity of the offence and the individual circumstances of the convicted person" (Article 23).

Part 4, Section 2 of the ICTR's Rules of Procedure and Evidence describes the process of appointment of defence counsel to those who have been brought into custody at the ICTR's detention facility in Arusha. While there are other provisions of the Rules of Procedure and Evidence that bear on issues related to defence, such as the required disclosure of evidence, this chapter is limited to examining those procedures pertaining to assignment of defence counsel.

The qualifications for practicing before the ICTR are actually quite few. An attorney only need demonstrate that she is allowed to practice law in her home country, or is a university professor of law (Rule 44) and can speak one of the two working languages of the Tribunal (English or French [Rule 44 bis]). For indigent defendants, the Registrar keeps a list of counsel who 1) qualify to practice before the ICTR as in Rule 44; 2) have indicated their willingness to accept assignment; and 3) who have at least 10 years relevant experience. Defendants must demonstrate their indigence to the Registrar's Office, which then selects attorneys for them from this list. In practice most defendants plead indigence. Defendants are entitled to one attorney, but in many cases they have also been allowed to hire additional counsel, as well as legal and investigative assistance. The Registrar also determines the payment schedule for these attorneys. Defence Counsel are subject to a code of ethics developed by the Registrar's Office.

We are interested in the extent to which the legal and national background of defence attorneys and their level of experience at the ICTR will affect the likelihood of obtaining successful judicial outcomes-either not guilty verdicts or lighter sentences for their clients. The hypotheses are tentative since very little theoretical work has been done on this subject. First, we are interested in determining if defence lawyers from particular legal systems enjoy any advantages in obtaining favourable verdicts and sentences for their clients. Perhaps the argumentative abilities of lawyers from common law backgrounds aid in their ability to influence the judges, or perhaps civil law lawyers are more adept at the compilation of large amounts of evidence that judges evaluate for its probative value.

As civil law judges are involved in significant amounts of investigating and weighing evidence to arrive at the truth-a trait shared by judges at the ICTR-civil law defence attorneys may enjoy greater success. On the other hand, the intermingling of these two systems within the ICTR places a distinct disadvantage on outsiders who have only trained within the confines of one of these two dominant legal systems. This effect tends to be negated within the institutional structure of the ICTR Office of the Prosecutor where actors can draw on a wealth of experience from colleagues from multiple legal traditions, and who tend to participate in multiple trials while at the ICTR. However, defence attorneys tend to work on one or two person teams where both attorneys may be from the same legal background, and where prior trial experience at the ICTR may be lacking. In theory the advantage of experience in multiple legal backgrounds enjoyed by the Prosecution ought to hinder those defence teams that are not similarly intermixed.

We used the ICTR website to determine the names of the attorneys, and for most, their country of origin. In the few cases where country of origin could not be determined on the ICTR web site, we relied on web searches using the individual's name and title. Once we ascertained national background, we used information from the University of Ottawa's "World Legal Systems" web site to identify national legal system as 1) common law; 2) civil law; 3) customary law3; 4) Islamic law.4 We created a series of dichotomous variables to measure each defence attorney's background. In cases where attorneys hailed from nations with multiple legal systems, we measured each type of system represented.

Judicial systems are characterised not just by the label we can apply to the legal structure, but also by the extent to which they provide for the rule of law in practice as well as in theory. Nations that value the rule of law provide for a transparent, efficient, and fair set of judicial institutions and procedures. Criminal and civil disputes are resolved within the system instead of extra-legally, while judges and courts are granted independence from politics. International criminal tribunals, like the ICTR, have largely copied these sorts of protections and rights from domestic systems. Thus, defence lawyers who have practiced in judicial systems where judges are independent decision makers and defendants are accorded fair trials may be better placed to defend their clients at the ICTR. Conversely, those defence attorneys hailing from nations without such protections where judges are subject to political pressure and where plaintiffs' rights are infringed upon to safeguard governmental interests-may be disadvantaged in the alien environment of the ICTR.

We use two indicators to measure judicial independence and fair trial protections from Linda Keith. Ranging from 0-16, the Keith measure of judicial independence considers judicial review, tenure in office, and ability to adjust compensation, among a variety of factors that tend to increase the independence of judges. Keith analysed constitutions from nations around the world to make these determinations. Each indicator of judicial independence ranges from "0" where there are no such guarantees; "1" where there are qualified guarantees; and "2" where a nation has fully guaranteed a specific element of judicial independence in the constitution. The scores are summed to create a 16-point scale indicating a regime's degree of judicial independence. Her variable measuring fair trial protections is a similarly constructed scale that ranges from "0" where there are no fair trial protections; "1" where there are qualified protections; and "2" where a nation has full, fair trial protections.

The level of democracy and protection of civil liberties in a society is also likely to have a profound impact on the professionalisation of defence attorneys. Attorneys who practice in a political culture where the people freely choose governments and their freedoms are protected may be at an advantage in international criminal tribunals. If the freedoms their nations afford them provide for broader and deeper experiences in the judicial system, they ought to be more skilled than attorneys who come from nations where such opportunities are limited. To measure these variables we use the Freedom House indicators of nations' political rights and civil liberties. Quoting from the Freedom House web site: "Political rights enable people to participate freely in the political process. This includes the right to vote and compete for public office and to elect representatives who have a decisive vote on public policies. Civil liberties include the freedom to develop opinions, institutions, and personal autonomy without interference from the state." Each measure ranges from "1" to "7" where "1" represents the most favourable conditions for political rights and civil liberties, and "7" the least favourable.

Yet, we must allow that it is quite possible these national background characteristics will have no impact on decision making by the judges at the ICTR. If defence lawyers are more nearly a product of an internau'onal legal culture rather than a domestic one, national differences may lose their influence as lawyers gain exposure to this culture. If what matters most is the professionalisation that occurs within this community, the differences that might have existed between attorneys because of their previous background may have already diminished considerably by the time they practice before the ICTR. Rather, their individual skill and the pool of resources available to them may be more consequential.

Some ICTR critics have asserted that the, "tribunals are resource biased in favour of the prosecution." As noted in the Harvard Law Review. In the absence of uniformly effective representation, even a robustly prodefendant statutory and regulatory framework would tend to result in an uneven prosecutorial record, prejudicing defendants whose attorneys do not effectively litigate their claims and simultaneously privileging other defendants of equal culpability who can afford, or are fortunate enough to be provided with more effective attorneys.

Typically at the ICTR the defence team consists of two lawyers who rarely have served on a previous defence team, while the prosecution typically is made up of three or more "repeat players" who have served on multiple prosecution teams. The potency of the Office of the Prosecutors' mandate, coupled with these perceived differences in prosecution and defence team experience, may create an "inequality of arms."

Analogously, research on U.S. courts has shown that repeat players enjoy a number of advantages that enhances their ability to win favourable outcomes.10 Such actors (e.g., "upperdogs") are often more likely to win in court because they possess greater resources, expertise in the legal process, and familiarity with the judicial system. This description might well apply to prosecution attorneys at the ICTR.

In order to determine if the number of prosecution lawyers and their assumed greater levels of experience at the ICTR have any bearing on judges' verdicts and sentences, we gathered data on the number and experience of lawyers from each side. First, we determine how many lawyers for each team participated in a completed case at the ICTR from the final indictment located at the ICTR website. Each case is then assigned a numeric total for the number of prosecutors and the number of defence lawyers. Second, we track the total amount of experience that individual lawyers bring to each team.

Each lawyer's name, from all completed cases, is catalogued and tracked in order to observe in how many previous cases she or he has participated. Based on the date located on the final indictment, we count the number of cases argued by these attorneys previously (and including the current case).

Analysis

To better understand how the background of defence attorneys affects verdicts and sentences, we make a preliminary assessment of these relationships on the various counts on which defendants have been charged. Although the ICTR judges have issued a number of verdicts, their work still continues. Thus, results are preliminary and conclusions tentative at this point. Verdicts are either decisions of "guilty" or "not guilty" (we code verdicts the judges dismissed as not guilty) issued on each individual count on which an individual is charged and judged. We measure sentences as either life (coded "1"), or not life (coded ("0").

Since January, 2005, 20 defendants have been tried before the ICTR while three individuals have entered guilty pleas prior to a trial. Only three individuals who have stood trial have been found innocent of all charges. Individuals have been cumulatively charged with 197 counts of violations of international law and have pled or been found guilty on a total of 82 (42 percent). They have been found guilty of 38 out of 77 counts of genocide (49 percent) and 43 out of 85 charges of crimes against humanity (51 percent). Thus, although most defendants have been found guilty of at least one charge, they are also often found innocent of other charges. If we leave out cases where individuals pled guilty, we see that there have been 185 counts on which defendants were tried. They were found guilty on 70 out of 185 charges (38 percent). They have been found guilty of 32 out of 71 counts of genocide (45 percent) and 37 out of 79 charges of crimes against humanity (47 percent).

Of those 20 individuals who have been found guilty of at least one count of genocide or crimes against humanity, 11 have received a life sentence on at least one or more counts. Sometimes judges impose one global sentence on a defendant; in other cases they provide separate punishments for each guilty count. Those individuals who did not receive a life sentence have been sentenced on average to 244 months in prison for the various counts on which they were found guilty. The minimum sentence on a guilty count has been 84 months in prison, while the longest non-life sentence has been 420 months.

Of the 38 convictions on charges of genocide, defendants have been given a life sentence on 24 of those counts (63 percent). Those who did not receive a life sentence for a particular count were punished with sentences ranging from 120-420 months. Of the 43 convictions on charges of crimes against humanity, defendants have been given a life sentence on 18 of those counts (42 percent). Those who did not receive a life sentence for a particular count were punished with sentences ranging from 84-420 months.

Excluded from the analysis of verdicts are those cases where the defendant pled guilty and there was no trial (those results are in the first two columns), and thus we analyse the verdicts in the cases of 20 individuals. In the second set of columns where we examine the relationships between our variables of interest and sentences, we look at the punishments handed down to all individuals who have pled or been found guilty (20 individuals). We exclude from this set of correlations those cases where the defendants were found innocent of all charges and add those cases where the defendants pled guilty. We calculated correlation coefficients between our two dependent variables and all of our measures of defence attorney background and the number and experience of lawyers from both the prosecution and defence. We distinguish between the first and second listed attorneys of record for those instances where an individual is represented by more than one attorney. We note, however, that the order in which attorneys are listed in ICTR cases does not necessarily always have any substantive implications.

We begin by analysing the relationship between the legal background from which defence attorneys hail and its impact on their ability to obtain not guilty verdicts and lighter sentences. The national legal background of the first listed attorney of record-civil law, common law, Islamic law, or customary law-does not appear to make a difference in the likelihood of obtaining a not guilty verdict. However, when we analyse the relationship between the backgrounds of the second attorney of record (assuming there is one), we find that common law lawyers tend to fare poorly. The correlation between this background type and the likelihood of the lawyer's client receiving a guilty verdict is positive common law lawyers do not fare as well. In contrast, when the second attorney comes from an Islamic law background, there is a negative relationship, which indicates they are more likely to obtain not guilty verdicts. We would point out, however, that the perfect record attorneys from Islamic law societies have in obtaining not guilty verdicts is due to the outcomes in only one case of seven counts.

The results are more interesting when we look at the impact of national legal background on the ability of the attorney to obtain a sentence of less than life imprisonment. We find that given the data available, first attorneys of record coming from customary law backgrounds are best able to obtain lighter penalties for their clients. The correlation coefficient for this variable is negative and statistically significant. None of the other measures for common law, civil law, or Islamic law attorneys exercised any meaningful and statistically significant impact. The same results are obtained when we look at the legal background of second attorneys. Lawyers whose origins are in customary law countries seem to do a better job at helping their clients escape life imprisonment.

Thus, despite our expectation that attorneys from the dominant legal cultures in the world might perform better, it appears that it is customary law background that better predicts success. While we cannot offer any more than speculation regarding this finding, it may be that since many of these customary law lawyers are from African nations, which is where many of the ICTR judges hail from as well, that they are better versed in developing arguments that appeal to the trial chambers. Future research will need to pay much closer attention to these findings.

It should be reassuring, however, that experience in one of the two predominant legal cultures of the world does not guarantee an especially advantageous advocacy at the ICTR. For if some experts are concerned this tribunal, and perhaps others, are biased in favour of common or civil law experience, the limited evidence here suggests that such concerns may not be warranted. Still, it is possible that the international tribunals are developing their own hybrid systems that utilise best practices or best-suited practices from all the world's legal cultures. If this is the case then it may be that professional background in just one legal system is not sufficient. Perhaps the best defence combines talent from both civil, common law, and other systems.

Mixed Teams

To investigate this possibility we created several new measures of mixed teams of defence lawyers. The first "mixed team" variable we created measures the presence of a common law lawyer and a civil law lawyer on the defence team. Again, our results are somewhat counter intuitive We find that such teams were statistically more likely to obtain guilty verdicts, but that such combinations improved the likelihood of the client receiving less than a life sentence. The correlation coefficient for the first relationship is .17 ($p. < .01$); while for the second it is -.24 ($p. < .05$). We also created two other mixed team variables where we combined common and civil law attorneys with customary law defence lawyers. When the team consists of a civil law attorney and a customary law attorney, the correlation with verdicts is .10 (p. > .10) and statistically insignificant, while the correlation between such teams and the likelihood of obtaining a life sentence is -.29 (p. <.01). When the team consists of a common law lawyer and a customary law lawyer the respective correlations with verdicts and sentences are .13 (p > .05) and -.42 (p. < .001). These tentative findings seem to suggest that while mixed teams fare no better than homogenous teams when it comes to verdicts, mixed teams appear to perform decidedly better than others in obtaining lighter sentences for their clients.

Additional Results

Some of the more unusual results concern the relationship between the extent of political rights and civil liberties in the defence attorneys' home nations and the decisions of the judges. We should note that the political rights and civil liberties variables are scaled from 1 - 7, where "1" represents the most political rights and civil liberties and "7" represents the least such rights.

First, we see that attorneys from states with the most political rights and civil liberties appear to be better able to obtain not guilty verdicts for their clients. But, second, we see that those lawyers coming from the least democratic states with the fewest civil liberties are better able to protect their clients from life sentences. Could it be that lawyers from democratic states perform better in the somewhat more objective determination of their client's liability because of their greater skill at advocacy in a transparent and fact-based judicial system (as opposed to the more politicized judicial systems one is apt to find in undemocratic nations)? Defence attorneys from undemocratic states may be advantaged in the more subjective determination of punishment because their advocacy skills are more oriented toward appeals to political judgment rather than objective fact. At this point, we only have such speculation to offer. We also find no evidence to suggest that attorneys from states with more judicial independence or fair trial protections are better able to secure not guilty verdicts or lighter sentences for their clients.

Next, we see that neither the number of prosecution or defence attorneys, nor their previous ICTR experience, exercises a statistically significant impact on guilty verdicts. After a guilty verdict is obtained, however, the number of prosecution lawyers does have a statistically significant and positive effect on the probability that the Tribunal issues a life sentence. The total experience of the prosecution team demonstrates no statistically significant relationship when measured against the probability of a life sentence. The total experience of the defence team is positively related to the probability of a life sentence. Perhaps individuals with the most difficult cases to defend seek more defence counsel, albeit to no avail as ultimately the ICTR punishes them severely regardless.

Generally, the advantages the ICTR prosecution teams are perceived to enjoy in their depth of experience and resources do not apparently translate into greater success in the courtroom. Still, these findings are only tentative and obviously do not even begin to get at such issues as the quality of the counsel, the level of effort put forth, and other intangible factors.

Our findings provide some preliminary, yet unique insights into the relative success of defence attorneys at the International Criminal Tribunal for Rwanda. In the data collected to date, the type of national background these lawyers come from plays an important, though limited, role in their abilities to obtain not guilty verdicts and sentences less than life for their clients. Those teams of defence attorneys that appear to enjoy the greatest success at the ICTR consist of at least one lawyer from a customary law nation. Further investigation is needed to better understand what kind of skill set customary law lawyers are bringing to the Tribunal and whether such skills can be gained by lawyers from other national, legal backgrounds.

We also note that the extent of protections for political rights and civil liberties in defence lawyers' home states appears to play an important, if not always expected, role in judicial decision making. Those from the most politically free nations appear to do a better job of obtaining not guilty verdicts, while those from more authoritarian governments with fewer freedoms seem to do better in obtaining lighter sentences for their clients. This finding too requires further examination, principally through a more multivariate analysis where we can also examine the impact of other factors on sentencing decisions, such as the severity of the crimes committed and the guilty party's level of power in the genocidal regime in Rwanda at the time.

As the world increasingly moves toward the prosecution of those who violate international humanitarian law, it also becomes increasingly important that steps be taken to ensure the adjudicatory process is as fair and impartial as possible. Noticeable in this regard is the creation of a unit within the International Criminal Court for issues pertaining to defence counsel. As well, an International Criminal

Bar now represents the interests of defence lawyers that practice before the ICC. As the work of the ICC begins in earnest, the efforts of this association and the ICC's personnel involved in defence issues will be critical in maintaining a substantial body of defence lawyers trained and experienced in international humanitarian law. This, in turn, is critical for the legitimacy of the ICC and ultimately the success of international criminal law in holding accountable those who violate its tenets.

Chapter 4

Remaking of the Iraqi Legal System

One of the U.S. administration's main goals since overthrowing the Saddam Hussein regime has been the adoption of a new Iraqi constitution-befitting a new, democratic Iraq. The United States initially announced that it would turn over control to an Iraqi government only after the adoption of a permanent constitution and the conclusion of free and fair elections pursuant to that constitution. To assist with the administration of Iraq, on July 15, 2003, the United States-in the form of the Coalition Provisional Authority (CPA)-appointed a twenty-five member Iraqi Governing Council, whose "most important task was to organise a constitutional convention to write a new, permanent Iraqi constitution," after which the CPA would "return legal sovereignty to a government elected under the new constitution." The Governing Council was scheduled to announce a timeline for the constitutional process by December 15, 2003, with the United States aiming for the new constitution to be completed within six months thereafter.

By the fall of 2003, with the Governing Council unable to produce a timetable, the CPA concluded that this schedule was unworkable and that a constitutional process would require much more time than the United States had planned for the occupation of Iraq. On November 15, 2003, the CPA announced an alternative plan in the Agreement on Political Process: it would abandon the position that a permanent constitution is a necessary precondition to Iraqi sovereignty, and instead transfer sovereignty to an Iraqi Interim Government (Interim Government) on June 30, 2004. The Interim Government would operate under a transitional law, subsequently adopted on March 8, 2004, called the Law of Administration for the State of Iraq for the Transitional Period (Interim Constitution). According to the Interim Constitution, by the end of 2004 the Interim Government will have held elections for a National Assembly, one of whose functions will be both to draft a permanent constitution, and then to present it to a national referendum. If the people of Iraq adopt the proposed constitution by October 15, 2005, elections would then take place pursuant to it by December 15, 2005, to form a new permanent Iraqi government by December 31, 2005.

In order to consider the new Iraq successfully launched, the United States wanted Iraq to adopt a new constitution quicklywhile still incorporating all of the freedoms, rights, and guarantees of a democratic nation. This fast-track state was to be the first true democracy in the Arab world, with the new constitution as its hallmark. One major area of American concern for the new constitution, however, was the role of Islam. The United States warned that it would not tolerate an Iranian-style theocracy in Iraq, preferring instead a Turkish-style "Islamic democracy" as a model for Iraq.

These U.S. ambitions and concerns evince a simplistic understanding of the role of Islamic law in Iraq's current legal system and what role Islamic law might play in a remaking of that system. First, Iraq is unlikely to be guided by the example of either Iran or Turkey. Among nations with predominantly Muslim populations, Iran and Turkey represent the two opposite ends of the spectrum of possible state structures: Islamic law is the supreme law of the land in Iran, where a council of clerics routinely invalidates legislation adopted by the elected Parliament on the grounds that it contradicts the clerics' interpretation of Islamic law, while the Turkish state is so ideologically secular that some expressions of religion protected even in the United States are illegal in Turkey. The Iraqi population's diverse political, religious, and ethnic affiliations suggest that agreement will come only through negotiation and compromise among many different views, making the prevalence of any one extreme view on the role of Islamic law in the new Iraq unlikely.

Second, constitutional drafting will probably not establish precisely the role of Islamic law in the new Iraqi legal system. Since no evidence suggests that Iraq will adopt language such as in the Turkish constitution or an Iranian model, Islamic law provisions at the constitutional level can be expected to be general and open to substantial interpretation-the Islamic law provisions in the Interim Constitution already display this kind of vagueness. The experience of countries that have sought to incorporate Islamic law in their constitutions in some moderate way, such as Egypt, corroborates that generalised provisions in Iraq's Interim Constitution or the future permanent constitution regarding Islamic law will need extensive subsequent interpretation before their precise implications can be known. This Chapter addresses these two areas in depth-the role of Islamic law in the Iraqi legal system, and how the new constitution may deal with this question-and analyses, based on Iraq's history, current situation, and the experience of other similarly situated countries, how Islamic law may be retained or incorporated into the new Iraqi legal system.

This Chapter argues that the significant debates over Islamic law in Iraq have been and can be expected to continue to be played out at the substantive-law level, where the influence of Islamic law has been most tangibly felt. Since the significance of Islamic law provisions at the constitutional level can be understood only in conjunction with such relevant substantive laws (for example, family law), debates over constitutional wording must be seen as part of a larger framework of the role of Islamic law in the Iraqi legal system generally.

This Chapter discusses recent legal developments in Iraq and what they indicate about possible roles for Islamic law in the new legal system. Although the Governing Council has now been dissolved, it did make many official decisions during the period of its effectiveness as the principal Iraqi administrative body, and its former formal positions and expressions, along with the opinions of its former members, are still good indicators of some viewpoints held by the Iraqi people. This Part also surveys recent opinion polls from Iraq, paying particular attention to responses to questions about the desired role of Islamic law in the new legal system.

It addresses the cases of Turkey and Iran and the role of Islamic law in their legal systems, showing why neither is an appropriate model of governance for the new Iraq. Holding Turkey and Iran up as good and bad examples, respectively, only obscures issues Iraq actually faces. It identifies Egypt as a country that has historically incorporated Islamic law in ways similar to Iraq, and whose experience therefore provides a useful comparative tool to shed light on Iraq's current legal situation and the shape it may take in the future. For example, Egypt has incorporated reference to Islamic law in its constitution, and therefore the Egyptian Supreme Constitutional Court's construction of this language may offer a sense of what similar wording might mean in the Iraqi context. Already, the Iraqi Interim Constitution tracks some of the language from the Egyptian constitution. This Part also discusses the role of Islamic law in Egypt's civil code and personal status laws, where Islamic law has had its most palpable effects.

It considers possible interpretations of the Islamic law-related provisions in Iraq's Interim Constitution, and then discusses implications for the drafting of the permanent constitution. As in Egypt, in Iraq Islamic law has influenced the civil code and family law-both areas where the debate over Islamic law has been, and can be expected to remain, most heated. As an illustration: a recent low-profile resolution of the Iraqi Governing Council regarding family law has already shown that in the midst of high-profile constitutional planning, the crucial battles over Islamic law are already taking place in the context of specific laws.

Recent Developments in Iraq

During its tenure the Iraqi Governing Council adopted two significant pieces of legislation that raise Islamic law issues: the Interim Constitution, and Governing Council Resolution 137 (the Family Law Resolution). An Interim Government assumed sovereignty for Iraq from the CPA on June 28, 2004, two days earlier than planned, but as of the time this Chapter went to press, had taken few decisions of its own. The Governing Council's legacy with regard to Islamic law remains the significant source of decisionmaking in this regard. As background, this Part first describes the composition and function of the Governing Council and discusses recent opinion polls in Iraq on the role of Islamic law in the new legal system. This Part then turns to the specific details of the Interim Constitution and the Family Law Resolution, pointing out what these documents imply for future legal developments in Iraq. This Chapter will ultimately revisit these two items in Part FV for further historical and comparative analysis.

Governing Council

On July 13, 2003, the U.S. administration in Iraq appointed twenty-five Iraqis to form a Governing Council "as the principal body of the Iraqi interim administration, pending the establishment of an internationally recognised, representative government by the people of Iraq . . . ." The Governing Council had the right to issue decisions in areas of national policy, but they required the approval of the CPA to go into force.

The CPA appointed the individuals to the Governing Council intending that they would represent Iraq's ethnic and religious composition in a roughly proportional way.' Iraq's population of twenty-four million is believed to consist of sixty percent Shi'ite Muslims, thirty-two to thirty-seven percent Sunni Muslims, three percent Christian, and less than one percent Jewish and Yezdi. Ethnically, about seventy-five to eighty percent of the population are Arab, fifteen to twenty percent are Kurds, and less than five percent are Turkomans, Chaldeans, or Assyrians. Men make up slightly more than half of the population.

The composition of the Governing Council indicates some of the diversity within Iraq, although, as discussed below, some powerful points of view were not included. When first appointed, the Governing Council consisted of fourteen Shi'ites, nine Sunnis (five of whom are Kurds), a Christian, and a Turkoman. Three members were women, one of whom, Dr. Akila al-Hashimi, a Shi'ite, was fatally attacked and died on September 25, 2003. One observer's visual description of the Governing Council-at its first meeting with U.S., U.K., and U.N. officials-reads: "2 members wore the black turbans of Shiite Islamic clerics descended from the Prophet Muhammad and 2 wore the flowing robes and headdresses of tribal sheiks. Three women were among them, two in head scarves and one without. The rest, men of various political stripes, wore business suits."

Shi'ites formed a majority on the Governing Council, and while they have united on certain issues, they were in fact a diverse group. Four of the Shi'ites are religious leaders. Ibrahim al-Ja'fari is the spokesman of al-Da'wa (the Call), a group that formed in the 1950s in Iraq with the religious scholar Muhammad Baqir alSadr at its centre. This group went underground in 1980 when Saddam Hussein made membership in it punishable by death and then ordered the execution of Baqir al-Sadr and his sister, Bint alHuda. The late 'Izz al-Din Salim, who was assassinated in Baghdad on May 17, 2004, while serving as the Governing Council's rotating president, served as the head of that same group until his death.

Muhammad Bahr al-'Ulum, an elderly Shi'ite cleric, fled Iraq following the rise of the Ba'th party and, after time in Iran and Egypt, eventually arrived in London, where he established the charitable organisation AhI al-Bayt. Born in Iraq in 1927 to a learned family, Bahr al-'Ulum became a leading religious scholar in Najaf and collaborated with Ayatollah Muhsin al-Hakim, who was the most authoritative clergy member at the time. One of Bahr al-'Ulum's early publications on the role of Islamic law in Iraq is discussed.

The Supreme Council for the Islamic Revolution in Iraq (SCIRI) was represented on the Governing Council by Abd al-'Aziz alHakim, who is second in the group's hierarchy and the brother of its late leader, Muhammad Baqir al-Hakim. SCIRI was formed in 1982 in Iran by Iraqi Shi'ite leaders who fled due to growing oppression from the Iraqi regime. SCIRI was heavily patronized by the Iranian government, and this, along with al-Hakim's seeming willingness to support the structure of the Islamic state in Iran, has made other Shi'ite organisations such as al-Da'wa wary of SCIRTs intentions.

Shi'ite Governing Council members also included Hamid Majid Musa, secretary of the Iraqi Communist Party (ICP). The ICP was alternately courted and oppressed by the government depending on larger political concerns, such as the extent of Iraq's need for the support of the Soviet Union at any given moment. The ICP formally severed ties with the Iraqi regime in 1979, by which time most of its senior leaders had already fled the country. Ahmad Chalabi, the head of the Iraqi National Congress (INC), was also one of the fourteen Shi'ites. He founded the INC in 1992 and had long been favoured by the Pentagon, although he has recently severed ties with the CPA and the Pentagon ceased its monthly payments to the INC over accusations that Chalabi misled the CIA and betrayed U.S. secrets to Iran. Raja Habib al-Khuza'i, who was a Shi'ite Council member, runs a maternity hospital in southern Iraq. She studied and lived in Britain in the 1960s and 1970s and returned to Iraq in 1977. Another exiled doctor, Dr. Iyad Allawi, had fled to Britain after a conflict with Saddam Hussein and became a surgeon in London. Ahmad al-Barak is a Shi'ite and general coordinator for the Human Rights Association of Babel.

The two main Kurdish groups were represented by Masud Barzani of the Kurdistan Democratic Party (KDP) and Jalal Talabani of the Patriotic Union of Kurdistan (PUK). Salah al-Din Baha' al-Din comes from the newer Kurdistan Islamic Union, which has ties to the Muslim Brotherhood. The less prominent Kurdish Socialist Party, which had been operating from London, was represented on the Governing Council by Mahmud 'Uthman. Iraqi Court of Appeals Judge Dara Nur al-Din is also Kurdish. These five members are Sunnis, as are a great majority of Kurds, although they are typically identified as Kurds rather than Sunnis for purposes of discussing Iraq's interest groups generally, or the composition of the Governing Council specifically.

There were also four non-Kurdish Sunni members on the Governing Council. Nasir al-Chadirchi is the leader of the National Democratic Party (NDP). His father had formed the NDP in the monarchical period to advocate "social democracy and political reform by parliamentary means," but it was suppressed in the early years of the republic. Adnan Pachachi was foreign minister of Iraq from 1965-1967 and formed the Union of Independent Democrats. Shaykh Ghazi al-Yawar is a civil engineer and head of a tribe in northern Iraq. Finally, Muhsin 'Abd al-'Aziz is the secretary General of the Iraqi Islamic Party, which is the Iraqi branch of the Muslim Brotherhood. Songul Chapouk is from Kirkuk and from the Iraqi Turkomen community. The Assyrian representative was Yonnadam Kanna, of the Assyrian Democratic Movement.

Although the CPA designed the Governing Council to represent the range of diversity of Iraqis, it soon became clear that other viewpoints were left out. One of the most significant alternative voices to emerge was that of the most prominent Shi'ite cleric, Grand Ayatollah Ali Sistani. His insistence that the constitutional drafters be chosen in general nationwide elections has been credited with pushing the United States to adopt the alternative plan announced as the Agreement on Political Process on November 15, 2003. Others outside of the Governing Council framework, such as the young Muqtada al-Sadr, have been extremely vocal and active-though not participating directly in the constitutional process.

Opinion Polls

Opinion polls conducted in Iraq since the overthrow of Saddam Hussein reveal a broad range of opinions among Iraqis about the role of Islam and Islamic law in their new state structure, although opinion polls in Iraq must be used with some degree of skepticism. The Department of State Office of Research, in coordination with the Iraq Central Statistics Office and the Iraq Centre for Research and Strategic Studies, conducted interviews in the cities of Baghdad, Falluja, Ramadi, Basra, Najaf, Suleymania, and Erbil in the late summer of 2003 (these cities are indicated on the map below). The final report, issued on October 21, 2003, is based on 1444 interviews in these cities. Interviewees were asked to choose their preferred political system for Iraq from the options of "democracy," "mix of democracy and Islam," and an "Islamic state." The categories are problematic because, as discussed below, the terms "Islamic state," and "unique mix of democracy and Islam" are too broad to capture any specific meaning. Furthermore, it is not clear why the category of "democracy" excludes Islam. Nevertheless, the responses-which varied widely by geographic location-are a rough indicator of general views. In Erbil, in the north, sixty-six percent preferred a "democracy," and only five percent preferred an "Islamic state." In the holy city of Najaf, ninety-two percent preferred an "Islamic state" with just four percent supporting a "democracy."

These results are significant because they demonstrate the diverse conceptions among Iraqis of the appropriate role for Islamic law, indicating that there is no unified Iraqi vision for the role of Islamic law in the new state's legal framework.

Interim Constitution

On March 8, 2004, the Governing Council adopted the Interim Constitution as the fundamental law for Iraq, effective from the transfer of power to an Interim Government supposed to have taken place on June 30, 2004, until the election and formation of an Iraqi government pursuant to a new constitution (the Transitional Period). The Interim Constitution's drafting process was opaque, but the general understanding is that the Interim Constitution was composed by a small committee in consultation with the CPA and Governing Council. According to Nathan Brown, the Iraqi Governing Council:

> *Did not take up the constitutional draft as a body until February 2004, but some of its members have been active in drafting documents for the full body to consider. The first draft seems to have been circulated by Kurdish parties; in response, a second draft was circulated, apparently under the sponsorship of Council member Adnan Pachachi.*

It seems to have been the Pachachi-sponsored document-which was substantially the same as the Interim Constitution-that was published in the Kuwaiti daily paper al-Qabas on February 1, 2004 (the Pachachi Draft). This draft document and the Interim Constitution eventually adopted did not differ in substantial ways. Particular variations pertaining to Islamic law-related provisions are noted in the discussion of the Interim Constitution.

The adoption process of the Interim Constitution proved difficult. The Governing Council first attempted to sign the document on March 5, 2004, but was delayed by some Council members' objections to aspects of its content, thus pushing the signing ceremony forward to March 8, 2004. While the adoption was unanimous, "the celebratory mood was dampened by calls from the country's most powerful Shiite leaders to amend the new charter before it goes into force." Governing Council member Ibrahim al-Ja'fari, stating that he spoke on behalf of twelve of the thirteen Shi'ite members, announced that they "had endorsed the Interim Constitution in order to preserve the unity of the country" but that the Shi'ite leaders would seek to amend parts of it before its effective date of June 30, 2004, which they were not able to accomplish.

One of the Shi'ite leaders' main objections is to the process by which the future constitution is to be ratified: The Interim Constitution provides that it must be accepted by a majority of Iraqis, while also providing that opposition by two-thirds of the voters in three governorates (that is, provinces) can defeat it. The Shi'ite concern is that since three of the governorates are predominately Kurdish, this provision gives the Kurds veto power. Ayatollah Sistani reiterated this criticism of the ratification process-explaining that by giving any religious or political group with some measure of authority the ability to defeat the entire constitution, the process allows such a minority group to force the adoption of a constitutional provision that the majority of Iraqis would otherwise oppose. The Shi'ite Governing Council members also objected to the provision that amendments to the Interim Constitution may be made only by the future National Assembly, which is to be elected by the end of 2004. The Interim Constitution does not provide for an amendment mechanism prior to that time. The Interim Constitution provides that a new government is to be formed no later than December 31, 2005, at which time the Interim Constitution will expire, although there are some provisions for extensions.

The Interim Constitution contains several provisions relevant to the issue of Islamic law. These provisions-and reactions to them-are instructive, even though the drafting and adoption of the Interim Constitution included only a small, unelected group of Iraqis. Article 7 of the Interim Constitution is the most significant in this regard:

> *Islam is the official religion of the State and is considered a source of legislation (masdar li'l-tashri'). No law that contradicts the universally agreed upon immutable/unchanging tenets of Islam (thawabit al-Islam al-mujma' 'alayha), the principles of democracy, or the rights cited in Chapter Two of this Law may be enacted during this Transitional Period. This Law respects the Islamic identity (al-huwiya al-Islamiya) of the majority of the Iraqi people and guarantees the full religious rights of all individuals to freedom of religious belief and practice.*

Such language, which invokes Islam as a source of law, is not new in countries with Muslim populations-rather, it echoes constitutional language from Iraq's own history as well as that of other Arab countries. The two most prominent issues that Article 7 raises are the recognition of Islam as a source of legislation, and the prohibition against adopting laws in the Interim Period that contradict the universally agreed upon immutable tenets of Islam. These two issues are discussed more fully and FV, within the contexts of Egypt and Iraq, respectively.

The Family Law Resolution

On December 29, 2003, The Governing Council, by a narrow majority, adopted a resolution that would apply the Islamic Sharia to all matters of family law in Iraq-including marriage, divorce, custody, wills, and inheritance-according to the individual's specific religious affiliation within Islam. The resolution also declared invalid all previous laws, decisions, and directions regarding family law that contravene Islamic law. The Governing Council subsequently withdrew it, however, when Ambassador L. Paul Bremer, III, the chief U.S. administrator in Iraq, did not approve the resolution in order for it to go into effect.

It is unsurprising-and even predictable-that family law was the first area in which attempts were made to abrogate existing laws and turn to a heritage of Islamic law. This resolution now stands as only the latest in a series of controversial enactments in Iraq regarding matters of family law. And while the Family Law Resolution did not go into effect, Iraqis critical of it have expressed concern that the views it represents predominate within the country.

From the Edges: Turkey and Iran

This Part explains why Turkey and Iran are both inapposite models for the new Iraq, since they each represent outlying examples of the possible ways Islamic law has been incorporated into legal systems of countries with predominately Muslim populations.

Turkey

Turkey is often called an "Islamic democracy" without any attention to the precise meaning of this phrase. The vast majority of Turkey's citizens are Muslim, and officials are elected through a democratic process, but there is nothing particularly or uniquely Islamic about Turkey's democracy. In fact, religion is constitutionally prohibited from playing any role in state life. The possible results of Turkey's democratic process are bounded by strict rules against any religiously-oriented proposals or policies, the result being that Turkey's political system is, in fact, more secular than a secular democracy such as the United States.

The state of Turkey was born out of the collapse of the Ottoman Empire following World War I. General Mustafa Kemal was the leading military figure during the war, and he went on to declare the formation of the new Republic of Turkey and the promulgation of its new constitution on October 29, 1923. Mustafa Kemal, who became known as Ataturk, "father of the Turks," expressed his policies in terms of six principles: republicanism, nationalism, secularism, statism, populism, and revolutionism.

Secularism was one of the most important of these principles, and all signs of Islam's political role from the era of the Ottoman sultanate were erased. Religious officials and courts were abolished, and laws based on Islam were abandoned in favour of laws derived from the Swiss civil code. In 1928 a constitutional amendment removed the provision in the 1923 constitution that identified Islam as the religion of the state. Islam was reduced to personal belief, but even in this regard there were limitations. Certain items of religious dress could be worn only inside places of worship, and while Ataturk did not attempt to abolish the veil for women, he encouraged women to abandon it.

Legislation, however, could not force a wholesale change in people's beliefs, and a great number of Turks continued to practice their religion to the extent they could and did not support the aggressive secularization of the state. Other fundamental tensions remained in political life, causing the military to intervene three times-in 1960, 1971, and 1980-and take control of the government temporarily until the situation stabilised and civilian rule could return. The 1980 crisis was due to the inability of the politicians and the nation's police force to control increasing political violence, which stemmed in particular from opposition in Kurdistan and from demands for a stronger role for Islam in the country. Encouraged by the 1979 Iranian revolution, Islamists in Turkey were calling for the return of Islamic law, which presented a direct challenge to the nation's fundamental principle of secularism.

The army's 1980 intervention resulted in a new constitution, approved in a national referendum on November 7, 1982, which is the constitution in force today. Article 2 identifies the Republic of Turkey as a "democratic, secular and social state governed by the rule of law." Per Article 4, Articles 1 through 3 are not subject to amendment, nor may their amendment even be proposed. Article 24 addresses freedom of religion and conscience, and provides that:

> *Everyone has the right to freedom of conscience, religious belief and conviction.*

Acts of worship, religious services, and ceremonies shall be conducted freely, provided that they do not violate the provisions of Article 14. ....

No one shall be allowed to exploit or abuse religion or religious feelings, or things held sacred by religion, in any manner whatsoever, for the purpose of personal influence, or for even partially basing the fundamental, social, economic, political, and legal order of the State on religious tenets.

Article 14 provides, in part, that:

> *None of the rights and freedoms embodied in the Constitution shall be exercised with the aim of... placing the government of the State under the control of an individual or a group of people, or establishing the hegemony of one social class over others, or creating discrimination on the basis of language, race, religion or sect, or of establishing by any other means a system of government based on these concepts and ideas.*

These provisions amount to a careful defining of the scope of religion in public and private life. Fundamental tensions remain, however, between adherents to the state's secularism, and citizens who want some role for Islam in political life and greater tolerance for expressions of Islam in Turkish public life more generally. An "Islam-inspired" political party, the Welfare Party, gained supporters in the early 1990s and performed well in the 1994 local elections, with voters electing Welfare Party mayors for Istanbul and Ankara. In the 1995 national elections Welfare Party members won the largest number of seats in the national parliament. The party's supporters were diverse, including not only "conservative townspeople and poor urban migrants, but also up-and-coming professionals, intellectuals, and wealthy industrialists." Their political interests ranged widely as well, "from social and economic reform to replacing the secular state system with one founded on Islamic law."

In 1997 the Turkish army pressured Welfare Party Prime Minister Necmettin Erbakan to hand over office to Tansu Ciller of the conservative True Path Party, on the grounds that the Welfare Party was helping to spread the influence of Islamic fundamentalism. State prosecutors sought a ruling in the Constitutional Court that the Welfare Party was aiming to violate the principle of secularism and, as such, should be banned. The army then filed its own petition with the Constitutional Court, charging that Erbakan had accepted foreign funding in his efforts to undermine the secularism of the state.

The Constitutional Court banned the Welfare Party in 1998, on the grounds that it violated the principle of secularism. Parliamentarians formerly affiliated with the Welfare Party then established the Virtue Party, while the Turkish chief prosecutor made it clear that he would seek to close the new party if it seemed to be a direct continuation of the Welfare Party. One Virtue Party member was Tayyip Erdogan, who was elected Mayor of Istanbul. Thereafter he was tried in a state security court for inciting the public to enmity through exploitation of religion, and subsequently sentenced to ten months in prison. In 1999 the Chief Prosecutor filed a case with the Constitutional Court seeking to close the Virtue Party, contending that its members "are like vampires which feed on nothing but blood, exploiting people's religious beliefs." Two years later, the Constitutional Court closed the Virtue Party, again due to activities violating the principles of secularism.

In August 2001 Erdogan-released from jail but still prohibited from holding public office-formed the Justice and Development Party (AKP, per its Turkish acronym), supported by the more moderate members of the former Virtue Party. Members of the AKP said that "they will not stress their religious beliefs as much as they had in the past but will attempt to establish a moderate right-wing party." In the 2002 parliamentary elections AKP won the highest percentage of votes, 34.3%, with Ataturk's former party, the Republican People's Party, winning only 19.4%. Still under a ban from public office, Erdogan was not able to take the position of prime minister, as the head of the winning party usually does, so AKP member Abdullah Gul assumed the position. In March 2003 Erdogan's ban was lifted and he was able to assume the position of prime minister.

The AKP rejects the label "Islamist" and the party platform does not even mention Islam. Party leaders describe themselves as "Muslim Democrats," along the lines of Germany's centre-right Christian Democrats. Erdogan's government "has put its weight clearly behind Turkey's bid for European Union membership and has not attempted to pass any measures on the most obvious reforms its supporters would like to see, such as lifting bans on the wearing of Islamic-style headscarves." But the army and public prosecutors are watching for any signs of impermissible activity.

Noah Feldman vividly explains the secularism of the Turkish system:

> *The radical form of the separation of church and state, backed by the authority of the military, goes well beyond the separation in, say, the United States. If Erdogan wanted to found the Justice and Development Party in the United States, he could do it, even if its principles were identifiably Islamic. If-to extend the hypothetical scenario-Erdogan became president and his party controlled Congress, President Erdogan could announce that Islamic values were important to him. He could tell interviewers that he prayed about important decisions, and he could replace Billy Graham, a regular feature of every inauguration since President Nixon's, with the imam of his choice.*

Of course, unless the Constitution were amended, there would be a range of laws that the Justice and Development Party could not enact. Under current American constitutional law, the party could not enact laws designed to support mosques or Islamic education in particular. It could not make Islamic law into the law of the state, or make the government pay for public-service announcements touting the virtues of an Islamic lifestyle. But Erdogan could run for office on a platform of amending the Constitution to make the United States an Islamic country, and if he had the votes, then, under Article V of the Constitution, he could do it. The military would not intervene, or, at least, under the Constitution it would not be allowed to intervene. Separation of church and state is subject to amendment, like the rest of the Constitution.

This hypothetical scenario demonstrates that the permissible role of religion in Turkey's political sphere is carefully circumscribed. It is unlikely that Iraq will seek Turkey's legal system as a model, for numerous reasons. From the earliest days of the selection of Iraq's Governing Council, albeit by the United States, it was clear that Iraqis would not accept a Governing Council full of secular reformists that even appoached Mustafa Kemal's outlook. Opinion polls and the Interim Constitution are also signs that an aggressively secular agenda is not under consideration. The United States can point to Turkey as an example of a Muslim country that has embraced democracy, but the limits of what the democratic process may produce in Turkey are carefully circumscribed and tightly controlled. Referring to Turkey as a model puts the focus on ways to separate religion and state and exclude Islam from the legal structure-an unrealistic objective in Iraq. The real and difficult question facing Iraqis is not if, but how Islamic law will be retained and incorporated into the constitution and legal system.

Iran

In Iran, the current constitutional structure, with regard to the role Islam plays in the legal system, is the opposite of Turkey's, and also an unlikely path for Iraq. The Islamic revolution of 1978-1979 in Iran resulted in the formation of an "Islamic republic"; subsequently, revolutionary leaders drafted a constitution in which they elaborated on the details of the state structure. The key to understanding what makes Iran an Islamic republic is in the complex arrangement of the state's components and the ultimate subjugation of all state activity to review by the country's highest religious leaders according to the concept of velayet-e faqih (guardianship of the jurist).

Article 1 of the Iranian Constitution states that "the government of Iran is an Islamic republic, endorsed by the people of Iran on the basis of their long-standing belief in the administration of truth and justice in the Qur'an." The practical effect of this language is that:

> *All laws and regulations pertaining to civil, penal, financial, economic, administrative, cultural, military, political and other spheres must be based on Islamic rules and standards. This chapter governs absolutely and generally all articles of the Constitution, as well as all other laws and regulations, and the duty to ascertain this matter devolves on the jurists of the Guardian Council. As for religious belief, Article 12 provides that "the official religion of Iran is Islam, and the sect followed is Twelver Ja'fari Shi'ism, and this principle is never subject to change."*

The highest political office in Iran is that of the Supreme Leader, the guardian jurist. This office was first held by Ayatollah Khomeini, who was "recognised by a decisive majority of the people for leadership," and since his death by the current Supreme Leader Ayatollah Khamene'i. The Supreme Leader has direct control over the armed forces and internal security forces; he appoints half of the members of the Guardian Council; and he appoints the highest judicial authorities.

Closely linked to the Supreme Leader is the Guardian Council, composed of six experts in Islamic law appointed by the Supreme

Leader, and six lawyers from various fields of law nominated by the judiciary leaders and accepted by the parliament (the National Consultative Assembly (Assembly)). The Guardian Council has tremendous power: it must approve candidates before they can run in Presidential or Assembly elections, and may reject candidats on the basis of their ideological beliefs. Furthermore, the Guardian Council also reviews all legislation passed by the Assembly; the six Islamic jurists pass on its compliance with Islamic law, and the entire Council reviews it for consistency with the Constitution.

The Iranian people do have some voice through presidential and Assembly elections. The executive function is fulfilled by the president, who is elected by the people in nationwide elections and fulfills those executive duties not delegated to the Supreme Leader. Muhammad Khatami was elected to a second four-year term in 2001 with seventy-seven percent of the vote. Considered a reformer, his efforts have been stymied to a large extent by the Guardian Council's veto. Reformers and moderates likewise won a majority of the Assembly's 290 seats in the general 2000 elections. For the 2004 Assembly elections the Guardian Council rejected a record percentage of candidate applicants, leading to a temporary standoff between the president and the Guardian Council. Reformers in turn called for a boycott of the elections, and the elections took place with record-low voter participation. As a result, reformist voices decreased in the Assembly.

If the Assembly and the president adopt legislation that the Guardian Council will approve, then the legislative process could work smoothly. The Assembly and the president, however, have been interested in reform beyond that which the Council is willing to tolerate and as a result are at a virtual deadlock with the Guardian Council. A recent example is the Assembly's approval on July 23, 2003, of a bill authorising Iran's acceptance of the Convention on the Elimination of Discrimination Against Women (CEDAW). The Guardian Council subsequently vetoed this acceptance on the ground that it violated the constitution and Islamic law. The result of vetoes such as this has been increasingly frequent popular demonstrations in the streets of Iran protesting the strict control of the Supreme Leader and Guardian Council.

The growing tension in Iran between reformist politicians and the ruling clerics, and the increasing dissatisfaction of Iranians with their governmental system, cannot be missed by Iraqi Shi'ites. Furthermore, the concept of guardianship of the religious scholar, velayet-e faqih, is not widely accepted among the leading and influential Shi'ite clerics.

Additionally, the population of Iraq is much more diverse than that of Iran, with a sizeable Sunni population as well as Shi'ites whose perspectives are not sympathetic to Iran's system, such as secularists, liberals, and communists. Holding up Iran as the example of what Iraq should not become, therefore, avoids the more central question of how Iraq may seek to include Islamic law in a democratic structure. It has also led the United States to neglect some Shi'ite leaders in Iraq, such as Ayatollah Sistani, on the assumption that as a high ranking Shi'ite cleric he would endorse an Iranian model for Iraq. To approach the question of Iraq's legal future in more depth, the next Part examines how similar issues have played out in Egypt.

An Apposite Frame of Reference: Egypt

Egypt exemplifies an intermediate approach to the incorporation of Islamic law in a legal system, and its legal history resembles Iraq's own. The balance is perhaps not ideal for Egypt; the government has been fighting a battle with Islamists and has striven to prevent critics of the government from serving in the national assembly. Egypt's legal framework, and the tensions within it, are instructive for Iraq's situation. The constitution, civil code, and family law are the key areas in which Islamic law is referenced.

More specific terminology is necessary to discuss the details of Egypt's legal system here and that of Iraq in Part FV. The English term "Islamic law" is misleadingly simple and suggests, incorrectly, that Islamic law refers to an established body of substantive law that could be applied in any particular jurisdiction, as if it were, for example, the Uniform Commercial Code. Two Arabic words are often translated as Islamic law: Sharia and fiqh; and while the meanings of these two terms overlap to a large degree and are used by some scholars interchangeably, it is useful to note their main distinctions. Sharia means divine law, or God's law. It is the system of rules that God intended for humans. The textual manifestations of the Sharia are considered to be the Qur'an, as the word of God, and the reports of the acts and speech of the Prophet Muhammad (sunnd). The meaning of any particular provision of the Qur'an or sunna may be unclear, or a particular issue or question may not seem to be covered by either of these two sources.

The question, then, is how can humans best access and understand God's law? Rules of the Sharia are understood, or derived, in a process called ijtihad, meaning, literally, exertion or effort. Using interpretive tools that are themselves the subject of an extensive field of legal study, scholars of Islamic law interpret and elaborate the texts of the Sharia to produce legal doctrine. The Arabic term for this legal doctrine is fiqh, which means discernment or comprehension. The relationship between Sharia and fiqh is significant: while Sharia is divine law, fiqh is human knowledge or supposition about the Sharia. Scholars of Islamic law strive to understand the Sharia and in doing so often come to different conclusions. So, whereas there is one God's law, there can be multiple human understandings. A basic assumption exists, however, that knowledge of the Sharia is generally ascertainable by humans.

Over time differences in opinion about the contents of the Sharia tended to coalesce around leading scholarly proponents, and so-called schools of law (madhhab) formed. In Sunni Islam there are four main schools today: Hanafi, Shafi'i, Maliki, and Hanbali. Historically, school affiliation among Sunnis was more important than it tends to be today. In Shi'ite Islam, there are three main branches: Twelvers, Ismailis, and Zaydis. These branches are larger than schools of law, but include the types of legal differentiations found among the Sunni schools of law.

The process of ijtihad requires extensive knowledge of the sources of the Sharia as well as the relevant means of interpretation. In Sunni Islam, there are very few scholars who would identify themselves by the associated title, mujtahid. Those learned to a lesser degree might serve as religious judges and answer questions on matters of Islamic law, but they would typically follow the prevailing opinions of their school and not undertake a fresh study of the primary sources for themselves. Thus, when a legal system seeks to apply the Sharia, it is unclear precisely what this means in practice. Sharia as interpreted by whom? Using which interpretive tools? Following which particular school? Or operating independently of the established schools? The interpretive issues can be substantial, and must be considered when discussing Islamic law, especially in the context of modern efforts to incorporate Islamic law into a legal system when several sources of law may be involved. In Iran, for example, Guardian Council members come to their own conclusions about Islamic law, and their belief that CEDAW violates the Sharia may not be shared by a scholar of Islamic law in Malaysia, Pakistan, or Egypt, or even by other religious scholars within Iran itself.

The Egyptian Way

With a clearer sense of the complexities involved with the Sharia and how humans seek to understand it, this Part now turns to the role of Islamic law in the Egyptian legal system. The three key areas for this examination are the constitution, the civil code, and family law (personal status laws).

The Constitution

The current constitution of Egypt was promulgated in 1971, as the country's fourth constitution since the 1952 military coup that ended the monarchy. The document was produced under Anwar Sadat's authority after he emerged as the new President following Gamal Abd al-Naser's death. The 1971 Constitution was amended in 1980.

Article 2 of the constitution, as amended, states that Islam is the religion of the state, Arabic is the official language, and "the principles of the Islamic Sharia are the main source of legislation." Proclaiming the official religion of the state seems only to recognise the religion of the vast majority of Egyptians, but the full significance of the phrase is unclear. (Perhaps it underpins issues such as state holidays, school curriculum, and the like.)

The final clause, declaring that "the principles of the Islamic Sharia are the main source of legislation," ("mabadi' al-shari'a alislamiya al-masdar al-ra'isi li'l-tashri'") has been the source of extensive controversy. The first issue is the meaning of "principles." This is on its face not a reference to the fiqh of any one particular school-such as the prevailing Hanafi or Shafi'i schools of Egyptor even more broadly to the Sharia to be interpreted by religious authorities in Egypt without adherence to any one particular school. As will be seen in the interpretive case law discussed below, there is no well-defined set of "principles" in Islamic law that corresponds to the plain meaning of this term. The vagueness seems to have been intentional. As Vogel notes, Article 2 of the Egyptian Constitution "carefully avoids using various terms which in their ordinary usage are nearly synonymous with the ones it does use but which also have technical Islamic legal meanings."

The second interpretive issue concerns the use of the definite article preceding the word "main." The 1971 constitution provided that the principles of the Islamic Sharia are "a main source of legislation," implying that there were other sources not identified in the constitution. In the drafting phase of the 1971 constitution, there had been considerable debate over whether and how Islamic law should be referenced. One proposal was: "The Islamic Sharia is a main source of legislation." Without the term "principles," this phrase is broader in that it refers to all rules that could be considered part of the Sharia-including but not limited to a general set of principles. For some critics, though, this direct reference to the Sharia was not Islamic enough because it did not specify how this source would appear in laws, and a modification was proposed to make the Sharia the source of legislation. Others found the language "the Islamic Sharia is a main source of legislation" far too definite and feared that it would lead to broad changes in the laws of the country to bring them into conformity with some interpretation of the Sharia. These discussions about the phrasing indicate that the final version, stating that "the principles of the Islamic Sharia are a main source of lawmaking," was adopted as a compromise but without a clear sense of its meaning.

In 1980 the "Islamic-ness" of the constitution was enhanced when Article 2 was amended to read "the principles of the Islamic Sharia are the main source of legislation." Since the significance of the original phrasing was still unclear at that time, it was an even larger question as to what the amendment would mean. The Supreme Constitutional Court (SCC), which was established in 1979, has provided interpretive guidance through a series of decisions, taking a fairly reserved approach to the meaning of Article 2 these rulings are relevant to the constitutional process in Iraq because the Egyptian experience gives a sense of similar language that has been used and its resulting interpretation. A selection of cases involving Article 2 is discussed here to provide a general sense of how the SCC has interpreted it.

The first Article 2 case the SCC heard was a claim brought by alAzhar University that Article 226 of the 1949 Civil Code, which requires payment of post-judgment interest, is unconstitutional. The University had been required to pay post-judgment interest on a court judgment for commercial debt and claimed that this payment amounted to usury, and as such was prohibited by the Qur'an. The University argued that the article of the Civil Code providing for such interest payments was in conflict with the principles of the Islamic Sharia and thus in conflict with Article 2 of the Constitution.

The SCC determined that the Article 2 amendment applied only to legislation issued after the date of the amendment, May 22, 1980. It did not have retroactive force and, thus, did not apply to the 1949 Civil Code. The SCC relied upon the report of the legislative committee that proposed the Article 2 amendment, which said that the amended language "requires the lawmaker to resort to the rulings of the Islamic Sharia-and not to any other source-to investigate the compatibility of any legislation under consideration with the Sharia." According to the SCC, this means that when passing new legislation, the lawmaker is restricted, as of the date of the amendment, to that which conforms to the principles of the Islamic Sharia.

The SCC subsequently heard challenges to legislation adopted after the date of the amendment and articulated a test for constitutionality. In case 8 of Judicial Year 17, decided May 18, 1996, the SCC heard a challenge to a Ministry of Education decree prohibiting girls from attending school while wearing a niqab, a face covering. The hair covering, the hijab, was permitted. The father of two girls who were denied entry to their secondary school for wearing the niqab challenged the decree on the ground that it violated Article 2 of the Constitution. His argument was that because he believed the niqab to be required in Islam, the prohibition of it was a violation of the principles of the Sharia.

The SCC stated that the Article 2 language, "the principles of the Islamic Sharia are the main source of legislation," means that no legislation may violate rules of Islamic law that are "definite in terms of their authenticity and meaning" (al-ahkam al-qat'iya fi thubutiha wa dalalatiha). Such rules, according to the SCC, neither need nor permit interpretation (ijtihad) because their meanings are absolutely clear. Because they are absolutely clear, they do not change with time. The SCC did not invent the wording of this test but rather adopted the phrase from classical fiqh sources that discussed texts of the Qur'an and sunna that classical religious scholars could show to "have only one meaning and to be, beyond doubt, historically accurate and authentic." This is, then, a two-part test: (1) the authenticity of the text must be proven beyond doubt; and (2) there must be one absolutely clear meaning of the text.

As for part one of the test, the authenticity of the totality of the Qur'an is accepted, so this part of the test applies only to the sunna, about which there is extensive debate and disagreement as to its authenticity. Part two is a real issue for both the Qur'an and sunna, for which, as discussed above, there can be and are multiple opinions. The SCC's two-part test is directly related to:

> *Law's fundamental methodological stance that, while God alone is the true legislator, his law can only be known from the revealed texts themselves, meaning the Qur'an and the authenticated Sunna. This means that, when these texts are uncertain in their authenticity or*

> *their meanings and thus leave room for interpretation, the residual uncertainty cannot be reduced merely by human opinion. One learned person's ijtihad, if done according to the proper method (usul al-fiqh) [jurisprudence], has as much a claim to divine truth as that of any other such scholar. No one may declare an ijtihad of a qualified person to be totally wrong. Accordingly, and as the maxim asserts, a judgment based on ijtihad cannot be reversed. When, however, revealed texts are both unambiguous and authentic, then God's law is known to a certainty. As to these there can be no valid ijtihad, and the decision of any judge or mufti, however qualified, contradicting what God has commanded may be reversed by any other judge.*

Due to the expression by the SCC of the test it would use for these cases, the SCC's interpretation of "the principles of the Islamic Sharia" that it will protect is fairly narrow and gives the executive and legislative powers a good amount of discretion in this regard, because "as even classical scholars of usul al-fiqh [jurisprudence] have acknowledged, few texts of the revelation can be said to have only one possible meaning or interpretation, and few sunna texts to be authenticated beyond doubt (the Qur'an alone is considered authentic in its entirety)." The Qur'an will easily pass part one of the test, while texts of the sunna will be much more difficult. Part two of the test is also a high hurdle for provisions of both the Qur'an and sunna. As a result, the SCC has seldom invalidated legislation for contradicting Article 2.

Yet, as Vogel has noted, the SCC has on several occasions upheld legislation from an Article 2 challenge and, while explaining why the particular law does not violate the clear meaning of a Qur'anic provision, has mentioned as dicta propositions that the SCC does consider definite in terms of meaning and authenticity. These propositions include:

> *that polygamy is a right of the husband; that, apart from exceptional circumstances, wives must have the consent of their husbands to leave the marital home; that women must cover most of their bodies, if not everything but their face and hands; that women have no immunity from state interference in the matter of religious requirements as to dress; that it is the father alone (and not the mother) who has the responsibility for the maintenance of minor children; that (in a case*

falling outside personal status) interest is prohibited in an agreement to extend a debt.

These propositions were not at issue in the cases in which they were mentioned, of course, but what they say about the SCC's interpretation-and other possible interpretations-of "principles," is instructive.

The specific wording of Article 2, the SCC's jurisprudence, and the other possible ways in which Article 2 could have been interpreted provide important lessons for Iraq. The Interim Constitution of Iraq includes the phrase: "Islam is the official religion of the State and is considered a source of legislation (masdar li'l-tashrie)." The "source of legislation" concept and language is the same as in Egypt's Article 2, yet the substance of that source for Egypt is "the principles of the Islamic Sharia" whereas for Iraq it is the larger category of "Islam." For Egypt those principles are "the main source of legislation" while the Iraqi wording tracks Egypt's original wording, "a source of legislation." Unfortunately for our ability to predict the potential meanings of the Iraqi phrase, when the Egyptian constitution was promulgated in 1971 there was little sense of the meaning of "a source of legislation," nor was there constitutional interpretation of that phrase. Egypt's experience illustrates the necessity for interpretive guidance before the meanings of such phrases, and the tests used to determine legislative compatibility, will be ascertainable. In the case of Egypt, the SCC proved to be a powerful institution, and has remained remarkably independent from the government. In Iraq, it remains unclear what body will be responsible for interpreting constitutional questions and how independent this body will be from other governmental pressures.

Also significant to this discussion is that there was nothing inevitable about the SCC's tests for determining Article 2 disputes. Egypt's amended Article 2 wording could have been-and may still be-interpreted in many ways. For example the SCC could have adopted an even stricter definition of the principles of the Islamic Sharia, leaving lawmakers unfettered in terms of Islamic-ness and protecting only a few of the most certain rules. The SCC could also have taken a much broader view of the principles it would protect, accepting, for example, any Islamic rule or principle in any fiqh work, even if held by only a single scholar, correspondingly striking down a substantial number of laws. The judges then move from acting as identifiers of the certain provisions-for which the main legal books can probably suffice-to legal scholars seeking any one opinion that might contradict a law, and then to mujtahids themselves, exercising their own independent reasoning to determine whether a law is valid in Islamic terms. In this final, extreme sense, the judges would function similarly to the Guardian Council in Iran.

The Civil Code

The Civil Code is relevant to the issue of the role of Islamic law in the legal system because the drafting and adoption of Egypt's (and Iraq's) civil code involved extensive discussion of the code's Islamic credentials. One approach to Egypt's legal framework would have been to avoid any reference to Islamic law in the constitution but leave the matter to the legislature to incorporate it as they see fit. This was the case in Egypt prior to the 1971 constitution and in Iraq until the Interim Constitution was adopted. Under this model, so long as the people desire a role for Islamic law in their legislation, they would elect representatives (or have representatives appoint themselves) who promised to carry out this task. Determinations of the Islamic credentials of legislation would be made in the legislature and not by a court. This Part discusses the experience of the Civil Code in Egypt in order to illustrate some of the issues that will arise regarding the Iraqi civil code, and to show that while the civil code may seem an unlikely area for a potentially heated discussion of the integration and retention of Islamic law, it is actually an important forum on this point.

Egypt's current civil code (Civil Code) was adopted in 1948 and went into force in 1949. The project to produce the Civil Code was launched in the mid-1930s as part of the construction of a unified court system that would have jurisdiction over all of Egypt's residents. At that time Egypt was using two civil codes: the Civil Code for the Mixed Courts, adopted in 1876, and the Civil Code for the National Courts, adopted in 1883. The Mixed Court Code was French in origin, and the National Code was based mainly on the French code and in small part on a codification of Sharia done by Qadri Pasha. When the Civil Code project began, there were several competing proposals for it, including calls for a code based fully on codified Sharia.

In 1938 the Ministry of Justice appointed Egyptian University law professor Abdel Razziq Sanhuri and his former advisor at the University of Lyon, Edouard Lambert, to head a constitutional committee. Sanhuri went on to be not only Egypt's most prominent scholar of modern jurisprudence and the main drafter of the Civil Code, but also well known for his work with legal systems throughout the Arab world. He was the main drafter of the civil codes in Iraq and Libya, for example, and worked on the constitutions of Sudan and Bahrain.

Egypt's Civil Code involves the issue of Islamic law in two ways: First, the Sharia is a residual source of law to be used by a judge if the Civil Code is silent on a particular issue. The second issue is the degree to which the Code's substantive provisions conform to some interpretation of the Sharia.

Article 1 of the Civil Code explains the general use of Sharia in the absence of other laws:

(1). The provisions of the code apply to all matters that they address literally or in meaning.

(2). If there is not a provision that can be applied, then the judge rules according to custom ('urf); if this does not exist, then according to the principles of the Islamic Sharia; if these do not exist, then according to the principles of natural law and rules of justice.

The phrase "principles of the Islamic Sharia" is, of course, the exact same wording that was later used in the 1971 Constitution. Ranking custom ('urf) before the principles is a minor slight to Islamic law in favour of customary practice in Egypt, especially since Sanhuri reversed the order in the Libyan and Syrian codes, placing Sharia before custom. (The Iraqi code is like the Egyptian code in this regard.) The legislative history of the Civil Code indicates what other phrasings were considered for Article 1. Some members of the Egyptian drafting committee, for example, wanted to add to the phrase "principles of the Islamic Sharia" the provision that these are not to be restricted to any one school of law in Sunni Islam. Sanhuri objected on the ground that "principles" will be so widely accepted as not to differ among schools, so that adding this extra phrase would be redundant.

Sanhuri was explicit in stating that his goal was to make the Sharia suitable for and compatible with the modern age, asserting that the drafting committee borrowed much from the general theories of the Islamic Sharia and its detailed rules. A Western commentator who sought to identify the role of the Sharia in the Civil Code also found that a desire to incorporate the Sharia influenced choices the drafters made among concepts on which modern European codes were divided. Still, in Egypt there are those who find the Civil Code lacking in terms of its "Islamic-ness"; the cases brought to the SCC challenging the Islamic credentials of provisions of the civil code and other laws are evidence of this.

The Particular Case of Personal Status Law

If vagueness in the Egyptian constitutional provision regarding Islamic law is matched by moderate specificity in the articles of the Civil Code, then Islamic law is detailed, tangible, and highly controversial in the area of law referred to as "personal status." Personal status law deals primarily with marriage, divorce, child custody, inheritance, and other family-related matters; historically, it has been the area of law regulated by the state that is most closely tied to Sharia and most resistant to secularization. As Frank Vogel summarises the situation in the Muslim world: "Everywhere but in Turkey, personal status law has remained fiqh in content."

Related to specific laws is the judicial forum for personal status cases. These cases were usually the last remaining type of case to be heard in Sharia courts before their dissolution, which, in Egypt, occurred in 1955. A basic understanding of Sharia courts is thus necessary to follow Egypt's, and later Iraq's, legal histories with regard to personal status. "Sharia court" refers to the traditional type of court in Muslim areas, in which the judge is a religious scholar and the applicable law is the Sharia, as ascertained and applied by the judge. In the case of Egypt, Sharia courts continued to have wide jurisdiction throughout most of the period of Ottoman rule in Egypt, and these courts encompassed civil and criminal law and administrative matters. These courts heard disputes between Muslims, between a Muslim and a non-Muslim, between non-Muslims of different denominations, and even between non-Muslims of the same denomination if they agreed to its jurisdiction.

Toward the end of the nineteenth century, Egypt began to introduce a national system of civil courts for Egyptians, and with the arrival of increasing numbers of foreigners in Egypt, introduced special "mixed" tribunals for disputes between foreigners of different nationalities, and for disputes between a foreigner and an Egyptian. These courts increasingly took over jurisdiction from the Sharia courts, which, by 1880, had jurisdiction only over personal status, succession, religious endowments, gifts, and homicide. An 1880 law specified that Sharia court judgments should be based on the most approved opinions of the Hanafi school, except in cases of homicide. While much of the population of Egypt was Shafi'i, the Ottomans were Hanafi and this preference shows their influence.

The new national and mixed tribunals also prompted the development of new civil, criminal, and commercial codes. A dichotomy began to develop between Sharia courts, which continued to apply mostly non-codified Sharia, and the national and mixed courts, in which judges with civil legal training applied western-inspired codes. In Law 462 of 1955, the government abolished these remaining Sharia courts and provided that all cases formerly in their jurisdiction would thereafter be heard by a personal status division of the national courts. As for the law applicable in this personal status division of the national courts, Law 78 of 1931 continued to apply, which stated that the Sharia, and particularly the fiqh of the Hanafi school, would be the applicable law, except when there is a positive law (qanun) applicable to the issue before the court. In such cases the qanun applies, and recourse to Sharia is not permitted.

Essentially, the role of Sharia in the legal system has been narrowed considerably over the past century from its original position as the sole source of law in most cases brought to the courts in Egypt. Now, it is only a supplemental source of law in limited types of cases. It is also susceptible to further reduction according to decisions of the lawmaker to adopt new laws to supersede the Sharia.

Despite the codification of much of personal status law and the exercise of its jurisdiction by regular civil courts, albeit in the personal status division, there is still a special sensitivity to regulating in the area of personal status, particularly when the laws appear to deviate from Islamic precedent. Attempts at reform oriented legislation are discussed in section (a) below. The hierarchy of the sources of law in personal status cases, which allows resort to Sharia in absence of a relevant positive law, adds further complication to this area. A dramatic recent court case presented in Section (b) below demonstrates the effect this residual usage can have on the interpretation of personal status law.

Codified Personal Status Law

Egypt's personal status law is still very much fiqh in substance. Historically, its form was uncodified Sharia, and then piecemeal reforms followed with legislation in certain areas. A series of reform laws was adopted in the 1920s, beginning with Law 25 of Year 1920, which gave women the right to sue for divorce in certain narrow circumstances; formerly this had been solely a male prerogative. Law 25 of 1929 expanded the scope of the grounds on which a woman could sue for divorce to include "harm," which could be mental and physical cruelty, non-support, or other forms of marital neglect. A lull in reforms of this kind ensued for the next several decades, and then more active discussions began after Anwar Sadat became President in 1971. Parliamentary and general public opinion was not as receptive as reformers had hoped, however, and parliamentary debates throughout the 1970s did not result in any new personal status legislation. Frustrated by this inaction, Sadat issued a presidential decree while parliament was in recess, adopting Law 44 of 1979, which was also known popularly as "Jihan's law" after the name of Sadat's wife. The provisions of Law 44 included the wife's right to sue for divorce if her husband marries a second wife and she feels harmed thereby. Law 44 sparked controversy in diverse circles, including criticism by reformers that the law did not go far enough in improving the situation of women, and accusations from other groups that the law violated the Sharia by giving women excessive rights.

Sadat was assassinated by an Islamic movement within Egypt in 1980, and any efforts to reform the personal status laws slowed. "Jihan's Law" was then challenged by a husband defending a suit for divorce who claimed that the law violated the Sharia. The SCC heard the case but did not address the Article 2 issue, deciding that the law did not meet the criteria for passage by presidential decree, since it was not a matter of sufficient urgency, and was therefore invalid. It was not until 1985 that a new law of personal status was adopted. While still not a full code, it implemented some of the rules of the 1979 law. This was followed by Law 1 of Year 2000, but there is still no comprehensive unified code governing family law.

Residual Role of Sharia and the Case of Nasr Abu Zayd

A recent high-profile and highly controversial case illustrates the significance of Sharia as the second source of law in personal status cases. The details of the relationship between positive law and Sharia as played out in this case are complicated but well worth examining as an illustration of fundamental tensions in Egypt's legal system. The case also shows that when a state is considering the desired role of Islamic law in the legal system, it must consider not only what it wants to include but also what it wants to exclude.

The case began with an event anyone close to academic circles can appreciate: In May of 1992, Nasr Abu Zayd, an assistant professor of Islamic studies and literature at Cairo University, was denied promotion to full professor. Details began to leak: the departmental committee voted against him by only a seven-to-six margin, and two of the three evaluations from outside the university were in Abu Zayd's favour. The key opponent on the departmental committee had been Dr. 'Abd al-Sabur Shahin, who had a particular animosity towards Abu Zayd's use of contemporary methods of textual criticism in the study of the Qur'an and other religious texts, and had managed to prevail in the committee meeting.

The University rector "chose to regard the affair as an everyday case of a failed academic promotion rather than a threat to academic values and freedoms" and quietly advised Abu Zayd to wait and re-submit his application at a later point when conservative voices might not have as much power within the department. Instead, Abu Zayd went to the Egyptian media with his story, and Shahin went to the mosques. On April 2, 1993, Shahin proclaimed from the pulpit that Abu Zayd was nothing less than an apostate, while the more liberal-leaning newspapers supported Abu Zayd's academic freedom. Tensions rose, ultimately leading to a lawsuit that made its way to the Court of Cassation, Egypt's highest court.

A group of seven plaintiffs filed the case against Abu Zayd and his wife in a Cairo (Giza) court of first instance for matters of personal status on May 25, 1993; this is the personal status division in the national courts as discussed above. The plaintiffs all had some connection to the opposition to Abu Zayd that Shahin had been leading at Cairo University and in the mosques. In their complaint the plaintiffs argued that Abu Zayd's works constitute apostasy, and because an apostate man cannot marry a Muslim woman according to most fiqh opinions, the plaintiffs sought a court decision pronouncing a divorce between Abu Zayd and his wife, Ibtihal Younes. The claimants were by no means purporting to be acting on Younes' behalf; she believed her husband to still be a Muslim and wanted to remain married to him. The case came under the jurisdiction of the personal status courts because the plaintiffs were seeking divorce, which is a personal status action.

The complaint first triggered the issue of standing. The plaintiffs brought the case on the grounds of an Islamic legal concept called hisba, best defined as "commanding right and forbidding wrong." This concept has been addressed m fiqh, from the early period of Islam to the present. The basic idea is that each Muslim has the duty to enjoin other Muslims both to do what is right, and to forbid others from committing what is wrong. Historically, fiqh treatises do provide for a "claim of hisba," according to which a Muslim could bring to public attention a complaint of wrongdoing against another Muslim. On this basis, the plaintiffs claimed that when they saw textual evidence of apostasy in Abu Zayd's writings, they had the right to bring him to court to stop his wrongdoing. The plaintiffs had to contend with the fact that the doctrine of hisba does not appear in Egyptian codified law (qanun). They referred to the rule governing cases of personal status: Shariaand in particular the fiqh of the Hanafi school-is the source of law in personal status cases except when there is a qanun on point, in which case the qanun applies. They argued that because no codified law addressed the doctrine of hisba they could look to Hanafi fiqh on hisba and rely on that in bringing the case. Because the Hanafi school recognised the "claim of hisba" they should likewise be allowed to bring such a claim before the court.

The court of first instance did not accept this standing argument and dismissed the suit. The court found that the rule of Sharia's applicability in the absence of a codified law was only meant to apply to the substantive law in cases of personal status. For procedural questions, such as standing, the Civil and Commercial Procedural Law is the sole applicable law. This law provides that in order to bring a suit, the plaintiff must have a direct and personal interest recognised by law in the claim. This court, therefore, did not rule on the question of whether Abu Zayd's writings evidenced apostasy.

The plaintiffs appealed the court's decision to the Court of Appeals. The Court of Appeals reversed the lower court's decision on June 14, 1995, finding against Abu Zayd. Abu Zayd then appealed the decision, which was affirmed-with elaboration on the appellate court's reasoning-by the Court of Cassation. The Court of Cassation held that the fiqh of the Hanafi school is the source of law in matters of personal status except when there is a qanun on point. Merely because the legislature did not specifically provide for the claim of hisba does not mean it is not available; rather, the judges must determine the availability of a hisba claim within the Hanafi school historically. By implication, the judges found that the codified procedural law does not preclude the possibility of a claim based on hisba. The court then concluded that according to Hanafi fiqh, all capable Muslims had the duty of commanding good, and forbidding wrong vis-à-vis all other Muslims.

Abu Zayd argued in his defence that, as a professor of Islamic studies at Cairo University, he was learned to the level that entitled him to conduct his own independent reasoning on matters of law, in accordance with the concept of ijtihad.' He claimed that in his case, his publications were merely the exercise of his own ijtihad, which he was entitled to conduct in his capacity as a scholar of the Qur'an.

The court rejected this claim, holding that ijtihad is permitted only with regard to textual provisions of the Qur'an whose meanings have not yet been definitively determined. According to the court, Abu Zayd's views contradicted clear and certain interpretations-such as the rule that women receive one-half of the inheritance of men and that the testimony in court of one man is equal to that of two women. His writings thus constituted apostasy, and he is considered an apostate.

After the decision at the trial court level, the government saw the potential ramifications of the case, and the potential for Islamists to initiate other similar cases. First by executive order, followed by legislation from the parliament, attempts were made to eliminate the availability of hisba claims. On January 29, 1996, the legislature adopted Law No. 3, which gave the public prosecutor the sole power to bring a claim on the basis of hisba. This law includes the provision that the public prosecutor automatically becomes the plaintiff in any existing hisba claim for which a judgment had not yet been rendered. The Court of Cassation found that the law was inapplicable to Abu Zayd's appeal, since a judgment in the case had already been rendered by the trial court and court of appeals.

Since the time of the adoption of Law No. 3, the Egyptian government has not been requesting the public prosecutor to bring charges on the grounds of hisba, but this may not always be the case. An aggressive petitioner could try to use a hisba claim as a threatening device, since the case would have to appear before a judge before it could be dismissed. This is exactly what happened to the prominent Egyptian feminist author, Nawal al-Sa'adawi, who was brought to court by individuals on the same type of charge that was made against Abu Zayd. She expected that the court of first instance would immediately dismiss the charges because Law No. 3 limited hisba cases to the public prosecutor and it was a private individual-not the public prosecutor-who brought the case. Yet the court did not do so, and instead, the judge required her to appear in court a second time; it was not until several weeks later that the court dismissed the charges at the request of the public prosecutor.

The case of Abu Zayd shows that the special nature of family law can lead to unexpected-and even unintended-results. These examples also show that legal drafters need to decide not only what to include from the heritage of Islamic law, but also what to exclude and how to accomplish that exclusion. The family law discussion highlights the complexities regarding Islamic law in parts of the legal system often overlooked in high-profile discussions on the constitutional level. Yet, considering that virtually all Egyptians will encounter the rules of family law at some point in their lives, those rules arguably have greater social impact than Article 2 of the Egyptian Constitution-at least as it is currently interpreted. And not surprisingly, family law is one of the first areas where debates over Islamic law are already taking place in Iraq, as discussed below.

Iraq's Legal Making and Remaking

Structurally, Islamic law had already played a role in the Iraqi legal system in ways similar to Egypt. While Saddam Hussein concentrated all power in his own hands, subsuming law to his own personal decisions, there is still an underlying corpus of laws that was adopted before his rule, which was the product of accommodation among many interests that still exist today. The role of Islamic law in the Iraqi legal system historically is instructive for the context that made-and will likely continue to make-such inclusion possible or desirable. An historical view also identifies traditional fault lines that suggest areas of future debates and controversies.

The Constitution—Pre-Independence

The pre-independence 1925 constitution states that "Islam is the official religion of the state." As in the Egyptian constitution, this seems merely to recognise the religion of the majority of the state's population, without any clear meaning beyond that:

> *The 1925 constitution provided for three types of courts: civil, religious, and special. Religious courts were composed of Islamic Sharia courts and confessional courts for non-Muslims. Islamic courts had jurisdiction over claims involving the personal status of Muslims and the administration of Islamic endowments. Decisions in these courts were to be made according to the rules of the Sharia particular to each of Sunnis and Shi'ites, and then the different schools within the Sunnis. The constitution also required that a judge appointed for a particular area should be of the school of the majority of the residents of that area, while there should always be both Sunni and Ja'fari Shi'ite judges in Baghdad and Basra. This system already reveals the additional religious complexity of Iraq, as there are both Shi'ites and Sunnis to accommodate. After the U.S. invasion in*

2003, some commentators in and outside Iraq proposed that Iraq's 1925 constitution be used as a working model for a new constitution, since it was the most protective of human rights of all of Iraq's constitutions as a modern state.

Post-Independence

The declaration of Islam as the religion of the state is not just a relic of the colonial period. The brief post-revolution constitution of 1958 also recognised that "Islam is the religion of the state." The second Ba'th revolution of 1968 was followed by the more extensive 1970 constitution. The 1970 constitution defines Iraq as a democratic people's republic, the main aim of which is to establish a unified Arab state and a socialist system. It identifies the Iraqi people as the source and legitimacy of power. Language from the 1958 constitution was repeated: "Islam is the religion of the state." The 1970 constitution was adopted as a provisional constitution but remained the working constitution of the country. In 1990 a new constitution was drafted, but its adoption was uncertain because a referendum that confirmed Saddam Hussein as president did not specifically also ratify the proposed constitution. The same language referring to Islam as the religion of the state was included in this proposed 1990 document. This language was retained in the Interim Constitution: Islam is the official religion of the state.

Islamic law as a source of law had not been mentioned in the Iraqi constitutions before the Interim Constitution. The kind of public concern for the role of Islamic law that developed in Egypt in the 1970s and led to Article 2 of the Egyptian constitution, in original and revised form, did not occur or did not have the freedom to occur in Iraq. But significantly, the Interim Constitution does contain a source of law clause. Article 7 states: "Islam is the official religion of the State and is considered a source of legislation (masdar lil-tashri')." As discussed above, the Egyptian constitution provides that the "principles of the Islamic Sharia" are the main source of legislation, whereas the Iraqi phrasing makes Islam "a source of legislation." Thus, there are two main differences between the two documents: the "principles of the Islamic Sharia" are the main source of legislation in Egypt, whereas for Iraq, "Islam" is a source of legislation.

On the face of these two expressions, it is impossible to suggest what these differences will mean in practice. "Islam" in a legal context can be understood as the "Islamic Sharia," meaning the aspects of

Islam that pertain to rules and commands, so the difference in that phrasing is probably not significant. And since the predecessor of the Egyptian SCC did not interpret the meaning of "the principles of the Islamic Sharia are a main source of legislation," we have little historical and comparative record by which to evaluate the possibilities for the current formulation of Iraq's choice of language.

It is noteworthy, nevertheless, that "Islam" in the Iraqi Interim Constitution is not limited by "principles" or any other qualifier, which literally means that any aspect of Islam could be a source of legislation. Yet it is not clear what aspects of Islam that are not legal in some way might be considered a source of law. If the drafters had in mind principles or maxims of the Sharia, even though these are still vague expressions, one could reasonably expect to see this language in the document. The use of merely "Islam" could have been strategic; it might have been broad enough to be acceptable to the diverse members of the Iraqi Governing Council, yet not so specific as to be objectionable to those who might have wanted a weaker or stronger role for Islamic law in the document.

The choice of "Islam" instead of the "Islamic Sharia," or even "principles of the Islamic Sharia" for the source of law clause may be related to Paul Bremer's aim to maintain the role of Islam at the minimal level announced by the Governing Council in its political program in July 2003. Yet, by the time of the Interim Constitution drafting process in February 2004, the Governing Council's then-president Abdel Hamid "insisted Shariah must form the 'principal basis of law' . . . and his views were quickly seconded by three other council members." Commentators concluded that the Governing Council's "uncompromising position, and the fact that Sunni and Shia leaders appear to be in agreement, posed a serious challenge for the provisional authority."

Bremer announced to the Governing Council his limits of toleration: The "draft of the interim constitution, due to take effect at the end of February, would make Islam the state religion and 'a source of inspiration for the law' but not the main source for that law." Bremer, while visiting at a women's centre in Kerbala, was asked what would happen if the Governing Council were to include in the Interim Constitution that Sharia is the principal basis of legislation. "Our position is clear," Mr. Bremer replied. "It can't be law until I sign it." In several other similar statements, Bremer repeated this reference to "Islam as inspiration for law," stating in mid-February, for example, that the "current draft of the constitution would make Islam the state religion of Iraq and 'a source of inspiration for the law.'" The use of the term "inspiration" suggests an indirect, or at least weak, relationship between the rules or principles of "Islam" and "law." Perhaps the aim was to deemphasize actual rules of Islamic law or of the system of the Sharia in general, while still respecting Iraqi calls to value religion in their new constitution.

The ambiguous final wording of Article 7 of the Interim Constitution also suggests that it was negotiated in order to be acceptable to the range of views of the Governing Council and the CPA. In the earlier Pachachi Draft, Article 7 stated: "Islam is the official religion of the country and is considered a fundamental source among the sources of legislation . . . ." While the difference is slight, the recognition that there are other sources of legislation, of which Islam is just one, is a slightly weaker formulation in terms of the emphasis on Islam than the one that ultimately appeared in the Interim Constitution. It emphasized that other sources-such as custom, jurisprudence from other nations like Egypt, and international instruments-would be sources of law alongside Islam.

Iraq's Interim Constitution in Article 7 also includes the phrase: "No law that contradicts the universally agreed upon immutable/unchanging tenets of Islam (thawabit al-Islam al-mujma' 'alayha) . . . may be enacted during this Transition Period." The Pachachi Draft did not contain this contradiction clause. (Recall that the Transitional Period began June 30, 2004, and lasts until an Iraqi government is elected pursuant to a permanent constitution, which shall be, except in circumstances as provided by the Interim Constitution, no later than December 31, 2005). "Thawabit" means elements that are stable, permanent, and unchanging, whereas its opposite " mutaghayyiraf are those things that are unstable and subject to change. These terms were initially used in modern Arabic literary theory-not jurisprudence-but entered legal discussions in the modern period, and thus have no traditional meanings.

The Chief Mufti of Egypt, 'Alijuma', one of the highest-ranking religious figures in that country, stated that in Islamic law, "thabit" (the singular of "thawabit") refers to any constant for all Muslims, at all times, and at all places. He likened this category to those rules and practices accepted by Muslims as a matter of consensus (ijma1). Some examples he gave of thawabit include: prayer; the zakat tax; the pilgrimage; fasting during the month of Ramadan; purifications as a precondition of prayer; the rules governing the legality of sales contracts and marriages; the rules of annulment, divorce, and retaliatory punishment; the punishments specified in the Qur'an (hudud); and others whose status as rules or principles in Islamic law are agreed upon by Muslims. Juma' essentially said that one would have to be "under a rock" not to know that theft, adultery, murder, aggression, wine, pork, and carrion are all prohibited in Islam.

Yet the argument this Chapter seeks to make is that even the opinion of 'AIi Juma'-a highly-esteemed religious figure-is the view of just one scholar, albeit an important one. There is no clear sense in Islamic jurisprudence that the thawabit refer to a fixed and widely known list of rules or principles, just as was the problem with the "principles" in Article 2 of the Egyptian Constitution. There does appear to be some similarity between the Iraqi use of "thawabit" and the Egyptian SCC's interpretation of "principles" in Egypt's Article 2, since the SCC determined that "principles" are so certain that they do not change with time. These interpretations suggest something permanent and inviolable in the principles and the "fixed things"-but they are not defined nor is there a widely agreed list of what they include. The Iraqi phrase includes yet one more complicating factor, the provision that the "thawabit" must be "universally agreed upon." This clearly refers to the idea that these tenets must not only be immutable, but also universally agreed upon, and in the context of Iraq, this means by Sunnis and Shi'ites alike. Given the basic concepts of Islamic law regarding consensus as a source of law, those who must agree to form a "universally-agreed-upon principle" would be legal scholars, not every individual Sunni and Shi'ite.

This ambiguity in the Iraqi Interim Constitution is all the more problematic when considered in conjunction with Article 12, entitled "Fundamental Rights." Article 12 includes the provision: "All Iraqis are equal in their rights without regard to gender, sect, opinion, belief, nationality, religion, or origin, and they are equal before the law. Discrimination against an Iraqi citizen on the basis of his or her gender, nationality, religion, or origin is prohibited." This provision has been pointed to as evidence of the progressiveness of the Interim Constitution, and it is first in the list of excerpts from the law that the CPA is championing Iraq's "Bill of Rights."

The interplay between Article 12 and Article 7 of the Interim Constitution indicates in yet another way the level of compromise and negotiation that must have taken place to reach agreement between the Governing Council and the CPA. In addition to the statement in Article 7 that "no law that contradicts the universally agreed upon immutable/unchanging tenets of Islam (thawabit al-hlam al-mujma' 'alayha) . . . may be enacted during this Transitional Period," the drafters affirmed, in the same sentence, that neither may any law "contradict the principles of democracy, nor the rights cited in Chapter Two [the bill of rights] of this Law . . . during this Transition Period." Nathan Brown points out the oddity of this language:

> *This seems to be a strange nod in the direction of those who feared the language on Islam would somehow negate the rights provisions. I describe the language as strange because of its obvious redundancy: affirming the rights provisions in this manner adds nothing to their effectiveness. The language in Article 7 simply affirms rights that are affirmed elsewhere. In sum, the language of this chapter seems to say that it is unconstitutional to pass an unconstitutional law.*

Article 7 can be read as an effort to emphasize the point that the respect for the universally-agreed-upon immutable/unchanging tenets of Islam may not be used to trump other rights stated elsewhere in the constitution. Yet, perhaps this is not a redundancy at all, because it is possible to read this as a subtle attempt to provide that rights expressed would take priority over a universally-agreed-upon immutable/unchanging tenet of Islam in the case of a conflict.

If Article 7's protection of the universally-agreed-upon immutable/ unchanging tenets of Islam is not clear on its face, then how can it be reasonably known when an immutable principle conflicts with one of the protections of Article 12?

It is not difficult to imagine a proposed law to implement one of Article 12's guarantees challenged because it contradicts an immutable principle of Islam, as understood by an individual or group of Iraqi scholars. Without a clear sense of the meaning of these phrases, the Interim Constitution, even in its short lifespan, will undoubtedly generate both healthy debates and bitter conflicts.

The Civil Code

As in Egypt, the Civil Code in Iraq is the fundamental legislation and thus significant to the role of Islamic law in the new legal system. The Egyptian professor Sanhuri was already well known in Egypt for his law teaching and scholarship, and well on his way to recognition as the Arab world's preeminent legal scholar, when he was invited to Baghdad in 1935 to establish the curriculum for the new College of Law. While teaching in the College that he established, the Iraqi

Ministry of Justice asked him to participate in the drafting of a new civil code.

The drafting committee, headed by the Minister of Justice, debated the source of law for the code, considering two basic concepts: The first possibility was to follow Turkey's and Egypt's example. In 1926 Turkey had adopted the entire Swiss Code with minor modifications and eliminated Sharia law from the legal system. Egypt at that time was still using the 1883 Civil Code for the national courts with a separate Civil Code, adopted in 1875, for the Mixed Courts; both of these were based on the French Code. The second option, which the committee chose, was to synthesize the Sharia and new concepts of Western legislation in order to facilitate relationships with Western nations.

The drafting project was suspended in 1936 due to a coup against the Iraqi monarchy, and it was not until 1943 that Sanhuri returned to Baghdad to resume work on the code. In the meantime, he had begun drafting the Egyptian Civil Code, working with the same intention to blend Islamic law with laws of other systems, based on the Egyptians' choice to do so. In 1943 Sanhuri brought his expertise with the Egyptian Code to his work on Iraq's code, and as a result there are similarities between the two codes. Sanhuri's Iraqi partner in the drafting of the Iraqi Civil Code, Professor Munir al-Qadi, later wrote a commentary on the code in which he explained that it was a product of the combination of Islamic and Western laws.

The result of Sanhuri's efforts in Iraq is the 1951 Civil Code (Iraqi Civil Code). It begins almost identically to the Egyptian Civil Code:

> *Article 1(1). The provisions of the code apply to all matters that they address in letter or spirit. (2) If there is not a provision that can be applied, then the court rules according to customary practice ('urf); if this does not exist, then according to the principles of the Islamic Sharia most consistent with the provisions of this law but without being bound by any specific school of jurisprudence; if these do not exist, then according to the rules of equity. (3) The courts shall be guided in all of this by judicial decisions and by the jurisprudence of Iraq and then by the jurisprudence of other countries whose laws are similar to those of Iraq.*

The main difference from the Egyptian code is the provision that the principles could come from any school, which is an explicit recognition and inclusion of Sunni and Shi'ite jurisprudence. In Egypt Sanhuri had objected to such a clause on the grounds that it was redundant in a country of Sunnis, since a principle by definition rose to the level of uniform acceptance across the Sunni schools. In the case of Iraq, however, the failure of a Sunni-dominated government to include such a provision would be understood as an intentional and unacceptable exclusion of Shi'ites.

Personal Status Legislation

As in Egypt, the Sharia was most prominent in Iraq in the area of personal status law. Like the Egyptian Civil Code, the Iraqi Civil Code did not cover personal status matters, on the grounds that identifying and codifying an applicable rule for each issue was impossible at that time. Instead, personal status matters were still governed mainly by uncodified Sharia, and were heard in Sharia courts.

The first personal status code for Iraq was issued by the revolutionary regime in 1959, which had overthrown the monarchy the previous year in a violent coup. This code was intended to end a long-standing controversy over the unification and codification of personal status laws, and it produced a fairly radical code. This code is discussed more fully below, but first it is useful to understand its legislative history. A draft Code of Personal Status, covering marriage, testamentary disposition, and inheritance was proposed in 1947 by the Committee for Judicial Affairs of the Iraqi Chamber of Deputies, but no advances were made towards its adoption.

This draft attempted to accommodate differences between Sunnis and Shi'ites within the single code. It consisted of 177 articles, ninety-one of which were applicable to all Muslim Iraqis. In eighty-six of the articles, the differences between Sunnis and Shi'ites were preserved and two sets of rules were provided. It would be the judge's responsibility to apply the appropriate law depending on the person's affiliation. Sunnis were treated as a group and differences among the Sunni jurisprudential schools were not included.

For the rules on marriage, for example, fifty-seven articles contained unified rules while twenty-seven contained alternatives. For inheritance, only ten rules were unified and the remaining fifty-four contained alternatives. For the provisions that were either common to both or applicable to Sunnis alone, the rules were often similar to contemporary legislation in the Sunni Middle East. The Iraqi draft personal status code was lengthy and detailed, sacrificing simplicity for the sake of respecting legal rules particular to Shi'ites and Sunnis. In July 1958 a military coup in Baghdad overthrew the monarchy and established a republic, led by 'Abd al-Karim Qasem as Prime Minister.

No personal status code had yet been adopted. The intention to unify the country under the banner of Ba'thism involved a rejection of the draft code and its accommodation of diversity. On February 7, 1959, the Ministry of Justice established a committee to produce a unified code that would be "derived from those rules in the Sharia which were generally agreed and those enactments of Muslim countries which were accepted, together with the settled jurisprudence of the Iraqi courts."

The result was a code issued on December 30, 1959, that provided unitary rules, eliminating differences between the Sunnis and Shi'ites (Ja'faris), and in some cases provided rules that radically departed from any past practice in Iraq (the "Iraqi 1959 Family Code" or the "Code"). This Code did not cover many topics from the draft code. The new government clearly wanted to issue a code quickly, that reflected the principles of the revolution-a unified system for a unified state. The authors of the Iraqi 1959 Family Code drew upon both Sunni and Ja'fari views, so it was not a simple case of the wholesale imposition of all rules of one community upon the other. The Code also created rules without any precedent in any Islamic jurisprudence. The significance of the new Code was that all Muslim Iraqis were subject to all of its provisions, regardless of whether their personal beliefs would require otherwise.

The new Code instructed the judges of the Sharia courts that if the Code did not cover a matter before the court, they should give judgment "according to those principles of Islamic law which are most suited to the provisions of this code." Furthermore, "the courts shall be guided in all this by the law established by legal precedents and Islamic jurisprudence in Iraq and in the other Muslim countries whose legislation approximates to that of Iraq." As in Egypt's personal status laws, and in contrast to the civil codes of the two countries, the "principles of Islamic law" are the first residual source of law for matters of personal status, whereas in the civil codes they are the second residual source, after custom.

Two rules of the Iraqi 1959 Family Code were criticized at the time for deviating entirely from Islamic jurisprudence. First, in an attempt to reduce the number of polygamous marriages, the Code required a man to get judicial permission to marry a second wife. The judge was instructed to give this permission only when the husband was financially competent to support more than one wife and there was some lawful benefit involved in the second marriage. Even if these conditions were met, if the judge feared that the husband would not be able to treat his co-wives equally, then the judge should deny permission. A marriage concluded without judicial permission was invalid, and the husband was subject to punishment by imprisonment and a fine. Requiring a man to get judicial permission for a second wife was an innovation without precedent in Islamic jurisprudence at that time.

But the biggest departure from classical law, both Sunni and Ja'fari, came in the Code's rules on intestate succession. The general rule in Islamic law is that an individual may dispose of onethird of his or her estate in the will as the testator wishes, while the remaining two-thirds is distributed to the heirs according to the complex Islamic rules of inheritance. The prevailing view is that males receive shares twice as large as their female counterparts; this comes from the Qur'anic verse 4:II. The Code, in a dramatic departure from precedent, provided for equal inheritance by male and female heirs.

Opposition to the new code came from many sides. In response to criticisms about the new inheritance rules, Prime Minister 'Abd al-Karim Qasem responded that the Qur'anic verse providing the rule that male children should take twice the share of female children is only an exhortation, and not a command. Given this, he explained:

> *When the public welfare of the Iraqi people demanded equality between men and women in every respect, out of consideration for the rights of half the Iraqi people, apart from the fact that the schools of Islamic law hold variant views in regard to inheritance, and the principles on which it shall be reckoned and divided, and that the Iraqi people is made up of different religious sects: for all the foregoing reasons it is plain that the unification of the matter of inheritance, in the interests of half the Iraqi people, required legislation along the lines of this code.*

The Prime Minister was exercising what he may have believed to be his extensive powers of ijtihad or perhaps his sheer power as the successful leader of a military coup. As an indicator of how controversial this topic remains today, one of the grounds for the charge of apostasy made against Nasr Abu Zayd in Egypt was his own advocacy that changed circumstances in the world required that males and females receive equal shares in matters of inheritance. In Abu Zayd's case, the Court of Cassation concluded that since there is a clear Qur'anic text supporting the two-to-one ratio, ijtihad is not permitted with this text because the meaning is already absolutely clear.

More extensive criticism of the Iraqi 1959 Family Code came from Ja'fari leaders, who objected to the imposition of non-Ja'fari law on Ja'faris and also feared that their autonomy in legal matters would be lost to a Sunni-dominated judiciary. Prior to that time, the personal status court for each local community was headed by a religious judge with the same affiliation as the area's population. A unified code could easily mean encroachment by state-supported Sunni judges.

Bahr al-'Ulum-who was chosen a member of the Iraqi Governing Council-was one of the leaders of Ja'fari opposition to the Iraqi 1959 Family Code, and he published a critique of it in Najaf in 1963. His attacks on the substance of the Code centred on two main areas. First, he opposed the very concept of a code because it binds all judges of all generations to a single set of rules. This prevents the mujtahid judge from carrying out ijtihad and deducing the relevant law for any given case. It further prevents the judge who is not a mujtahid from doing what he is expected to do, which is to follow the established rules of his legal school. For this second scenario, he gives the example of a man who follows the Hanafi school and who divorces his wife while under duress or drunk. In the Hanafi school this is a valid divorce, while the Iraqi 1959 Family Code would consider it invalid. A Hanafi judge would not be permitted to recognise the man's divorce under the Code, and so would be prevented from following the established rules of his school, not to mention the confusion that could be experienced by the man and his wife.

In his second main criticism, which forms the bulk of his published critique, Bahr al-'Ulum reviewed each provision of the Code and identified it as belonging to one of the four Sunni schools of law, one of the Shi'ite schools, or having no basis in any school. His main point is that no one should be required to follow the rules of a school not his own, and so each provision of the Code is an affront on all whose school would take a different view. Even when a Code provision corresponds to aja'fari view, he still criticized it because when applied to a non-Ja'fari it is a violation of the more general concept that allows Muslims to follow the rules of their own school or the Sharia as interpreted by a mujtahid whom they follow.

In February 1963 Ba'thist officers with the assistance of Arab nationalists led a military coup against 'Abd al-Karim Qasem, overthrowing and executing him and his colleagues. After a short period of conflict among these new leaders, the new President 'Abd al-Salam 'Arif pushed out the Ba'th leaders and assumed complete control. 'Arif made efforts to show himself to be a pious Muslim, and was instrumental in the brief but significant amendment to the Iraqi 1959 Family Code that was issued on March 18, 1963. This amendment repealed the whole section on inheritance and modified the law on polygamy, so that while judicial approval was still a stated prerequisite to marry an additional wife, the additional marriage was valid even if such approval was not received, although the husband was subject to a penalty. 'Arif stated that the greatest distortion of the previous regime in terms of legislation was the abrogation of the Islamic rules of inheritance. This abrogation was unacceptable, he stated, because it contradicts a clear Qur'anic provision.

The Ba'thists made a successful return to power in 1968, and, having learned from their mistakes in 1958 and 1963, set out to consolidate their control and protect themselves from rivals. Hasan al-Bakr became president, with his young relative Saddam Hussein as a key aid. Bakr and then Hussein made few changes to the personal status laws. Law 21 of Year 1978 increased the possibility for women to obtain a judicial divorce, and gave women more rights in matters of child custody. Saddam Hussein subsequently changed the name of the Sharia courts to the courts of personal status but all other rules continued to apply.

With this understanding of the controversial history of personal status laws in Iraq, the significance of the Governing Council's Family Law Resolution 137 of Dec. 29, 2003 can now be appreciated fully. The decision called for the application of the Sharia, and abrogation of conflicting laws, in the areas of family law in accordance with each Iraqi's religious identity. This is a clear call for a return to the pre-code situation whereby personal status matters were governed by uncodified Sharia. The views espoused by Bahr al-'Ulum in his treatise are still powerful among some Governing Council members such that they made the Family Law Resolution one of their priorities even while many other major problems were on their agenda in late 2003. The adoption of the Family Law Resolution also indicates that these ideas have supporters among Iraqis as well.

This controversy over personal status law relates directly to the Interim Constitution and the future drafting of a permanent constitution. Quick and aggressive legislative actions at the level of the personal status laws may make later constitutional phrasing attempting to limit that legislation difficult to implement until an interpretive body has been established to interpret the Constitution ultimately chosen by Iraqis.

With the efforts to construct the "new" Iraq, Iraqis and the world community have quickly found themselves in the middle of a debate taking place in some parts of the Muslim world: What is the appropriate role for Islamic law in a state structure? Should an analysis of Iraq be framed in terms of Turkey's or Iran's current choices? This Chapter has shown that neither of these two models is a helpful way of thinking about Iraq's future. This leaves the most difficult and critical questions yet to be answered by Iraq: Should the Sharia be incorporated into a legal system in a highly positivized manner (such as the Iraqi and Egyptian civil codes) or left as a residual source (such as Egypt's personal status laws)? Will some Iraqis challenge the existing Iraqi Civil Code for its Islamic credentials? Who will be the ultimate arbiter of what constitutes Islamic law in Iraq, and how much diversity of opinion about it will be allowed? Will Sunnis and Shi'ites be the only two recognised categories? What if the Hanafis and Shafi'is have different rules on a key personal status matter?

If uncodified Sharia is used as the source or one source of law in particular areas of the law, will interpretive guidelines be legislated for judges and what kind of training in Islamic law will these judges have? Will the views of a particular school, or a particular jurist, be adopted as state law by a legislative body, or will the legislature perhaps patch together rules from several different schools, including Sunnis and Shi'ites, to produce a law or code whose component parts are Islamic in some way but where the overall product seems completely new? While the constitutional process in Iraq is still in the preliminary stages, and the attempt by the Governing Council to legislate in the area of family law was thwarted, such debates indicate the arguments that will expand and intensify in Iraq throughout the Transitional Period and occupy centre stage in Iraq and in the international community during the permanent constitution's drafting process, its subsequent national referendum, elections pursuant to that new constitution, and finally the administration of the first Iraqi government elected under the new Constitution.

To appreciate the key issues in Iraq's past, current, and future legal system, this Chapter has examined the Islamic-law related language of the Interim Constitution and considered some of the choices the drafters of the permanent constitution will need to make in the near future. This Chapter has also shown that exclusive focus on the constitutional level neglects areas in which Islamic law is more established, integrated, and tangible, and more likely to have immediate effects on the lives of Iraqis. While constitutional scholars may work carefully on constitutional language regarding Islamic law, the real battles are already being fought in the personal status laws, and will likely also take place with the civil code. Ultimately, the hope of the international community is that the Iraqi people will adopt a constitution that includes proper rights and protections for its citizens, and adheres to international norms and agreements. During the course of the Transitional Period, the drafting of the permanent constitution and its adoption, and the elections to the National Assembly, the international community must understand that there is no one model for a democracy of Muslim citizens. As U.S. Secretary of State Colin Powell recognised:

> *"We will have to accept what the Iraqi people decide upon," he said in an implicit concession that Washington's dreams of a year ago of a vibrant Western-style democracy may be crumbling fast. Asked if such a result was worth the loss of U.S. lives, he said the relatives of those who died "will see that the Iraqi people are interested in a democracy."*

The most effective way for the foreign community to engage with Iraqis in the remaking of their legal system is to work with and assist communities within Iraq who are struggling for security, safety, freedom, and democracy, for it is such local level groups who are best equipped to design the hardware of Iraq's democratic structure. At the same time, the international community must not lose sight of the ways in which aspects of the legal system can change quickly-and against the will of many Iraqis themselves-and be prepared to work with Iraqis who are also struggling to establish and maintain basic rights in their legal system, including gender equality. The Iraqi blend of democracy that ultimately emerges will be as much-if not more-a product of a "ground up" process than a "top down" one, although this still leaves ample room for international assistance and involvement in the building process. The Iraqis have had more than their share of dictates from above, and only a home grown democracy will be a genuine and sustainable one.

Chapter 5

The Dispute Settlement and World Trade Law

Over the course of several decades, Japan and the United States have engaged in acrimonious conflict over the issue of whether Japan has truly opened its economy in accordance with the disciplines of the General Agreement on Tariffs and Trade (GATT) and, now, the World Trade Organisation (WTO) trade agreements regime. These two countries have perhaps the most adversarial of relationships in the international trade arena, despite their close connections as strategic allies and their numerous other ties. The U.S. government has persistently tried to use a very hard stick to pound open Japanese markets that it alleges are closed. In most cases, the Japanese government seems to succumb to this pounding, and to enter into bilateral agreements with the U.S. government, although it is questionable whether these side agreements really result in trade liberalisation. One can trace cycles of such behaviour over the course of many years. Japan and the United States have engaged in bilateral trade negotiations, or perhaps more accurately, "renegotiation" between official WTO rounds. The behaviour of these two trading nations presents an intriguing study of the nature of the global trading system and its limitations.

Law & Policy in International Business

More recently, Japan and the United States have disputed measures affecting photographic film and paper. The dispute centred on the question of whether Japanese markets for camera film and paper for photographs were open to Eastman Kodak Company, a company headquartered in Rochester, New York. The United States contended that, for over thirty years, the Japanese government engaged in systematic and non-transparent measures designed to protect the two principal Japanese producers of film and paper, Fuji Photo Film

Ltd. and Konica Corporation, from international competition to keep Kodak out of the Japanese market and to counteract the tariff concessions that Japan made in several GATT rounds of multilateral negotiations.

On December 5, 1997, the WTO Panel on Japan—Measures Affecting Consumer Photographic Film and Paper issued an Interim Report deciding in favour of Japan. It was the first case that the United States lost before a WTO panel. The Panel Report was finalised in January 1998, circulated to WTO members on March 31, 1998, and adopted by the WTO Dispute Settlement Body (DSB) on April 22, 1998. In the WTO proceeding, the United States argued that, over the course of several decades, Japan engaged in a broad range of protectionist activities intended to circumvent tariff concessions that Japan agreed to in various GATT negotiating rounds. The activities can be classified into three categories: distribution countermeasures, restrictions on large retail stores, and promotion countermeasures. The United States first argued that Japan engaged in distribution countermeasures to encourage and facilitate the creation of market structures for the distribution of film and photographic paper that caused the exclusion of imports from distribution channels in Japan.

Second, a Large Stores Law, the United States argued, restricted the development of large retail stores in Japan. The United States argued that these large stores, if permitted to grow in accordance with market forces, would diminish the monopoly power of wholesalers and provide increased opportunities for the import of foreign film and paper into Japan. Finally, the United States argued that Japan implemented restrictions on the offering of advertising promotions in a manner that impeded international competition by prohibiting financially strong international competitors from engaging in marketing strategies designed to penetrate the Japanese market. The United States classified the three categories of countermeasures as "liberalisation countermeasures," meaning that Japan promulgated and implemented these measures to counteract and circumvent the concessions that Japan agreed to during the GATT negotiations. The United States argued that these measures, by themselves and in combination, contravened the WTO agreements. The United States argued that the measures violated Articles III, X, and XXIII:1(b) of the GATT.

Article III sets forth the national treatment obligations of the GATT. Article X sets forth requirements for the transparent publication and administration of regulations affecting international trade by

WTO member countries. Article XXIII:1(b) prohibits nullification or impairment of WTO obligations by WTO members by methods that do not expressly violate the WTO Agreement, but which "nullify or impair" the WTO obligations. Among other things, Article XXIII:1(b) prohibits nullification or impairment of WTO obligations by methods that do not expressly violate the WTO Agreement, but that evade basic WTO obligations. A claim before the DSB under Article XXIII:1(b) is called a "non-violation claim" because it asserts that a WTO member has nullified or impaired its concessions. It does not assert, however, any explicit violations of substantive WTO obligations. The DSB found that Japan had not violated these provisions and that the United States failed to prove its case.

The Kodak-Fuji case was the first post-Uruguay Round WTO dispute settlement panel case to consider a non-violation complaint under GATT Article XXIII:1(b). It remains the only post-Uruguay Round case to date that is decided on the basis of the non-violation provisions of Article XXIII:1(b). Article XXIII has the potential to play a significant part in the WTO dispute settlement regime. It has been on the books since the initial GATT came into existence in 1947, but there have been very few cases in which the GATT has considered the non-violation provision on its merits. Indeed, there have been only three successful cases based on the provision. The new dispute settlement regime, however, has the potential to expand substantially the operation of the provision.

Article XXIII, particularly the non-violation provision, has the potential to be an important piece of the WTO agreement architecture. It provides WTO members with the twin incentives of providing concessions to one another during successive rounds of multilateral negotiations and of avoiding circumvention of agreed-upon concessions after the conclusion of the negotiating rounds. The impracticalities related to the ability of WTO members to obtain adequate information about barriers to trade in the economies of other members, to reach agreement on concessions, and to monitor compliance makes Article XXIII necessary to encourage liberalisation and to deter evasion of agreed-upon concessions.

Despite its significant potential as a monitoring mechanism in the WTO system, many scholars have dismissed Article XXIII as setting forth dangerously broad language that should be construed narrowly. The cases in which non-violation nullification or impairment was found to exist all date prior to 1960 and were decided when the GATT was in its infancy. Moreover, for the most part, they deal with some fairly standard and straightforward questions of nullification or impairment, such as where a GATT contracting party has nullified or impaired the benefits of a tariff through a subsidy. In Kodak-Fuji, the United States asked the DSB to consider very novel claims. These claims, however, related to core issues relating to the structure of the institutions of the economy of Japan, a major trading nation. The U.S. claims were of the kind typically addressed in domestic law and policy regulating restrictive business practices. The United States asked the DSB for a great deal, given that the WTO does not yet regulate competition policy and restrictive business practices.

The Kodak-Fuji case appears to have been a test case for the United States and, to some extent, for other WTO members. The European Community and Mexico expressed their interest in the case as third parties. The United States apparently sought to determine whether the existing WTO agreements would sufficiently regulate anti-competitive behaviour in the absence of an explicit agreement within the WTO framework that deals with competition policy. The case is consistent with the United States' cautious approach to the question of whether the WTO should have an agreement dealing with competition policy. The great deal of discussion as to whether the WTO framework should include an international agreement that deals with competition questions has failed to generate any consensus. As a result of the Singapore Ministerial Conference, a Working Group on Trade and Competition Policy has been established to look at this question, but with no concrete results as yet.

This Chapter sets forth the main findings of the Kodak-Fuji panel report. It also examines the decision in the context of remedial activity that the United States attempted pursuant to its municipal law—the well-known Section 301 of the Trade Act of 1974, as amended by the Omnibus Trade and Competitiveness Act of 1988. The Article is based on the contention that detailed "case study" analysis of DSB panel reports assists substantially in understanding how the WTO DSU operates. This is particularly true for the first panel report to apply the non-violation provisions of Article XXIII:1(b).

It provides an analytical framework for thinking about Kodak-Fuji, specifically, and about non-violation claims under Article XXIII:1(b), generally. A substantial number of WTO scholars have argued that the non-violation provisions should be interpreted narrowly, particularly as the coverage of WTO agreements expands into new areas and covers old areas in greater depth. It examines the implications of the Kodak-Fuji decision and extends the analysis of the non-violation provision of Article XXIII:1(b). It first provides an analytical introduction to Article XXIII. It explores the meaning of Article XXIII and its role in the WTO system. It looks at six kinds of complaints that may be brought under XXIII in WTO dispute proceedings. Then it explores in detail "non-violation, nullification or impairment" claims that formed the basis of the U.S. claim in Kodak-Fuji and that seem to hold out the most promise for future DSB panel jurisprudence. Although the mainstream view would seem to be that Article XXIII:1(b) should be used in rare circumstances, this Article proposes a policy oriented jurisprudence for Article XXIII:1(b), infusing it with the ability to cover the fundamental problem of "domestic policy externalities" among WTO members. Although a controversial approach, the non-violation provision can address the regulation of domestic policy when domestic policy autonomy has a substantial adverse effect on obligations set forth in WTO agreements. Finally, Part III examines the WTO dispute settlement system as part of a policy evolution game. It uses positive political theory to show that WTO institutions will likely constrain the DSB to issue non-violation decisions that essentially conform with WTO member preferences. Indeed, policy development based on a common law jurisprudence may be helpful to the WTO in making policy in successive negotiating rounds.

This Chapter reaches the opposite conclusion of those reached by other scholars, who argue that Article XXIII should be interpreted narrowly. Although a panel report in favour of the United States in Kodak-Fuji, assuming it would have withstood an appeal to the WTO Appellate Body, would have provided the United States with a major victory and significant leverage in bilateral negotiations with Japan, this is not a reason to support the U.S. claim. Rather, a win for the United States would have been an important first move in a policy evolution game concerning the development of competition policy and dealing with the issue of transparency in the Japanese economy and in the economies of WTO members generally.

The Kodak-Fuji Proceedings

The Section 301 Proceeding

Under U.S. law, private parties may request that the U.S. government, through the U.S. Trade Representative (USTR), its principal organ in WTO matters, impose unilateral sanctions on a country that maintains measures that block free trade. Parties may seek such unilateral remedies when a country has violated or evaded a WTO obligation. Parties may also seek unilateral remedies to open markets in which a country maintains protectionist measures even though the measure does not constitute a violation or evasion of WTO obligations.

Section 301 of the Trade Act of 1974, as amended, provides the principal unilateral remedy. Section 301 is controversial. Some governments and commentators contend that it takes an overly aggressive approach that is ill-suited to the rule-based multilateral framework that has emerged from the Uruguay Round of multilateral trade negotiations. Kodak filed a petition under Section 301 with the USTR on May 18, 1995. Kodak's petition alleged that prior to 1976, Japan violated the bilateral U.S.-Japan Friendship Commerce and Navigation Treaty and the Organisation for Economic Co-operation and Development Code of Liberalisation of Capital Movements with restrictions on inward foreign investment. Kodak's petition further alleged that Japan instituted liberalisation countermeasures designed to maintain restrictions after they were removed under the WTO regime. The acting USTR initiated an investigation under Section 301 as of July 5, 1995.

On June 13, 1996, the acting USTR found the following:

> *Certain acts, policies, and practices of the Government of Japan with respect to the sale and distribution of consumer photographic materials in Japan are unreasonable and burden or restrict U.S. commerce. Specifically, the USTR found that the Government of Japan established and tolerated a market structure that impedes U.S. exports of consumer photographic materials to Japan, and in which practices occur that also impede U.S. exports of these products to Japan, thereby denying fair and equitable market opportunities. The USTR also concluded that there is reason to believe based on strong evidence that certain Japanese Government liberalisation countermeasures, including inter alia, distribution guidelines and related measures, the Law Pertaining to Adjustment of Business Activities of the Retail Industry for Large Scale Retail Stores (LSRS Law) and the Law Against Unjustifiable Premiums and Misleading Representations (Premiums Law) contravene Japan's obligations under the Multilateral Trade Agreements annexed to the Marrakesh Agreement Establishing the*

> *World Trade Organisation (WTO), and nullify or impair benefits accruing to the United States under the WTO agreements.*

Further details from the summary of the 301 proceeding are as follows:

> *The USTR found that when the Japanese Government gradually withdrew its formal restrictions on imports and inward investment following international pressure beginning in the late 1960s, it simultaneously implemented liberalisation countermeasures designed to restrict access of foreign capital and goods to the Japanese market. The capital and import liberalisation countermeasures implemented beginning in the 1960s, included measures to block or limit foreign direct investment in both new and established enterprises with the intent and effect, inter alia, of limiting market access for imported products. Because of the perceived need to protect the Japanese photographic materials industry from foreign products, the consumer photographic materials sector was among the last to be liberalised. Restrictions on foreign investment in existing enterprises remained in effect until the early 1980s. During the period of capital and import liberalisation countermeasures, the Government of Japan, in particular the Ministry of International Trade and Industry (MITI), took steps to restructure the distribution sector to prevent foreign products from making inroads into the Japanese market. For example, MITI promulgated distribution guidelines for photographic film, and the market structure and practices established under and promoted by these guidelines fostered a dependent and exclusionary relationship among Japan's major photographic materials manufacturer, the primary wholesalers (tokuyakuten), secondary wholesalers, and retailers. The distribution structure, retail sales environment, and business relationships in this sector that were established as a result of MITI's protection of the sector remain in place today.*

The USTR also uncovered significant evidence of anti-competitive activities that warrants full and thorough examination.

The Japanese government refused to participate in the 301 proceeding, although Fuji did participate. The following finding from the 301 proceeding encapsulates the U.S. position on the Japanese refusal:

> *At an October 3, 1995 meeting in Tokyo, U.S. Government officials were prepared to discuss the substance of the issues involved in the investigation, and they solicited the views of and information from Japanese officials concerning those issues. However, at that meeting and throughout the course of the investigation, the Government of Japan unreasonably refused to consult on the substance of the matters under investigation, despite repeated U.S. attempts to engage in consultations.*

The Japanese government took the position that the issues were inappropriate for resolution in a 301 proceeding and that Kodak should have brought its complaint to the Japan Fair Trade Commission because its complaint was essentially that Japan failed to enforce its Antimonopoly Law. The Japanese government argued that the dispute involved questions of competition law and not international economic law. Given that Kodak argued that the Japanese government was involved significantly in erecting trade barriers, and that the industrial policy of the country was designed to stop foreign firms from entering the Japanese market even after the Japanese government conceded to tariff reductions in various rounds of GATT multilateral trade negotiations, Kodak apparently was reluctant to seek a domestic remedy in Japan from the Japanese government. The acting USTR stated in the 301 proceeding that the United States:

> *immediately will seek recourse to the dispute settlement procedures of the WTO to challenge these measures and their application, as provided by the Trade Act and in accordance with Article 23 of the WTO Dispute Settlement Understanding (DSU). If, at the conclusion of dispute settlement proceedings, the WTO Dispute Settlement Body finds that Japanese government acts, policies or practices violate, or are inconsistent with, the provisions of, or otherwise deny benefits accruing to the United States under, any of the WTO agreements, and, unless Japan is taking satisfactory measures to grant the rights of the United States under the WTO agreements, has agreed to eliminate or phase out the affected act, policy or practice, or agreed to an imminent*

satisfactory solution to the burden or restriction on U.S. commerce, or provided satisfactory compensatory trade benefits, the United States shall take action under section 301 in accordance with the DSU.... The United States will request consultations immediately with the Government of Japan pursuant to arrangements for consultations on restrictive business practices adopted by the GATT Contracting Parties in 1960 and carried forward into the WTO.

The WTO Proceeding Contemporaneously with its decision under Section 301, the USTR, on June 13, 1996, requested consultations with the Japanese government under Article 4.4 of the WTO Dispute Settlement Understanding and Article XXIII:1 of the GATT. Japan and the United States held consultations on July 11, 1996. The consultations failed to result in a resolution of the dispute. The United States alleged that a large number of Japanese government proclamations and activities fell within the three categories of liberalisation countermeasures described above. The parties vigorously advocated their respective positions and devoted significant legal resources to dealing with the various issues in the dispute. The clearest and most succinct way to deal with the issues is to start with the law. The measures that the United States challenged and how the law applies to them will then be examined. The case is analysed in this fashion because the facts are so complex and dynamic, spanning over thirty years, and it is easier to deal with them once.

Procedural Issues

One of the principal issues in the Kodak-Fuji case was the level of detail the parties should be required to provide in the "pleading" or initial presentation of their claim before the Dispute Settlement Body. This has been a significant issue in a number of municipal jurisdictions, with the trend toward more relaxed "notice"-type pleading and the avoidance of forfeiture on the basis of technical pleading rules. It has also been the subject of several WTO panel reports.

Article 6.2 of the WTO Understanding on Rules and Procedures Governing the Settlement of Disputes provides in pertinent part that "the request for the establishment of a panel shall be made in writing. It shall indicate whether consultations were held, identify the specific measures at issue, and provide a brief summary of the legal basis of the complaint sufficient to present the problem clearly...." In this case, the United States admitted that its request for a panel did not contain eight measures. The initial submission of the United States to the panel and to Japan disclosed and discussed these measures. The issue thus was "whether the ordinary meaning of the terms of Article 6.2, i.e., that `the specific measures at issue' be identified in the panel request can be met ifa 'measure' is not explicitly described in the request." The panel provided the following guidance:

> *To fall within the terms of Article 6.2, it seems clear that a "measure" not explicitly described in a panel request must have a clear relationship to a "measure" that is specifically described therein, so that it can be said to be "included" in the specified "measure." In our view, the requirements of Article 6.2 would be met in the case of a "measure" that is subsidiary or so closely related to a "measure" specifically identified, that the responding party can reasonably be found to have received adequate notice of the scope of the claims asserted by the complaining party. The two key elements—close relationship and notice—are interrelated: only if a "measure" is subsidiary or closely related to a specifically identified "measure" will notice be adequate.*

Article 6.2 provides a general pleading requirement. Article 26 of the Rules and Procedures is a special provision for non-violation complaints. It states that, for non: violation complaints of the type described in Article XXIII:1(b), the complainant "shall present a detailed justification in support of any complaint relating to a measure that does not conflict with the relevant covered agreement." In other words, if the complainant alleges that the measure taken by the respondent nullified or impaired a WTO obligation without explicitly violating a WTO agreement, the complainant :must proffer a detailed justification for its complaint. The panel report states that Article 26.1 and WTO jurisprudence "confirm that this is an exceptional remedy for which the complaining part), bears the burden of providing a detailed justification to back its allegations." According to the panel, this detailed justification will establish a presumption that what is claimed is true, and that it would be for Japan to rebut any such presumption.

Substantive Issues: The Non-Violation Claim—General Considerations

Article XXIII:1(b) provides that a WTO member may seek dispute settlement in the following circumstances: "If any WTO Member should consider that any benefit accruing to it directly or indirectly under this Agreement is being nullified or impaired ... as the result of ... the application by another WTO Member of any measure, whether or not it conflicts with the provisions of this Agreement." This is known as a non-violation claim because the measures alleged to violate WTO obligations under this provision do not have to be an explicit breach of any provision in a WTO agreement or of any concessions made by the other WTO member.

A prior panel report, in the EEC—Oilseeds case, explained the purpose for the provision as follows:

> *The idea underlying [... Article XXIII:1(b)] is that the improved competitive opportunities that can legitimately be expected from a tariff concession can be frustrated not only by measures proscribed by the General Agreement but also by measures consistent with that Agreement. In order to encourage contracting parties to make tariff concessions they must therefore be given a right of redress when a reciprocal concession is impaired by another contracting party as a result of the application of any measure, whether or not it conflicts with the General Agreement.*

The panel considered that the main value of a tariff concession is that it provides an assurance of better market access through improved price competition. Contracting parties negotiate tariff concessions primarily to obtain that advantage. They must therefore be assumed to base their tariff negotiations on the expectation that the price effect of the tariff concessions will not be systematically offset. If no right of redress were given to them in such a case they would be reluctant to make tariff concessions and the General Agreement would no longer be useful as a legal framework for incorporating the results of trade negotiations.

The rationale for Article XXIII:1(b) thus provides countries with an incentive to make tariff concessions. The impracticalities for the parties to obtain adequate information about barriers to trade that exist in the economies of other parties, to reach agreement on tariff concessions, and to monitor compliance with concessions, makes the clause a needed incentive device to encourage negotiations in the WTO multilateral negotiations process. As explained in the panel report, this provision has been on the books of the GATT for almost fifty years, yet there have been very few cases in which a GATT panel or working party has considered the provision on its merits. On this basis, the panel report stated that the remedy should be approached with caution and as an exceptional remedy. As explained in the panel report, "the reason for this caution is straightforward. Members negotiate the rules that they agree to follow and only exceptionally would expect to be challenged for actions not in contravention ,of those rules."

The panel said that each case brought under Article XXIII:1(b)

should be examined on its own merits, bearing in mind the above-mentioned need to safeguard the process of negotiating reciprocal tariff concessions. Our role as a panel charged with examining claims under Article XXIII:1(b) is, therefore, to make an objective assessment of whether, in light of all the relevant facts and circumstances in the matter before us, particular measures taken by Japan have nullified or impaired benefits accruing to the United :States within the meaning of Article XXIII:1(b).

All but one of the cases prior to Kodak-Fuji concerned allegations that a subsidy to a firm that was consistent with the GATT, but that was provided subsequent to a tariff concession, nullified or impaired the tariff concession. There is no reason to limit Article XXIII:1(b) to such situations. As the panel report found:

> *We wish to make clear that we do not a priori consider it inappropriate to apply the Article XXIII:1(b) remedy to other governmental actions, such as those designed to strengthen the competitiveness of certain distribution or industrial sectors through non-financial assistance. Whether assistance is financial nor non-financial, direct or indirect, does not determine whether its effect may offset the expected result of tariff negotiations. Thus, a Member's industrial policy, pursuing the goal of increasing efficiency in a sector, could in some circumstances upset the competitive relationship in the market place between domestic and imported products in a way that could give rise to a cause of action under Article XXIII:1(b). In the context of a Member's distribution system, for example, it is conceivable that measures that do not infringe GATT rules could be implemented in a manner that effectively results in a disproportionate impact on market conditions for imported products. In this regard, however, we must also bear in mind that tariff concessions have never*

been viewed as creating a guarantee of trade volumes, but rather, as explained below, as creating expectations as to competitive relationships. b. The Elements of a Non-Violation Claim The panel report sets forth the following three elements of a claim under Article XXIII:1(b): (i) application of a measure by a WTO Member, (ii) a benefit accruing under a WTO agreement, and (iii) nullification or impairment of the benefit as a result of the application of the measure.

(i) What is a "Measure?"

The parties to the dispute vigorously litigated the question of what constitutes a "measure." In Japan, a great deal of government direction of private sector activity is accomplished through administrative guidance that, in formal legal terms, is non-binding, but that may be a very persuasive tool of the Japanese government. The panel report stated

The ordinary meaning of measure as it is used in Article XXIII: 1(b) certainly encompasses a law or regulation enacted by a government. But in our view, it is broader than that and includes other governmental actions short of legally enforceable enactments. At the same time, it is also true that not every utterance by a government official or study prepared by a non-governmental body at the request of the government or with some degree of government support can be viewed as a measure of a Member government.

The panel was mindful of the role of formally non-binding administrative guidance in Japan and found the following with respect to such guidance:

In Japan, it is accepted that the government sometimes acts through what is referred to as administrative guidance. In such a case, the company receiving guidance from the Government of Japan may not be legally bound to act in accordance with it, but compliance may be expected in light of the power of the government and a system of government incentives and disincentives arising from the wide array of government activities and involvement in the Japanese economy.

The panel concluded that "where administrative guidance creates incentives or disincentives largely dependent upon governmental action for private parties to act in a particular manner, it may be considered a governmental measure." The panel explained, however, that the examination of alleged measures must be performed in context and that the incentives/disincentives test is not the exclusive test of whether a government activity is a measure under Article XXIII:1(b). The panel found that it should be open to a "broad definition of the term measure for purposes of Article XXIII:1(b), which considers whether or not a non-binding government action has an effect similar to a binding one." An action must be taken by the government of a WTO member to be a measure. As explained by the panel:

> *As the WTO Agreement is an international agreement, in respect of which only national governments and separate customs territories are directly subject to obligations, it follows by implication that the term measure in Article XXIII:1(b) and Article 26.1 of the DSU, as elsewhere in the WTO Agreement, refers only to policies or actions of governments, not those of private parties. But while this "truth" may not be open to question, there have been a number of trade disputes in relation to which panels have been faced with making sometimes difficult judgements as to the extent to which what appear on their face to be private actions may nonetheless be attributable to a government because of some governmental connection to or endorsement of those actions.*

The panel concluded that an action is taken by private parties does not rule out the possibility that it may be deemed to be governmental if there is sufficient government involvement with it. It is difficult to establish bright-line rules in this regard, however. Thus, that possibility will need to be examined on a case-by-case basis.

Finally, an action must be currently applied to be a measure. Only an action that continues in operation, and not the market structure that resulted from past actions, constitutes a measure under Article XXIII: 1(b). This is based on the plain meaning of Article XXIII:1(b) and its use of the present tense, "if any Member should consider that any benefit accruing to it ... is being nullified or impaired ... as a result of ... (b) the application by another Member of any measure, whether or not it conflicts with the provisions of the Agreement." (ii) What is a Benefit Accruing under the WTO Agreements?

Article XXIII:1(b) provides that, to prove a non-violation claim, the complainant must show that a benefit accruing under a relevant WTO agreement is being nullified or impaired. The panel ruled that the concept of benefit in WTO precedent has been that of "legitimate expectations of improved market-access opportunities arising out of relevant tariff concessions." The panel also said that "for expectations to be legitimate, they must take into account all measures of the party making the concession that could have been reasonably anticipated at the time of the concession."

Japan argued that only the tariff concessions granted in the Uruguay Round, the latest round of multilateral negotiations, should be considered by the panel. Japan's argument was based on Article 30 of the Vienna Convention on the Law of Treaties, to the effect that in the event of a conflict, the provision that is later in time prevails. The panel disagreed, asserting that it could consider concessions going back to the 1967 Kennedy Round. The panel's decision was based on Paragraph 1 of the GATT 1994, negotiated as part of the Uruguay Round. Paragraph 1 provides that GATT 1994 incorporates "protocols and certifications relating to tariff concessions." The panel found that Article 30 did not apply because there is nothing inherently incompatible—in conflict—between the earlier and later agreed tariff concessions. Such a conflict would only seem to exist if the subsequent concessions were less favourable that prior concessions, which is not the situation in this case. Where tariff concessions has been progressively improved, the benefits—expectations of improved market access—accruing directly or indirectly under different tariff concession protocols incorporated in GATT 1994 can be read in harmony.

The panel explained, however, that the United States might have a very difficult case because it was based on expectations from rounds concluded eighteen and thirty years ago. A WTO member must "legitimately expect" to obtain a benefit as a result of tariff negotiations. One of the principal issues in making such a determination was what to do with measures that existed prior to a round. The panel report sets forth the following guidelines:

> *First, in the case of measures shown by the United States to have been introduced subsequent to the conclusion of the tariff negotiations at issue, it is our view that the United States has raised a presumption that it should not be held to have anticipated these measures and it is then for Japan to rebut that presumption. Such a rebuttal might be made, for example, by establishing that the measure at issue is so clearly contemplated in an earlier measure that the United States should be held to have anticipated it.*

However, there must be a clear connection shown. In our view, it is not sufficient to claim that a specific measure should have been anticipated because it is consistent with or a continuation of a past general government policy.

Second, in the case of measures shown by Japan to have been introduced prior to the conclusion of the tariff negotiations at issue, it is our view that Japan has raised a presumption that the United States should be held to have anticipated those measures and it is for the United States to rebut that presumption. In this connection, it is our view that the United States is charged with knowledge of Japanese government measures as of the date of their publication. We realise that knowledge of a measure's existence is not equivalent to understanding the impact of the measure on a specific product market. For example, a vague measure could be given substance through enforcement policies that are initially unexpected or later changed significantly. However, where the United States claims that it did not know of a measure's relevance to market access conditions in respect of film or paper, we would expect the United States to clearly demonstrate why initially it could not have reasonably anticipated the effect of an existing measure on the film or paper market and when it did realise the effect. Such a showing will need to be fled to the relevant points in time (i.e., the conclusions of the Kennedy, Tokyo and Uruguay Rounds) in order to assess the extent of the United States' legitimate expectations of benefits from these three Rounds. A simple statement that a Member's measures were so opaque and informal that their impact could not be assessed is not sufficient....

Third, for our purposes, we consider the conclusion of the tariff negotiations in the three Rounds to be as follows: In the case of the Kennedy Round, it appears that tariff negotiations continued until the very end of the Round and thus we will consider the date of the conclusion of the Round, i.e., 30 June 1967, as the relevant date. In the case of the Tokyo Round, the conclusion of the Round was 12 April 1979, although the relevant Protocol was formally dated 30 June 1979. We will address where appropriate the U.S. argument that the negotiations on film tariff reductions ended earlier. In the case of the Uruguay Round, tariff negotiations were substantially completed as of 15 December 1993, although the formal end of the Round occurred on the signing of the WTO Agreement in Marrakech on 15 April 1994. Accordingly, we will use the date of 15 December 1993 as the conclusion of the Uruguay Round tariff negotiations. (iii) Nullification or Impairment of Benefits: The Causation Requirement Article XXIII:1(b) provides that, for a WTO member to establish a non-violation claim, it must prove that a benefit under the WTO agreements is being "nullified or impaired as the result of" measures by another WTO member. The panel ruled that this means that "it must be demonstrated that the competitive position of the imported products subject to and benefiting from a relevant market access (tariff) concession is being upset by ... the application of a measure not reasonably anticipated."

Finding causation when both the government and the private sector are engaged in the activities in question presents one potential problem. The panel ruled that "the issue is whether ... a measure has made more than a de minimus contribution to nullification or impairment."

The proclamations of the Japanese government that were under scrutiny in this case were all facially neutral—they did not say anything about the origin of the goods. Japan argued that this was sufficient to find that there was no causal connection between the alleged measures and competitive conditions for film and photographic paper. The U.S. position was that the panel should examine disparate impact. The panel stated:

> *In our view, even in the absence of de jure discrimination (measures which on their face discriminate as to origin), it may be possible for the United. States to show de facto discrimination (measures which have a disparate impact on imports). However, in such circumstances, the complaining party is called upon to make a detailed showing of any claimed disproportionate impact on imports resulting from the origin-neutral measure. And, the burden of demonstrating such impact may be significantly more difficult where the relationship between the measure and the product is questionable.*

The parties disagreed in many cases about whether a specific measure was intended to restrict imports or to promote other policies. The Japanese government may have had a multitude of reasons for its activities. The panel found a potential connection between intent and causation. Although Article XXIII:1(b) does not require a proof of intent of nullification or impairment of benefits,

What matters for purposes of establishing causality is the impact of a measure, i.e. whether it upsets competitive relationships.

Nonetheless, intent may not be irrelevant. In our view, if a measure that appears on its face to be origin-neutral in its effect on domestic and imported products is nevertheless shown to have been intended to restrict imports, we may be more inclined to find a causal relationship in specific cases, bearing in mind that intent is not determinative where it in fact exists. It remains for the complaining party to show that the specific measure it challenges does in fact nullify or impair benefits within the meaning of Article XXIII:1(b).

Finally, the panel agreed with the United States that it should examine the impact of the measures in combination as well as individually. The panel said that "notwithstanding the logic of this theoretical argument, however, we are sensitive to the fact that the technique of engaging in a combined assessment of measures so as to determine causation is subject to potential abuse and therefore must be approached with caution and circumscribed as necessary."

The WTO Rulings on the Non-Violation Claim

In applying the law to the facts, the panel looked at all three factors, regardless of whether the case could be disposed of on the basis of a single factor. The panel thus did not apply established principles of judicial economy. Article XXIII:1(b) factors are cumulative, and all must be met in order for a claim to succeed.

Distribution Countermeasures—The Claim in Context

In the two most recent rounds of trade negotiations, the Tokyo and the Uruguay Rounds, Japan committed to substantial reductions in its tariffs and applied rates for photographic film and paper. Tariffs were eliminated completely in the Uruguay Round. The United States took the position that these tariff concessions were nullified or impaired by "the Japanese government's array of opaque, informal measures" designed to exclude foreign products and to support "single-brand distribution" for Japanese products only.

The United States advanced as a "general theme" of their entire case that there is a "unique relationship" in Japan between government and industry. The U.S. argument was that Japanese industrial policy relied substantially on "quasi-governmental entities, including, inter alia, fair trade councils, advisory committees, study groups, research institutes, and chambers of commerce." The United States argued that these entities engaged in a "concerted adjustment" process to restrict entry into the market by foreign competitors. As the panel report explained:

> *The United States argues that when the liberalisation of international trading conditions became imminent, MITI and Japanese industry recognised the superiority of foreign firms which could create serious competition for Japanese manufacturers and their products. MITI and Japanese manufacturers, it is argued, consequently devised a plan to streamline Japan's distribution system in order to bring it under the control of domestic producers. The basic US position is that MITI sought to strengthen vertical distribution channels that would handle the products of a particular domestic manufacturer exclusively.*

Japan countered that the United States engaged in distorted characterisation. Japan argued that the panel should examine each "measure" on its own merit without any "preconceived prejudice" against an alleged "unique" Japanese system. The panel considered the following distribution countermeasures on the merits:

(1) 1967 Cabinet Decision;

(2) 1967 JFTC Notification 17 on premiums to businesses;

(3) 1968 Sixth Interim Report on Distribution Modernisation Outlook and Issues;

(4) 1969 Seventh Interim Report on Systemisation of Distribution Activities;

(5) 1969 Survey Report regarding Transaction Terms;

(6) 1970 Guidelines for Rationalising Terms of Trade for Photographic Film;

(7) 1971 Basic Plan for the Systemisation of Distribution; and

(8) 1975 Manual for Systemisation of Distribution by Industry: Camera and Film.

The panel rejected the U.S. distribution countermeasures claim. The panel concluded:

> *The United States has not been able to show that the various "measures" it cites have upset competitive relationships between domestic and US film and paper in Japan, principally because single-brand distribution appears to have occurred before and independently of those "measures", but also because the United States has not demonstrated that these "measures" are directed*

at promoting vertical integration or single-brand distribution. In answering the timing problem, the United States has provided no convincing evidence or arguments that the cited "measures" in fact had the effect of reinforcing single-brand distribution. Equally, the United States has not explained why the vertically integrated, single-brand distribution structure of the film sector in Japan—a state of affairs that the evidence suggests is similar to that occurring elsewhere in the world (including in the United States)—would have broken down in the absence of continuing government intervention.

In addition, the panel ruled that the United States failed to show that a number of measures important to its case continued in effect. Indeed, the panel held that some "may be dated or have been formally revoked." With respect to such measures, the United States failed to prove that they "are today upsetting competitive relationships between domestic and U.S. film and paper in Japan." As to some measures, the panel was not persuaded that their major purpose was to block entry of foreign firms.

The Specific Alleged Distribution Countermeasures

The 1967 Cabinet Decision on Liberalisation of Inward Direct Investment

In the WTO proceeding, the United States characterised a 1967 Cabinet Decision Concerning Liberalisation of Inward Direct Investment of June 1967 (hereinafter 1967 Cabinet Decision) as a "watershed" in Japan's protection of film and photographic paper markets liberalised under the GATT/WTO framework. The avowed purpose of the 1967 Cabinet Decision was to determine what steps the Japanese government and Japanese industry should take to prepare for capital liberalisation and for the introduction of foreign enterprises into Japan. The Decision states the following three points as the basic justification of its "countermeasures" to deal with the presence of foreign investment in Japan: (1) prevent disorder that may arise from the advancement of foreign capital; (2) create the foundation to enable our enterprises to compete with foreign enterprises on equal terms; and (3) actively strengthen the quality of domestic enterprises and reorganise the industrial system so that they can fully compete with foreign capital.

In reading the portions of the 1967 Cabinet Decision set forth in the panel report, one is struck by what would seem to be policy conclusions that fly in the face of neo-classical economic theory and that seek "orderly" competition. For example, the 1967 Cabinet Decision states:

> *It would be necessary to restrain foreign enterprises coming into Japan after liberalisation from disturbing order in domestic industries, by resorting to the strength of their superior power, and from advancing into the non-liberalised sectors by evading control. The establishment of these "(counter)measures" for strengthening the capacity of our enterprises for international competition and for preventing foreign enterprises from disturbing order in our industries and market would be a basic necessity if the liberalisation is to be promoted and if our people are to enjoy its economic benefits.*

The 1967 Cabinet Decision asserted that the distribution sector required substantial improvement:

> *Modernisation lags behind most in the distribution sector. Here, the power of resistance against the inroad of foreign capital is weak, and the impact of foreign capital advancing into this sector will also pose significant impact on the production sector. It is necessary, therefore, to implement countermeasures in support of the efforts of industry with the objectives of modernising the distribution structure, fundamentally strengthening the enterprises in this sector, and establishing a mass sales system.*

The United States argued that the 1967 Cabinet Decision set a clear national priority in Japan to protect domestic industry from international competition. The United States also argued that, while Japan agreed on the international level to liberalisation, it began a process of restructuring Japanese industry through various countermeasures to offset the effects of international liberalisation. Japan responded that the 1967 Cabinet Decision was concerned with modernisation and efficiency in the Japanese distribution sector to prepare it for international competition. The panel report is vague on whether the 1967 Cabinet Decision is a measure. The panel found that the 1967 Cabinet Decision as a whole constitutes a measure, but it also found that the part of the Decision dealing with modernisation of the distribution sector "is more in the nature of a general policy statement than either a decision on particular government actions or a mandate to private industry to follow governmental policy by taking specific actions." The panel report is also vague on whether the Decision continued in force after December 1980, when the Cabinet Decision of December 26, 1980 expressly states that the 1967 Cabinet Decision was no longer in effect. The 1980 Decision, according to the panel, does not clearly abolish the 1967 Cabinet Decision.

The panel found that the United States could not claim any benefits accruing from the 1967 Cabinet Decision under the Tokyo and Uruguay Rounds. The 1967 Cabinet Decision was published in Kampo, Japan's official gazette, on June 21, 1967. The Kennedy Round concluded on June 30, 1967, but the Tokyo and Uruguay Rounds were far into the future at the time. Applying the principles set forth above, the panel ruled that the United States could not claim legitimate expectations of improved market access based on the Tokyo and Uruguay Rounds.

The United States also failed to demonstrate that the 1967 Cabinet Decision nullified or impaired its Kennedy Round benefits. The portions of the 1967 Cabinet Decision dealing with the Japanese distribution sector set forth general policy statements that do not provide for clear directions to the public or the private sector to undertake specific activities.

1967 Japan Fair Trade Commission Notification 17 on Premiums to Business

Notification 17, issued on May 10, 1967 by the Japan Fair Trade Commission (JFTC), prohibited manufacturers of certain goods, including film and photographic paper, to offer cash and other premiums in excess of 100,000 yen ($278 in 1967) annually as inducements to wholesalers and retailers to distribute and sell the products of the manufacturers or to agree to certain contract terms. The JFTC repealed Notification 17 in April 1996. The United States alleged that Notification 17 was both a distribution and a premium countermeasure.

The panel found that Notification 17 was a measure under Article XXIII:1(b), but only between 1967 and 1996. The United States argued that the repeal was ineffective because manufacturers were still required to comply with Designation 9 of JFTC Notification 15 of 1982, which banned "unjust inducements" in excess of "normal business practice." The panel concluded that Notification 17 was no longer in effect for two reasons. First, consideration by the panel of Designation 9 was inappropriate for the same reason that other measures were excluded from the panel's terms of reference: an insufficient relationship existed between Designation 9 and measures specified in the U.S. complaint. Second, the panel concluded that the United States failed to prove that "the policy underlying JFTC Notification 17 has been continued through ongoing administrative guidance."

The panel found that Notification 17 was not a benefit under the GATT/WTO framework. Notification 17 existed prior to the Kennedy Round. The panel ruled that "although we can conceive of circumstances where the exporting WTO Member may not reasonably be aware of the significance of a measure for or its potential disparate impact on imported products until some time after its publication, the United States has not demonstrated the existence of any such circumstance here."

Notification 17 applied to both foreign and domestic firms and did not contain any explicit discrimination against foreign firms. The United States argued that Notification 17 was nevertheless discriminatory. Because of restrictions on foreign investment in Japan until the 1970s, foreign firms could not set up their own distribution networks. They thus had to compete with domestic firms for existing wholesalers and distributors. The domestic firms were already entrenched in the distribution system. Notification 17, argued the United States, restricted the ability of foreign firms to compete with domestic firms on crucial terms such as price. The panel found that, although a JFTC press summary stated that "counteracting the influence of U.S. capital" was a purpose of Notification 17, the JFTC justified Notification 17 as necessary to deal with distortions in the domestic market and "cut-throat sales practices promoted by huge capital power." The panel ruled that, on balance, the evidence on the adoption of Notification 17 suggested that it "was directed against potential excesses of promotional activities in the distribution sector in general." The panel found that the United States failed to identify a single instance in which implementation of Notification 17 led to the upsetting of the competitive relationship between Japanese and U.S. film and photographic paper.

1968 Sixth Interim Report on Distribution Modernisation Outlook and Issues

The Sixth Interim Report of the MITI Industrial Structure Council Distribution Committee, entitled, "Distribution Modernisation Outlook and Issues," stated the following concerns about the potential for foreign enterprises to take control of Japan's distribution system:

1. There is a risk that growth sectors will fall under the monopolistic control of foreign capital, resulting from the difference in capital resources and the like.
2. There is a risk that the process of sales expansion by foreign capital affiliated distribution enterprises will aggravate excessive competition and hinder the smooth implementation of distribution modernisation plans and the established order of trade will be disrupted.
3. There is a risk that the manufacturing sector will be dominated by controlling the sales routes, bringing about the international subcontracting of Japanese industry.

The Sixth Interim Report was issued on August 5, 1968. The United States was concerned that the Sixth Interim Report would promote horizontal integration and make entry into the Japanese distribution system difficult for foreign firms. Japan responded that the Sixth Interim Report addressed modernisation of the distribution sector as a whole and was intended to deal with the concern that domestic firms would be restricted in using distribution channels that were subject to regulation, while foreign firms, in the wake of capital liberalisation, would be free to build modern and potentially exclusive distribution systems.

The panel ruled that the Sixth Interim Report was not a measure. It found that the Distribution Committee was established by the MITI Industrial Structure Council, which was an advisory council that was not comprised of government officials. The panel ruled that the Sixth Interim Report was not binding law or regulation, nor did it provide "incentives or disincentives to the private sector to take any particular action." It was essentially a "study report" to government, an examination of the status of the distribution sector that makes general recommendations to government. It does not tell the private sector to take any action.

The panel ruled that the Sixth Interim Report did not frustrate the legitimate expectations of the United States of a benefit accruing under GATT/WTO. Any such expectations could only exist with respect to Kennedy Round negotiations because the Sixth Interim Report was issued in 1968. The Tokyo Round concluded in 1979, and the Uruguay Round in 1994. The panel ruled that the United States failed to demonstrate causation and that the United States failed to prove that the Sixth Interim Report nullified or impaired benefits accruing to the United States under Article XXIII:1(b). The panel found the following to be influential in its ruling on lack of causation:

> *First, the report is an advisory report directed to the government, setting out non-binding policy options for the government; second, these policy options are directed to modernising and improving the overall efficiency of the distribution sector in Japan; third, they are not at all product-specific; and fourth, the United States has not been able to point to any specific government actions resulting from this policy options report, except perhaps for the 1970 Guidelines discussed below.*

The panel found "timing problems" with the U.S. argument because, by 1968, a good deal of the distribution sector for film in Japan was already single brand. The panel noted that the Sixth Interim Report was origin-neutral and listed advantages that would result from liberalisation and discussed potential disadvantages of cooperation among firms in the distribution sector. The panel also found that the United States failed to point to a single instance where the Sixth Interim Report upset the competitive relationship between foreign and domestic firms.

1969 Seventh Interim Report on Systemisation of Distribution Activities

The Seventh Interim Report of the MITI Industrial Structure Council Distribution Committee, entitled "Systemisation of Distribution Activities," proposed the following four ideas to "systematise" the distribution system: "(i) establishing a Distribution Systemisation Council; (ii) presenting guide posts and promoting standardisation; (iii) establishing a system for providing distribution-related information; and (iv) providing incentives in areas such as financing and taxation." The Seventh Interim Report was issued in July 1969.

The United States argued that the Seventh Interim Report was one of the "key foundation stones" of Japan's alleged plan to "systematise" the distribution sector in order to make it resistant to foreign involvement. The United States argued that the purpose of the Seventh Interim Report was to direct stronger vertical and horizontal ties within Japanese industry to exclude foreigners. Japan provided the familiar refrain that the Seventh Interim Report would facilitate the modernisation of the backward distribution system so that Japanese firms could compete with foreign firms. The panel ruled that the Seventh Interim Report was not a measure, that it did not relate to benefits accruing under GATT/WTO, and that the United States failed to show nullification or impairment, for reasons similar to those provided concerning the Sixth Interim Report.

1969 Survey on Transaction Terms

In 1968, MITI asked the Institute for Distribution Research, an "apparently private organisation," to survey transaction terms in several industries, including tile film industry. The purpose of the survey included the dissemination of "rational trade practices." In March 1969, the Institute submitted its survey report on the film industry. MITI thereafter published drafts and republications of this 1969 Survey Report. The 1969 Survey Report examined the terms and conditions of contracts, including terms dealing with discounts and rebates, delivery, returns, settlement of accounts, and promotional practices. The Report included the following findings:

> *There is a view and an impression that the industry of general use photographic film, based on an oligopoly of two domestic manufacturers [Fuji and Konica], is superficially in a stable and normal state in which contract formation and documentation of transactions are progressing. Consider, however, one postulate:*

(1) If the oligopoly of the two domestic manufacturers is broken up by a foreign company; and

(2) If a new distribution route emerges to compete against the route of photographic material dealers, which is the core existing route in the distribution market.

There may be very few observers who have a sense of crisis regarding (1) and (2) as realistic issues; however, they should now be considered as the most concrete and realistic problems.

The 1969 Survey Report recommended the following:

> *Given this situation, it is necessary to formulate measures before hand in order to minimise the anticipated disorder in the distribution market. This is why it is significant to rationalise and standardise transaction terms and to create an established order of distribution.*

The panel concluded that the 1969 Survey Report was not a measure for reasons similar to those provided for reaching the same conclusion about the Sixth Interim Report. The panel found that it was "in the nature of a factual survey conducted by an apparently private organisation at the request of the Government" and that, "while it is true that the report contains a few introductory pages (and concluding paragraphs) on the subject of what are irrational contract terms, the vast bulk of the 1969 Survey Report simply provides a description of existing practices." The panel found the 1969 Survey Report to be a "background report providing current factual information of the basis on which the government might later decide to act." The panel concluded that the 1969 Survey Report did not upset any legitimate expectations by the United States of a benefit accruing under GATT/WTO, for reasons similar to the reasons provided for the Sixth Interim Report, discussed above. The panel ruled that the United States failed to prove any nullification or impairment. The panel found that neither party to the dispute "submitted any evidence or argument regarding the impact of the 1969 Survey Report on U.S. market-access expectations ... beyond the type of arguments made in relation to the Sixth and Seventh Interim Reports."

1970 Guidelines for Rationalising Terms of Trade for Photographic Film

MITI established a Transaction Terms Standardisation Committee to examine the issue of standardisation of contract terms in industry. It focused on industry generally rather than solely on the film industry. In 1970, the Committee published "Guidelines for Rationalising Terms of Trade for Photographic Film." The United States argued that the 1970 Guidelines promoted vertical integration through terms and conditions in transactions within the film distribution sector, and that this vertical integration was designed to make wholesalers more dependent on Japanese manufacturers. Japan countered that it issued essentially the same guidelines to fifteen different industries in 1970. The panel reiterated that "MITI has been consistently concerned with rationalisation of trading terms in the distribution sector since the 1960s. What had hitherto existed, Japan maintains, were irrational business practices that were economically inefficient." Japan also argued that single brand distribution was the norm prior to the issuance of the guidelines and is common world wide.

The panel ruled that the 1970 Guidelines constituted a measure under Article XXIII:1(b). In the publication of the 1970 Guidelines, MITI said "that it intends to see to it that improvement of terms of trade will be implemented in accordance with this guideline" and that "we expect that the parties involved in transactions understand the need for trade rationalisation, and will make voluntary efforts to achieve this purpose." MITI also asked industry associations to formulate more specific trade terms based on the 1970 Guidelines, and, shortly after the publication of the 1970 Guidelines, the wholesalers' association for film and photographic paper published a "Transaction Outline" to implement its own guidelines that were promulgated in response to the 1970 Guidelines and reported these activities back to MITI. Subsequently, MITI and industry together published a "Model Contract" for the film industry. The panel concluded that "there is sufficient likelihood that the administrative guidance given by MITI in the 1970 Guidelines provides sufficient incentives for private parties to act in a particular manner such that it would have a similar effect on business activity in Japan as a legally binding measure." The panel concluded that the 1970 Guidelines "may still be in effect" because the Japanese government had not expressly revoked them, although it issued new guidelines in 1990.

As for benefits accruing under GATT/WTO, based on the standards set forth above, the panel found that the United States could have a legitimate expectation with respect only to the Kennedy Round and not for the Tokyo and Uruguay Rounds. The panel found no nullification and impairment of GATT/WTO benefits. According to the panel, the United States argued the following:

> *The standardisation of transaction terms chilled the ability of foreign manufacturers to offer competitive terms to Japanese wholesalers: first, by setting uniform transaction terms, limiting the ability of foreign enterprises to outbid their Japanese competitors; second, by establishing shortened payment terms that enhanced the financial strength of Japanese manufacturers at the expense of wholesalers, and positioned domestic manufacturers to better withstand foreign penetration; and third, by establishing standardised terms, in particular volume rebates, that were by their very nature more beneficial to Japanese manufacturers with large market share.*

Japan responded that the 1970 Guidelines did not require uniform transaction terms or identify specific transaction terms to be followed. Rather, the 1970 Guidelines simply suggested the adoption of "rational" transaction terms. According to Japan, it was up to industry participants to come up with their own terms. Japan argued that, in fact, the terms of the transactions of the manufacturers did vary, and that single-brand distribution is the common form of distribution in the film industry world-wide, including in the United States. The panel found the following with respect to causation:

In considering the purpose of the guidelines, we note that the introduction to the 1970 Guidelines states:

> *It goes without saying that rationalisation of terms of trade is essential to improving market conditions, assuring effective competition, creating efficient distribution activities, developing a large scale distribution system, systematising distribution activities, and facilitating the response to foreign capital.*

However, beyond this general introductory reference to facilitating the response to foreign capital, the recommendations set out in the 1970 Guidelines appear to be origin neutral, i.e., they do not formally differentiate as to the treatment of domestic and imported film and paper. We are not persuaded, therefore, that the 1970 Guidelines are directed at promoting vertical integration in the photographic materials distribution sector with a view to impeding market access for foreign products. Rather, as argued by Japan, they appear to be directed at generally improving transaction efficiency in this sector, a result that is not inherently unfavourable to imports. As noted above, the 1967 Cabinet Decision, the Sixth Interim Report, the Seventh Interim Report and the 1969 Survey Report provide context for the interpretation of the 1970 Guidelines. Our examination of those documents supports our view of the 1970 Guidelines. While the documents occasionally make reference to the imminent entry of foreign capital into Japan, in our reading of them, their main focus is clearly on improving the various inefficiencies and deficiencies in Japan's distribution system, as a means to address broader problems, such as the need to cope with inflationary pressures and labour shortages.

The panel did not rule out discrimination, even in measures that appear neutral on their face, but found that the United States did not provide a single instance of discrimination based on the 1970 Guidelines. The panel also found serious timing problems in the U.S. argument. Most of film wholesale activities were single-brand before 1970. Furthermore, Fuji started to tighten payment terms in 1966, prior to the issuance of the Guidelines. The panel also noted:

> *that single-brand wholesale distribution is the common market structure—indeed the norm—in most major*

> *national film markets, including the U.S. market. While the United States responds that the U.S. market structure was the result of private and not governmental actions, it is unclear why the same economic forces acting in the United States would not also exist in Japan.*

1971 Basic Plan of the Distribution Systemisation Promotion Council

On July 28, 1971, the Japanese government published the Basic Plan for the Systemisation of Distribution (hereinafter 1971 Basic Plan). MITI's Distribution Systemisation Promotion Council, which was formed in 1970 on the basis of a recommendation contained in the Seventh Interim Report, prepared the 1971 Basic Plan. The 1971 Basic Plan promoted the "systematisation and rationalisation" of the distribution sector. It was not limited to film and photographic paper.

The panel ruled that the 1971 Basic Plan was a measure under Article XXIII:1(b). The panel said:

> *Although the 1971 Basic Plan was authored and published by a quasi-governmental advisory body composed of academics, industry representatives and government officials, it nonetheless bears some hallmarks of a governmental measure in that the Distribution Systemisation Promotion Council was created by MITI and commissioned by MITI to prepare the plan. Moreover, as noted above, upon its publication senior MITI officials endorsed the plan and stated that MITI would work with the private sector to ensure implementation of the plan's recommendations. In light of these statements and actions by MITI, we consider that there is sufficient likelihood that the administrative guidance given by MITI in connection with the 1971 Basic Plan provides sufficient incentives for private parties to act in a particular manner such that it would have a similar effect on business activity in Japan to a legally binding measure.*

The panel found no evidence of abandonment of the 1971 Basic Plan by the Japanese government, although one may question whether the 1971 Basic Plan has relevance to the current market twenty-six years after its publication. The panel found a benefit accruing only under the Kennedy Round of the GATT, on grounds substantially similar as those set forth for the above measures. The panel found no impairment or nullification of a GATT/WTO benefit under Article

XXIII:1(b). The United States argued that the 1971 Basic Plan, along with the Seventh Interim Report, exemplified "Japan's intent to promote vertical keiretsu in its systemisation policy." The panel disagreed and found both that the 1971 Basic Plan was facially neutral and that the United States failed to carry its burden of proving that Japan applied the plan in a discriminatory fashion. Again, the timing problem plagued the U.S. case because single-brand distribution started well before 1971.

1971 Japan Fair Trade Commission International Contract Notification Requirement

Article 6 of Japan's Antimonopoly Law of 1947 provides:

(1) No entrepreneur shall enter into an international agreement or an international contract which contains such matters as constitute unreasonable restraint of trade or unfair trade practices.

(2) An entrepreneur who has entered into an international agreement or an international contract (limited to only such an agreement or contract that belongs to the types which are prescribed by the rules of the [JFTC] as tending to contain such matters as constitute unreasonable restraint of trade or unfair trade practices) shall, in accordance with the Rules of the [JFTC], file a notification thereof with the [JFTC], accompanied by a copy of the said agreement or contract (in the case of an oral agreement or contract, a document describing the contents thereof), within thirty days as from the conclusion of such agreement or contract.

The JFTC promulgated Rule 1 to implement the above Article 6.2. Japan contended that the Diet repealed the international contract notification requirement in June 1997 by amending Article 6(2) of the Antimonopoly Law and abolishing Rule 1. The panel did not consider the merits of the U.S. arguments on Rule 1 because the U.S. panel request had not identified it. The panel request referred to the Antimonopoly Law in connection with other measures and, therefore, did not put Japan on notice that Rule 1 would be under consideration.

1975 Manual for Systemisation of Distribution by Industry: Camera and Film

In March 1975, the Distribution Systematisation Centre published the "Manual for Systemisation of Distribution by Industry: Camera and Film," accompanied by actions taken to implement the recommendations. In accordance with the 1971 Basic Plan, the Distribution Systemisation Development Centre was formed in 1972 and had support from MITI. Its purpose was to facilitate the work of the Distribution Systemisation Promotion Council, and it was assigned to work with industry to produce industry-specific "Systemisation Manuals." The 1975 Manual was prepared by the Centre in collaboration with industry and with a MITI official in observer Status.

The panel found that the 1975 Manual was not the application of a measure under Article XXIII:1(b). The panel found the evidence "somewhat conflicting," but "on balance, in contrast to our conclusions on this issue in respect of the 1970 Guidelines and the 1971 Basic Plan, we consider that the evidence on this issue suggests that the 1975 Manual does not have sufficient government imprimatur to be considered a governmental measure in this case."

As for the issue of whether it nullified a benefit under the GATT, the panel ruled in the negative. As for the prior alleged measures, given the timing of the 1975 Manual, it could be a measure only with respect to the Kennedy Round. The panel found no causation. The 1975 Manual stated as an "urgent need" the improvement of the "structure" of Japanese manufacturers "to a capacity that will resist foreign capital affiliated firms." The panel concluded, however, that its assessment of the impact of this 1975 Manual is similar to that of the 1971 Basic Plan: the policy recommendations for systemisation and modernisation in the Japanese distribution sector are without regard to the source of the products involved. Also, even if one of the concerns expressed in the manual was to address `foreign capital affiliated firms,' this concern does not appear to be reflected in the actual analysis or recommendations advanced in the manual and the United States has not been able to point to any specific instances where such systemisation of the distribution sector in the Japanese film industry has undermined market-access conditions for U.S. film or paper." Moreover, timing problems continued to plague the U.S. case in that Fuji and Konica had nearly finished single-brand vertical integration of their wholesalers well before the publication of the 1975 Manual.

1976 Japan Development Bank Financing to Konica for Joint Distribution Facilities

The Japan Development Bank, a "quasi-governmental financial institution," provided funding in the form of subsidies to Konica so that Konica could establish joint distribution facilities with independent wholesalers. The panel did not consider the merits of U.S. claims with respect to such subsidies. The United States argued that Japan had adequate notice of the potential for the Konica subsidies to be raised because the subsidies related to the 1971 Basic Plan, which the United States raised in its panel request as well as in consultations. The 1971 Basic Plan refers to "positive support and guidance from the government." The panel concluded that there was an insufficient relationship between the 1971 Basic Plan and the Konica subsidization and that the statement from the 1971 Basic Plan by the United States was too vague and general to provide adequate notice to Japan that the Konica subsidies could be raised in the proceeding.

1967-77 Small and Medium-Sized Enterprises Act Financing

The Small and Medium-Sized Enterprise Agency (SMEA) is part of MITI. The United States made some relatively minor arguments that SMEA provided subsidies to various companies in the film and photographic paper industry. The United States used the same arguments for inclusion of assertions concerning SMEA financing in the proceeding as they did for the Konica financing, set forth above. The panel findings for refusal to consider the merits of the issues on SMEA financing were the same as for the Konica financing. The panel rejected discussion of SMEA financing on procedural grounds, finding inadequate notice to Japan.

Restrictions on Large Retail Stores: Japan's 1974 Large Stores Law as Amended

The Japanese Diet passed a Large Stores Law on October 1, 1973. By its terms, it became effective on March 1, 1974. The law set forth a mixture of notification and regulatory requirements that stores proposed in excess of a certain size were required to follow. The original law regulated stores in excess of 1500 square metres. A 1979 amendment lowered the threshold for application of the law to 500 square metres. The 1979 amendment also classified stores into two classes for regulation by different government entities. Class I stores, which were 1500 square metres and larger, were regulated by MITI; and Class II stores, which were between 500 and 1500 square metres, were regulated at the local level. The size for Class I stores was subsequently raised twice.

The law required advance notification of the building or opening of a store. The relevant government authority could recommend a reduction in size of the store, a delay in its opening and dictate opening times and store holidays. The purpose of the law, according to Japan in the WTO proceeding, was to preserve diversity and a balance of various sizes of retail outlets in the same area. The United States argued that the law imposed burdensome regulatory requirements that restricted the growth of alternative distribution channels for imported film. The panel explained the U.S. position as follows:

> *The United States claims that large retail stores remain one potentially significant alternative distribution channel in Japan for foreign film manufacturers despite the Japanese Government's alleged reorganisation of wholesale operations in the photographic materials sector. According to the United States, large retailers offered foreign manufacturers, foreclosed from the primary distribution network, a partial alternative to wholesalers. The United States also argues that large stores have carried imported products, including film, more frequently than small stores and have been less susceptible to pressure by domestic manufacturers. If such stores were permitted to proliferate across Japan, the United States argues, wholesalers would become less significant and foreign manufacturers could circumvent the bottle-necked distribution system. It was in response to this threat, the United States submits, that in 1967 and 1968 Japan began to impose controls on the expansion of large stores and finally enacted the Large Stores Law in 1973.*

Both parties agreed that the Large Store Law is a measure. The panel refused to find, however, that the United States could claim a benefit under GATT/WTO with respect to any round of negotiations other than the Kennedy Round, which applies only to black and white film. Japan argued that the United States could not even argue that it could not have anticipated the law prior to the 1967 Kennedy Round. Japan based its argument on the existence of the predecessor law of the Large Stores Law, the Department Store Law, which was promulgated in 1956. Japan alleged that the Large Stores Law simply extended the policy of the prior law to new types of stores, such as supermarkets and large discount stores, and was enacted to stop stores from circumventing long-standing policy. Moreover, according to Japan, the Large Stores Law was less stringent that the prior Department Store Law. The prior law required permission to open a store; the successor law only required notification. Other aspects of the successor law were less restrictive than the predecessor law. Japan argued that "even if one accepts, for argument's sake, that restrictions on large stores are unfavourable to imported products, there is nothing unfavourable to imports that the United States could not have anticipated at the time of the Kennedy Round tariff concessions."

The panel concluded, however, that because the Large Stores Law was introduced prior to the conclusion of the Kennedy Round in 1967, Japan had the burden of proving that the United States could have anticipated the passage of the Large Stores Law in 1979. The panel ruled that a broad notion of reasonable anticipation, as espoused by Japan, could have the effect of depriving this element of a non-violation case of its meaning. In our view, it is not sufficient to claim that a specific measure should have been anticipated because it is a continuation of a past general government policy.

The panel thus ruled that the United States could not have reasonably anticipated the Large Stores Law and its subsequent amendments as of the conclusion of the Kennedy Round. As for the Tokyo Round, the United States conceded its awareness of the law, but argued that it could not have known or appreciated its significance, particularly in combination with other countermeasures. The panel disagreed and found that the United States should have anticipated both the law and its 1979 amendment, based on the timing of the legislative processes, the Tokyo Round, and bilateral negotiations between the United States and Japan. As for the Uruguay Round, the United States had a particularly weak argument because the law was the subject of the U.S. government report "National Trade Estimate Report on Foreign Trade Barriers" and bilateral discussions and joint reports between the parties. Finally, the panel found no nullification or impairment. The panel summarised the U.S. argument on causation as follows:

> *The United States contends that the suppression of large stores under the Large Stores Law affects the distribution of foreign film in Japan in two respects. First, restricting large stores indirectly supports manufacturer domination of oligopolistic distribution structures. This structure depends on manufacturer dominance of wholesalers, and wholesaler dominance over retailers. Retailers with greater purchasing power and business sophistication could effectively play the various*

> *wholesalers and manufacturers off of each other to gain more favourable terms, and to resist attempts to hold the retailers under the control of a single manufacturer-wholesaler chain. Second, large stores provide an alternative channel to market film for foreign manufacturers excluded from the wholesale distribution system. With a sufficiently developed network of large stores, a manufacturer could reach a large portion of the Japanese market with a limited number of accounts. Consequently, the United States claims that Japan upset the competitive relationship between imported and domestic photographic film and paper by inhibiting the development of a viable alternative channel for the distribution and sale of imported film and paper.*

The panel examined two issues and found no nullification or impairment. First, it looked at the relationship of large stores and imported film and photographic paper. The panel found that the law was "clearly neutral as to products and the origin of products." The panel also found a lack of any evidence of a discriminatory implementation of the law. According to the panel, the real

motivating force behind opposition to the expansion of large stores in Japan, and in many other countries as well, is from small- and medium-sized stores concerned with the impact that such stores may have on them, and not because of a desire to hinder imports of foreign film and paper. As for the issue of discriminatory application of a facially neutral measure, the panel found conflicting evidence. The United States presented survey data showing that large stores are likely to carry imported film. Japan countered that the issue was whether or not a store carries a high volume of film, not the size of the store. The United States, however, contended that size controlled for this situation. The panel said:

> *It seems to us that even if there is a greater tendency for large stores to carry imported film, access to large stores is less important for film than for other imported products since film takes up very little shelf space even taking account that a full display of all film types is comprised of many rolls of film. This would seem to be confirmed by the Japanese evidence that high-volume sellers of film, whether large or small stores, are more likely to carry imported film. However, on balance we*

are left with conflicting evidence and no sure way to resolve the conflict.

The panel concluded that it was not necessary to resolve this issue, in light of its findings that the regulation of large retail stores had lessened over the years and that the trend was towards less regulation, with the result that the law was now more favourable to large stores than it was during the three rounds of multilateral negotiations. The panel noted the United States argument with "unease," finding it similar to the unsuccessful argument in Case C-145/88, Torfaen Borough Council v. B&Q PLC, that Sunday closing laws in the European Community were discriminatory and violated the EC Treaty. In that case, it was argued unsuccessfully that, because home improvement stores sell imported products and sell more products on Sunday, limitations on Sunday trading amount to import restrictions.

Finally, the panel noted that there were more large stores in Japan today than in 1982, the first year in which data was compiled. If the position of the United States was correct concerning the import friendliness of large stores, then U.S. products should have been in a better position. The U.S. argument seemed to imply that the market for imported film would be even better had the Japanese government not restricted large store growth. The panel explained:

In these circumstances, the argument would seem to be that the situation would be even better if Japan had not interfered with this favourable market evolution by slowing it. This raises the question of whether the United States can claim legitimate expectations related to expected market evolution, as opposed to expectations that the market situation at the time of a tariff concession will not be upset, e.g., by a grant of subsidies or implementation of measures that change existing competitive relationships or by restricting the use of previously permitted sales techniques. Normally, for competitive relationships to be upset, we would expect an adverse change in the situation existing at the time of the tariff concessions. In the case of subsidies, for example, a Member reasonably expects that subsidies will not be increased, not that they will be decreased. To the extent that the United States claim is viewed as being based on expectations about market evolution, the question becomes to what extent it must establish it had reasons to expect in ***1967*** *(or* ***1979*** *or* ***1993****) that there would be a relative expansion of the large-store segment of Japan's economy, taking into account the existing regulation under the Department Stores Law or Large Stores Law. Even assuming that such expectations would be protected by Article XXIII:1(b), the United States has not established that it had any such expectation in* ***1967, 1979*** *or* ***1993****.*

Promotion Countermeasures (i) The Claim in Context

The United States argued that the following eight promotion countermeasures nullified or impaired imports by restricting sales promotions by foreign firms in Japan:

(1) 1967 Cabinet Decision on Liberalisation of Inward Direct Investment;

(2) 1967 JFTC Notification 17 on premiums to businesses;

(3) 1977 JFTC Notification 5 on premium offers to consumers;

(4) 1981 JFTC Guidance on Dispatched Employees;

(5) 1982 Self-Regulating Rules Concerning Fairness In Trade With Business;

(6) 1982 Establishment of Fair Trade Promotion Council;

(7) 1982 Self-Regulating Standards Concerning Display of Processing Fees; and

(8) 1987 JFTC approval of the Retailers Fair Competition Code and the Retailers Fair Trade Council.

The United States argued that these promotion countermeasures reinforced the distribution countermeasures. Essentially, the United States argued that Japanese promotion countermeasures restricted the ability of new market entrants to use their capitalisation and competitiveness in combination with innovative marketing programs in order to capture market share in Japan.

The United States argued that Japan used these promotion countermeasures to nullify or impair trade liberalisation benefits that Japan agreed to in GATT/WTO negotiating rounds. Japan responded that the measures were typical consumer protection laws that encouraged firms to compete on the basis of price and quality and not on the basis of inducements or deceptive advertising. The promotion countermeasures were facially neutral because they applied to domestic and foreign firms alike.

As set forth below, the panel ruled in Japan's favour and found no nullification or impairment of GATT/WTO obligations.

The Specific Countermeasures

The 1967 Cabinet Decision

The United States argued that the 1967 Cabinet Decision was a promotion countermeasure as well as a distribution countermeasure. In June 1967, the Foreign Investment Council (FIC) Expert Committee, an advisory committee of the Japan Ministry of Finance, produced a report that the Japanese government had requested. The Report stated the following concerning the regulation of foreign capital:

(1) When foreign capital is brought into Japan, it is possible for a parent company to use vast amounts of capital to engage in dumping, offer premiums, and conduct large-scale publicity and advertising, etc. In the future, as liberalisation of direct investment in the domestic market progresses, such risk may conceivably be reinforced. Therefore, in such a situation, it is necessary to fully study whether these actions qualify as unfair trade practices as defined in Article 2 of the Antimonopoly Law and can be regulated pursuant to provisions under Article 19 of the said Antimonopoly Law or the Law Against Unjustifiable Premiums and Misleading Representations.

(2) For the application of the Antimonopoly Law, while one may not specifically select foreign capital affiliated firms for differential treatment, foreign capital affiliated firms nevertheless have the strong capital and technological background of the parent company and are usually in an economically strong position. Consequently, it is believed that they will often become the object of regulation of the Antimonopoly Law. On this point, we must be able to apply standards to deal with any disorderly activities by foreign capital because existing standards of regulation of unfair trade practices are not necessarily clear and we may, for example, clarify them by making use of a special designation or some other method.

Concerning the use of "fair" competition codes, the report stated that, "for the provision of large-scale premiums, it is believed that establishing fair competition codes pursuant to the [Premiums Law] with assistance from the industry that might be affected, would be an effective countermeasure." The United States argued that the Japanese government adopted the recommendations of the Expert Committee to the effect that the Premiums Law should be the basis of premium countermeasures in the nature of fair competition codes. Article 10 of the Premium Law provides for the establishment of such codes by industry.

The panel found that the 1967 Cabinet Decision was a measure in the context of U.S. arguments about promotion countermeasures for the same reasons that it found it to be a measure in the context of U.S. arguments about distribution countermeasures. Moreover, for reasons similar to those set forth when the 1967 Cabinet Decision was considered in the context of the U.S. argument that it was a distribution countermeasure, the panel found that the United States could claim legitimate expectations of a benefit accruing under GATT only for the Kennedy Round.

Again, the panel found no impairment or nullification to be caused by the 1967 Cabinet Decision, for reasons substantially similar to the reasons cited in its examination of the 1967 Cabinet Decision as a distribution countermeasure. The 1967 Cabinet Decision set forth "very general policy statements," and the United States failed to identify specific actions from the 1967 Cabinet Decision that discriminated against imports. The panel said that "at most, in our view, the 1967 Cabinet Decision is part of the context for later actions taken by Japan."

1967 JFTC Notification 17 on Premiums to Business

The United States alleged that JFTC Notification 17 was a promotion countermeasure as well as a distribution countermeasure. The panel, however, found that Notification 17 was not a measure after 1996 for the same reasons that it cited in considering Notification 17 as a potential distribution countermeasure. The panel found that Notification 17 did not impair any benefit accruing under GATT. The publication of Notification 17 by the Japanese government occurred prior in time to the conclusion of the Kennedy Round. The United States, moreover, failed to demonstrate any situation in which it could not have known of the effect of Notification 17 until some time after its publication. The panel noted that

> this is particularly true given that, as of 1967, the current structure of the Japanese film market was largely in place, i.e., there were only a few primary film wholesalers anti single-brand distribution of film was typical, it would seem that the United States should have been

able to assess the impact of this measure, if any, on the Japanese market for film at the time it was introduced.

The panel also found no impairment or nullification for reasons substantially similar to those that caused it to find no impairment or nullification when it considered Notification 17 as a potential distribution countermeasure.

1971 JFTC Notification No. 34 on Open Lotteries

On procedural grounds, the panel excluded from consideration Notification 34 on Unfair Trade Practices Offering Economic Benefits by Means of Advertising Lotteries, etc., promulgated by the JFTC on July 2,1971. Notification 34 declared that lotteries held by sellers of film and other products that offered "excessive economic benefits" were unfair and unlawful. Guidelines promulgated by the JFTC set yen limitations on what was an excessive economic benefit. The United States argued that Notification 34 restricted the ability of importing firms to introduce and market their products.

The panel excluded Notification 34 from consideration because the U.S. panel request failed to identify it as a measure and because it was not adequately related to other alleged measures identified in the request. Japan, therefore, would not have adequate notice. Notification 34 was promulgated pursuant to Article 2(7) of the Japanese Antimonopoly Law, which the United States did not identify as a measure in their panel request. According to the panel, the identification of other articles of the Antimonopoly Law in the panel request was insufficient to charge Japan with notice because the law was broad and covered a multitude of issues unrelated to lotteries.

1977 JFTC Notification 5 on Premiums to Consumers

On March 1, 1977, the JFTC issued Notification 5 on "Restriction on Premium Offers to Consumers." Notification 5 provided in pertinent part:

> *The value of a premium offered to general consumers, excluding those by lotteries or prize competition, shall be within 10 percent of the transaction value involved in the premium offer (provided that if the amount is less than 100 yen, the limit shall be 100 yen), and which is found reasonable in the light of normal business practices.*

The United States argued that Notification 5 unduly restricts the offering of premiums on photographic film and paper to consumers, particularly given the low price of film and paper. Premiums would have to be a token amount to remain lawful under Notification 5. The panel found that Notification 5 was a measure still in effect. The panel also found, however, that Notification 5 related to a benefit accruing under the GATT only with respect to the Kennedy Round, if at all.

Finally, the panel found no nullification or impairment. Notification 5, on its face, does not discriminate against foreign products or firms. Notification 5 appears to limit only one form of promotional activity-the value of premiums offered by manufacturers as a percentage of the value of the purchase. The panel found it "significant" that Notification 5 and other measures alleged by the United States "did not limit general advertising expenditures or price competition in general."

The United States argued that it was essential that foreign firms have the ability to offer premiums directly to customers because Japanese wholesalers and retailers refuse to pass discounts on to customers. The panel found this to be a weak argument, based on one example of Kodak's advertising, which increased market share during the Nagano Olympic Games. The panel accepted Japan's argument that the ability to give premiums is not essential to succeeding in the Japanese retail market for film. The United States, moreover, did not argue that the Japanese government was involved in any cartel-like behaviour to refuse to pass on price reductions to consumers. The United States also failed, according to the panel, to identify instances in which Notification 5 was applied in a discriminatory fashion.

1981 JFTC Guidance on Dispatched Employees

The Distribution Sector Office is part of the JFTC. It was established in October 1979 with the approval of the Japanese Cabinet. Its purpose is to "administer duties pertaining to unfair trade practice designations related to distribution." In December 1981, this Office made findings and recommendations to "camera, photographic materials, colour photo laboratories and related industries" in an article entitled "The Status of Distribution of Cameras." In this chapter, the Office advised the industry to deal with "problems" that resulted from the dispatching of employees by manufacturers to large retail stores. The article stated:

> *The JFTC is issuing guidance to the camera, photographic accessories, colour photo lab and related industries to examine the use of self-regulating measures with respect to the permanent dispatch of sales people*

> *so as not to go too far as manufacturers' sales promotion methods or as acts based on the buying power of volume sales stores.*

The United States asserted that the dispatch of manufacturers' employees to retailers and wholesalers constituted a "unique form of economic inducement" that "reduce costs for wholesalers and retailers and thereby allow for increased sales based upon cost or price reductions passed down the line of distribution." Japan replied that the photographic industry worked on self-regulating measures even before the JFTC published the above article. The panel found that the article constituted a measure. It was classic Japanese administrative guidance. The panel explained:

> *The relevant statement of the JFTC official makes explicit reference to "guidance" and advises the photographic materials industry (or a substantial part of it) "to examine the use of self-regulating measures with respect to the permanent dispatch of sales people". Given this explicit statement of guidance to the photographic materials industry from the government body charged with implementation of the Antimonopoly Law and the Premiums Law, we think it reasonable to assume, in the absence of substantial argument to the contrary, that this JFTC Guidance on Dispatched Employees meets the standard for governmental measures that we laid out in our general discussion of Article XXIII:1 (b). This result is supported by the fact that the guidance was acted upon.*

The guidance led to the Self-Regulating Measures discussed in the succeeding section. There was also no indication from Japan that the measure had been withdrawn. The panel found the measure to still be in effect, although its significance may have been minimal given the existence of the Self Regulating Measures. The panel found that the 1981 Guidance could relate to benefits accruing under the Kennedy and Tokyo Rounds, given that it was promulgated subsequent to the conclusion of those rounds. The United States, however, failed to demonstrate any circumstance that would make it unaware of the guidance for the Uruguay Round, which concluded in 1994.

The panel found no nullification or impairment. First, it was unclear whether the guidance was directed at film and paper, because it refers only to "camera, photographic accessories, colour photo lab and related industries." Second, the guidance applied to only one type of activity involving promotion. Third, the United States failed to demonstrate how the measure restricted the sale of imported film in Japan. Fourth, the measure was facially neutral and the United States presented no evidence of discriminatory application.

1982 Self-Regulating Rules Concerning Fairness in Trade with Business and 1982 Establishment of Fair Trade Promotion Council

The panel considered the U.S. arguments concerning "Self-Regulating Measures concerning Fairness in Trade with Business," issued in June 1982, and the establishment of the Fair Trade Promotion Council on December 23, 1982 together because they were closely related. The Self-Regulating Measures regulated the dispatch of employees for sales promotion and other marketing activities and provided financial standards for promotions. The Fair Trade Promotion Council, established by the industry on December 23, 1982, policed the "fairness" of transactions in the photographic industry and implementation of the Self-Regulating Measures. The panel found that the Self-Regulating Measures and the establishment of the Fair Trade Promotion Council were measures. Although the documentation on the Self-Regulating Measures and on the Fair Trade Promotion Council indicated that they were "largely the product of decisions by private industry associations," there were several references in various laws and documents that indicate a "substantial connection" among the JFTC, the Self Regulating Measures, and the Fair Trade Promotion Council.

With respect to benefits accruing under the GATT/WTO, the panel applied its standard approach and looked at the dates of the negotiating rounds and the alleged measures to determine whether the alleged measures would relate to benefits accruing under the Kennedy and Tokyo Rounds but not under the Uruguay Rounds. The panel found no nullification or impairment. The United States argued that the Fair Trade Promotion Council held a wide range of enforcement powers over competition for film. The United States provided an example, the Kodak VR Trial-Pack campaign, that it contended was seriously hindered by actions of the Council. The United States contended that the Council, at the request of the retailers association and with the prompting of the JFTC, determined that Kodak had engaged in misrepresentation in its advertisements, and the campaign was thus "cut back" and "muted." In addition, the United States asserted that, in July 1996, the Council issued a "directive" to Kodak stating that the Council "decided in July 1995 to request [Kodak's] co-operation in continuing to reduce dispatched employees" and that Kodak is to "immediately report the status of your company to this Council."

Japan replied that the actions of the Council, and the Self-Regulating Measures themselves, were private actions and did not involve the Japanese government. Moreover, Japan argued that the dispatch of employees is not of major concern in the marketing of film or paper: for film, consumers decide which brand to buy on their own, and the consumers of paper are adequately informed professionals. Finally, Japan argued that Kodak's VR campaign had nothing to do with dispatch of employees and disagreed with the characterisation of events by the United States concerning the sales campaign.

The panel agreed with Japan that the VR campaign had nothing to do with dispatch of employees or promotion money, the two key areas controlled by the Self-Regulating Measures. The panel also agreed that the dispatch of employees was a minor issue in the film and paper market. The panel disagreed with the Japanese characterisation of the Self Regulating Measures and the operations of the Council and the retailers association as purely private actions. The panel explained:

> *The evidence advanced by the two parties shows that the action against the VR trial pack had its origins with Zenren, the photo retailers' association, putting pressure on Kodak's distributor (Nagase) to limit promotion, in particular its pricing discounts on this new type of film. Indeed, the evidence suggests that Zenren succeeded in persuading Kodak to reduce the scope and duration of this promotional discount scheme. In addition to this private initiative by Zenren, however, the evidence also suggests that JFTC officials, at the urging of the Fair Trade Promotion Council, issued guidance to Kodak concerning potential issues under the Antimonopoly Law in relation to operation of the VR campaign.*

The panel found, however, that "it is not clear to us that compliance with most of these terms would seriously hinder the VR campaign." The panel concluded:

> *Considering all the evidence taken together, it appears that the pressure put on Kodak's subsidiary by Zenren was by far the major factor impacting the VR campaign.*

> *The pressure from Zenren has not been shown to have emanated in any way from the JFTC. Thus, we find that the United States has not come forward with a sufficient demonstration of how statements made to Kodak representatives by JFTC and council officials in relation to the VR campaign could be said to have impaired competitive market-access conditions accruing to the United States. According to the evidence of record, it appears that Kodak did carry out a successful if somewhat abbreviated VR campaign.*

Finally, the panel found theft the VR campaign was a "14 year-old incident" and was the only one proffered by the United States.

Self-Regulating Standards Concerning Display of Processing Fees for Colour Negative Film

In May 1984, the Fair Trade Promotion Council promulgated "Self-Regulating Standards Concerning Display of Processing Fees for Colour Negative Film." The 1984 Self-Regulating Standards regulate representations to consumers of price and price information relating to film developing and printing of pictures. Japan argued that the 1984 Self-Regulating Standards were intended to protect consumers from misleading representations by firms who offer inexpensive printing charges but, in fact, charge customers expensive fees for developing pictures. The 1984 Self-Regulating Standards, according to Japan, addressed an asymmetric information problem. The United States argued the Fair Trade Promotion Council used the 1984 Self-Regulating Standards to impose and enforce a broad range of restrictions on price competition to the detriment of foreign firms in Japan.

The panel ruled that the 1984 Self-Regulating Standards constituted a measure under Article XXIII:1(b), noting that the Fair Trade Promotion Council "has elaborate links to the JFTC." The panel found that the 1984 Self-Regulating Standards were based in part on instructions from the JFTC:

> *Even though the 1984 Self-Regulating Standards were apparently not formally approved by the JFTC, in view of these express references to the dependence of the Fair Trade Promotion Council on liaison with the JFTC for the establishment of these standards, we consider that there is a sufficient likelihood that private parties will act in conformity with the 1984 Self-Regulating*

> *Standards to consider them administrative guidance attributable to the Japanese Government. Thus, the 1984 Self-Regulating Standards, as such, have sufficient connection to the Japanese Government to warrant a finding that they are a measure within the ambit of Article XXIII:1(b).*

Although the Standards stated that they were temporary until the establishment of a Fair Competition Code, the panel, due to the lack of evidence on withdrawal of the standards, assumed that the 1984 Self-Regulating Standards were still in effect. The panel ruled that the 1984 Self-Regulating Standards related to a benefit accruing only under the Tokyo Round. The 1984 Self-Regulating Standards applied only to colour film; the Kennedy Round was thus irrelevant because it set forth tariff concessions only for black and white film. Further, the 1984 Self-Regulating Standards were promulgated prior to the conclusion of the Uruguay Round, and the United States presented no evidence, according to the panel, to indicate that it should not have known of the significance of the 1984 Self Regulating Standards prior to the Uruguay Round.

Finally, the panel found that the 1984 Self-Regulating Standards caused no nullification or impairment. The panel stated that "In essence, this measure appears directed at consumer protection, in particular, preventing misleading price representations in the film-processing industry." The panel also found that the United States did not show how the 1984 Self Regulating Standards, which are neutral on their face, were applied in a manner that discriminates against foreign firms.

1983 JFTC Guidance on Establishment of Rules on Loss-Leader Advertising and Dumping

The United States challenged what it contended was the JFTC's administrative guidance in recommending that industry promulgate rules on dumping and loss-leader advertising. The United States referred to an article in Zenren Tsuho in May 1983, quoting a speech by Yamada Akio, the Director of the Premiums and Representations Guidance Division of the JFTC. The United States alleged that Mr. Akio said:

> *In any case, it goes without saying that rule abiding sales practices and fair competition must be established. Fortunately, the photo industry has its "self-regulating standards for normalising trade". Nevertheless, it is of*

critical importance to develop rules one by one against dumping and loss-leader advertising. With the regard to loss-leader advertising, if the photo industry will clarify what the problems are, how we should apply the law will become clear.

The panel excluded this guidance from consideration on procedural grounds. The United States identified the guidance in response to a question asked by the panel, subsequent to the United States' initial submission in the proceeding. Japan objected to consideration of the merits of the guidance. The panel ruled that the guidance, "which is difficult to comprehend in any event and is in part subject to a translation dispute, probably is not a measure" and is apparently unrelated to any measure alleged by the United States in its panel request.

1987 JFTC Approval of Retailers' Fair Competition Code and the Retailers Fair Trade Council

On March 31, 1987, the JFTC approved a Fair Competition Code and its enforcement body, the Retailers Council. The Fair Competition Code states that its purpose is "to protect the general consumers' appropriate product selection, prevent the unfair inducement of customers, and thereby to secure fair competition." The Code contains rules on marketing representations made by retailers. The United States argued that the Fair Competition Code and its enforcement vehicle, the Retailers Council, operated in a manner that led to discriminatory treatment of foreign firms attempting to import film into the Japanese market.

The panel found that the Fair Competition Code and actions of the Retailers Council were measures of the Japanese government. The panel examined "the status these actions are given in the eyes of the Japanese Government and the photographic industry." Article 10(1) of the Premiums Law states that trade associations may obtain JFTC approval to establish fair competition codes. Article 10(3) states that the JFTC has supervisory powers over the codes and the councils. Article 10(5) states that the firms and trade associations operating under the codes are exempt from the Antimonopoly Law. According to the panel, these provisions made it "difficult to conclude" that the Retailers Council conducts "purely private actions of a private trade association" under the Fair Competition Code. The text of the Code itself, which references the role of the Premium Law and the JFTC, confirms this finding.

The panel found that the Fair Competition Code and the Retailers Council could impair benefits accruing under the Kennedy and Tokyo Rounds, because they did not predate those rounds, but could not do so for the Uruguay Round, because they did predate that round. The United States identified no extenuating circumstances for the Uruguay Round. The panel found no nullification or impairment caused by the Fair Competition Code or the Retailers Council. In reaching this conclusion, the panel examined three issues. First, it was unclear whether the Code and Council covered film. The Code, by its terms, applied to the "camera category" according to the Japanese translation, and to "cameras and related products" according to the U.S. translation. Second, the panel analysed whether the origin marking requirements discriminated against imports. The panel ruled:

> *While being sensitive to the possibility that a discriminatory country-of-origin designation requirement could result in impairment of competitive relationships, we initially note that GATT Article IX specifically allows origin-marking requirements. Thus, we hesitate to condemn automatically the requirements in the code, although they go beyond marking. Moreover, we note that the code requires indications of origin in respect of certain domestic, as well as imported products, and that Japan has provided an explanation for treating domestic and imported products differently with respect to country-of-origin designations. More significantly, the United States has failed to demonstrate how such a designation requirement in the code has upset competitive relationships between domestic and imported film or paper.*

Japan explained that the country of origin identification simply provided information to consumers. The third issue that the panel considered was whether Japan applied the Code in a discriminatory fashion to imported goods. The panel found that the United States failed to offer examples with a "clear connection" to the JFTC approval of the Code nor to the activities of the Council.

The United States argued that the "overlapping enforcement mechanisms" of the JFTC, the Fair Trade Promotion Council, the Retailers Council, and other "fair trade councils" and trade associations, considered along with the myriad rules restricting promotions, have imposed a "chilling effect" on importers. The panel found that this argument was too general.

The Combined Effects Analysis

The panel rejected the U.S. argument that all of the above alleged countermeasures in combination i.e., as a whole resulted in a violation of Article XXIII:1(b). The panel summarised Japan's counter-argument as "nothing combined with nothing is still nothing." The panel articulated the following standard for assessing the U.S. claim:

> *It is not implausible that individual measures which do not impair benefits when considered in isolation, could nonetheless have an adverse impact on conditions of competition when considered collectively. However, for such a legal theory to be shown to have factual relevance in the present case, the United States must adduce relevant specific evidence and provide a detailed justification showing how this evidence supports the theory. In considering the U.S. allegations in relation to "combined effects", we recall our discussion of the facts that (i) the various "measures" cited by the United States—distribution and promotion "measures" and restrictions on large stores—were introduced over a period of several decades, and (ii) a number of these "measures" are no longer in effect. We also recall our discussion of the timing problems as between the issuance of the "measures" and the emergence of standard transaction terms and single-brand distribution in the Japanese market. Against this background, to the extent that the United States claims that various "measures" in the areas of distribution, promotion and large stores set in motion policies which are said to have a complementary and cumulative effect on imported film and paper, we consider that it is for the United States to provide this panel with a detailed showing of how these alleged "measures" interact with one another in their implementation so as to cause effects different from, and additional to, those effects which are alleged to be caused by each "measure" acting individually.*

The panel found that the United States failed to meet this standard. It addressed each type of countermeasure alleged by the United States and found no proof of combined effect. As explained above, the panel found that none of the distribution countermeasures alleged by the United States individually upset the competitive conditions for importing film and paper. The panel also noted a "timing problem" for each of the alleged distribution countermeasures because the vertical integration of the market into single-brand distribution occurred before the adoption of the measures asserted by the United States. The panel found that this timing problem applied to the distribution measures as a set of measures. The panel ruled that the United States failed to present additional arguments and evidence to prove that the alleged measures operated in combination to impair competitive market access for imported film and paper.

As for the Large Stores Law, the United States relied on a MITI survey on transaction terms. The United States asserted that the MITI survey demonstrated that MITI was concerned that large stores threatened the oligopoly of Fuji and Konica in Japan. Japan countered that the survey actually expressed fear that new retail stores would introduce "irrational business practices" into the distribution sector, and that the United States failed to interpret the survey in the proper context. The panel found that the United States failed to present the requisite detailed justification and convincing evidence:

> *On the basis of the evidence and arguments presented by the two parties, and taking into account the additional portion of the MITI Survey Report mentioned by Japan, we consider that the MITI survey report cited by the United States, when correctly translated and read in context, does not sufficiently support the U.S. proposition in relation to the alleged role of the Large Stores Law (and related "measures") in supporting what the United States claims is an oligopolistic distribution system for film and paper in Japan. Rather, the evidence would seem to suggest that MITI was mostly concerned with avoiding the reintroduction of what MITI viewed as irrational business terms. To the extent that the U.S. claim is that the Large Stores Law "created" manufacturer-dominated, vertically integrated distribution in Japan, it suffers from the timing problem referred to above, i.e., such a distribution structure existed prior to the adoption of the Large Stores Law in 1973. The United States offers insufficient evidence as to how the Large Stores Law played a role in keeping this already-existing vertically integrated structure in place.*

The panel also ruled that the United States failed to demonstrate that the Large Stores Law, in addition to maintaining the oligopoly of Fuji and Konica, also restricted an alternate route for the marketing of imported products. The panel next rejected the U.S. claim that promotion countermeasures worked in combination to restrict the market for imported film and paper. The United States failed to prove that the alleged countermeasures had any effect individually, provided only a few examples, over many years, in which Kodak was restricted in promotional activities, and failed to provide additional evidence or arguments as to how the alleged promotion countermeasures in combination restricted competitive market access.

Finally, the panel rejected the U.S. claim that all three of the countermeasures worked together to restrict market access of imported film and paper. The panel found that none of the alleged countermeasures individually restricted market access, and the United States presented no additional evidence or argument that the combination of measures restricted market access.

The Violation Claims—The National Treatment Claim

Article III:4 of the GATT sets forth the basic national treatment requirement found in the WTO system. It provides in pertinent part as follows:

> *The products of the territory of a Member imported into the territory of any other Member shall be accorded treatment no less favourable than that accorded to like products of national origin in respect of all laws, regulations and requirements affecting their internal sale, offering for sale, purchase, transportation, distribution or use.*

The panel set forth the following requirements that the United States would have to meet to prove a violation of the national treatment obligation by Japan:

> *We consider that in line with GATT/WTO precedent, under this provision the United States is required to demonstrate the existence of: (a) a law, regulation or requirement affecting the internal sale, offering for sale or distribution of imported film or paper; and (b) treatment accorded in respect of the law, regulation or requirement that is less favourable to the imported film or paper than to like products of national origin.*

The panel also found that Article III: 1 was relevant to the proceeding. It provides:

> *Members recognise that internal taxes and other internal charges and laws, regulations and requirements affecting the internal sale, offering for sale, purchase, transportation, distribution or use of products, and internal quantitative regulations requiring the mixture, processing or use of products in specified amounts or proportions, should not be applied to imported or domestic products so as to afford protection to domestic production.*

The panel cited the WTO Appellate Body in Japan—Alcoholic Beverages, where it said that "Article III obliges Members of the WTO to provide equality of competitive conditions for imported products in relation to domestic products." Moreover, under Bananas III, the WTO Appellate Body explained that a determination of whether there has been a violation of Article III:4 does not require a determination of whether a measure "affords protection to domestic production." The United States argued that distribution countermeasures that Japan allegedly had undertaken violated the WTO national treatment obligation. As for the first issue, whether the alleged countermeasures are "laws, regulations or requirements," the panel stated:

> *A literal reading of the words all laws, regulations and requirements in Article III:4 could suggest that they may have a narrower scope than the word measure in Article XXIII:1(b). However, whether or not these words should be given as broad a construction as the word measure, in view of the broad interpretation assigned to them in WTO jurisprudence, we shall assume for the purposes of our present analysis that they should be interpreted as encompassing a similarly broad range of government action and action by private parties that may be assimilated to government action.*

For purposes of analysis, the panel decided to treat all of the distribution countermeasures cited by the United States as laws, regulations, or requirements, even though it only found four of them to be measures in the prior analysis, and only three of them to be in effect. The next issue for the panel to consider was whether these laws, regulations, or requirements accorded less favourable treatment to imported film and paper than to domestic film and paper. The panel applied the "effective equality of competitive opportunities" test set forth in U.S.—Section 337 as follows:

the "no less favourable" treatment requirement set out in Article III:4, is unqualified. These words are to be found throughout the General Agreement and later agreements negotiated in the GATT framework as an expression of the underlying principle of equality of treatment of imported products as compared to the treatment given either to other foreign products, under the most favoured nation standard, or to domestic products, under the national treatment standard of Article III.

The words "treatment no less favourable" in paragraph 4 call for effective equality of opportunities for imported products in respect of the application of laws, regulations and requirements affecting the internal sale, offering for sale, purchase transportation, distribution or use of products. This clearly sets a minimum permissible standard as a basis.

The panel found no "significant distinction" between the "upsetting the competitive relationship" standard of Article XXIII:1(b) and the "upsetting effective equality of competitive opportunities" standard of Article III:4, except that the latter "calls for no less favourable treatment for imported products in general" and the former "calls for a comparison of the competitive relationship between foreign and domestic products at two specific points in time, i.e., when the concession was granted and currently."

The panel's findings on the national treatment claim were similar to its findings on the non-violation claim. The eight distribution countermeasures alleged by the United States did not discriminate on a de jure or a de facto basis—they did not discriminate on their face or by their terms, nor were they applied on a discriminatory basis.

The panel reiterated that the distribution countermeasures alleged by the United States did not promote vertical integration to impede market access of foreign firms, and that the U.S. argument suffered from serious timing problems.

Finally, the panel reiterated that single brand distribution is now the "common market structure" and "indeed the norm" in national film markets, including the U.S. market. "It is unclear why the same economic forces acting to promote single brand wholesale distribution in the United States would not also exist in Japan."

The Transparency Claim

GATT 1994 Article X:1 provides:

> *Laws, regulations, judicial decisions and administrative rulings of general application, made effective by any contracting party, pertaining to the classification or the valuation of products for customs purposes, or to rates of duty, taxes or other charges, or to requirements, restrictions or prohibitions on imports or exports or on the transfer of payments therefore, or affecting their sale, distribution, transportation, insurance, warehousing, inspection, exhibition, processing, mixing or other use shall be published promptly in such a manner as to enable governments and traders to become acquainted with them.*

The issue presented by the United States was whether administrative rulings of the Japanese government are "administrative rulings of general application." The United States argued that Japan breached Article X:1 in the following two situations: (1) the failure to publish decisions that relate to the enforcement of the Premiums Law and fair competition codes when those decisions set or amend rules that apply to future cases; and (2) the failure to publish guidance in which applicants for a new or expanded store under the Large Stores Law are required to coordinate their plans with competitors and that require prior explanation prior to the filing of a notification under the Large Stores Law. The panel found that the meaning of "general application" was addressed in the WTO panel report in United States—Restrictions on Imports of Cotton and Man-Made Fibre Underwear, in which the panel stated that "if, for instance, the restraint was addressed to a specific company or applied to a specific shipment, it would not have qualified as a measure of general application." The panel also found that there were no WTO precedents directly on point. The panel explained:

> *In our view, it stands to reason that inasmuch as the Article X:1 requirement applies to all administrative rulings of general application, it also should extend to administrative rulings in individual cases where such rulings establish or revise principles or criteria applicable in future cases. At the same time, we consider that it is incumbent upon the United States in this case to clearly demonstrate the existence of such unpublished*

administrative rulings in individual matters which establish or revise principles applicable in future cases.

The panel summarised the United States arguments concerning the alleged non-transparent enforcement of the Premiums Law by Japan as follows:

The United States argues that Japan's enforcement of its premium and representation provisions is "shrouded in secrecy" resulting from the use of informal, unpublished enforcement actions. According to the United States, the problem is exacerbated due to the multitiered nature of Japan's enforcement system, with the JFTC, the prefectural governments and deputized private sector councils all having authority to enforce the Premiums Law. The confusion for companies attempting to do business in Japan primarily arises from Japan's failure to publish a large percentage of administrative rulings and enforcement actions and the difficulty in obtaining what information may be available. The United States submits that since the Premiums Law was enacted in 1962, the JFTC has initiated relatively few formal enforcement actions but has issued many "administrative guidances" or warnings, the overwhelming majority of which are unpublished. The lack of transparency is compounded, the United States maintains, by the fact that Japan's 47 prefectural governments take thousands of informal actions.

The panel found that "the primary difference between the parties is on whether or not such enforcement actions—i.e., unpublished enforcement actions that establish or modify criteria applicable in future cases—exist." The panel rejected the U.S. claim, explaining as follows:

We agree with the United States that the vast majority of individual enforcement actions are unpublished. However, we note that there is a pronounced lack of evidence as to the nature of any alleged unpublished enforcement actions effecting changes to JFTC enforcement criteria. We agree with Japan that the record is devoid of any specific allegation by the United States as to any JFTC enforcement action that is at odds with

> *already published policies. We acknowledge that the nature of the U.S. claim makes it difficult to cite examples—if a ruling is unpublished how can the United States know that it effects such changes? The United States maintains it has made repeated requests for information on enforcement activities from the Japanese Government, the respective enforcement councils and relevant photographic trade associations, but that, almost without exception, these requests have been denied. Nonetheless, it would seem that the United States should be able to cite examples of changed policies that it believes were in fact implemented first in unpublished decisions. Otherwise, we have no basis for finding that there are such decisions. Even if the rate of published-to-unpublished actions is low, we have nothing before us that suggests what it should be. We cannot find that Japan should publish "more" decisions in the absence of specific examples of the types of decisions that should be published, i.e., administrative rulings establishing or modifying criteria applicable in future cases.*

According to the U.S. allegations, four bodies in the Japanese private sector engage in enforcement based on delegations from the JFTC: (1) the Retailers Fair Trade Council, (2) the Promotion Council, (3) the Manufacturers Fair Trade Council, and (4) the Wholesalers Fair Trade Council. The United States complained that none of these enforcement bodies publishes its enforcement actions. Because these private bodies and the fair competition codes they maintain are created pursuant to Section 10 of the Premiums Law, and they are supervised by the JFTC, the United States argued that they engage in governmental action and that Article X:1 requires publication of enforcement actions that have ramifications for future cases. Again, the panel ruled against the United States, maintaining that the United States failed to present evidence

as to the nature of any alleged unpublished enforcement actions effecting changes to JFTC or code enforcement criteria. The record is devoid of any specific allegation by the United States as to any action taken by any of the councils that is at odds with the basic principles set forth in the codes. In these circumstances, we find that the United States has failed demonstrate the existence of any such administrative rulings by any of the councils, establishing or modifying criteria applicable in future cases, the non-publication of which could be viewed as a violation of Article X:1.

As for measures taken under the Large Stores Law, the panel found that there was "conflicting argument and evidence on whether or not there is unpublished administrative guidance promoting continuation through informal means of the formally abolished government policy requiring "prior explanation" by large stores." The panel framed the issue under consideration, however, as "whether or not such administrative rulings are rulings of general application." On this limited issue, the panel concluded: (i) the Japanese Government at the national level has published a directive formally eliminating the "prior explanation" requirement under the Large Stores Law, but (ii) there is anecdotal evidence of certain continued guidance at the subnational level in Japan urging large stores owners to continue the practice of prior explanation and adjustment.

The United States failed to convince the panel that the continued guidance establishes or modifies criteria applicable in future cases, or otherwise constitutes administrative rulings of "general application."

The U.S. Response: Litigation Strategy and Japanese "Commitments"

The U.S. response to the panel report was predictable. The USTR issued a press statement saying that we are obviously extremely disappointed in the WTO panel decision.... It is impossible to reconcile the realities of the marketplace with that decision. It is our intention to outline steps in the very near future to ensure that the Japanese market in this sector is indeed open and competitive.

The United States did not appeal the decision, however. Apparently, the United States decided as a matter of litigation strategy not to appeal to the WTO Appellate Body, which has competence only over matters of law. Rather, the U.S. approach was to characterise the representations that Japan made during the proceeding as "commitments"—something like a party admission in domestic U.S. litigation. The USTR explained that, "by making these statements to a WTO panel, Japan has committed itself before an international tribunal to implement its wholesale and retail distribution measures and enforce its competition laws in a manner consistent with its own representations and findings." The United States thus treated the panel report and Japan's representations in the case as part of bilateral negotiations between the countries concerning so-called structural impediments in the Japanese economy. Some have asserted that the panel proceeding was simply the part of the dispute between the countries that was not settled, and that the United States did not have a significant interest in winning or losing the case. MITI responded that the U.S. characterisation of Japan's representations in the dispute were unreasonable and that the United States has tried to "unilaterally create new future obligations." MITI said:

> *The U.S. position is untenable. Like all submissions to the WTO dispute settlement panels, Japan's submissions in the film dispute were representation of historic factual circumstances and legal principles at issue in the particular case. The U.S. characterisation of these factual representations about the past as future "commitments" attempts to unilaterally create new future obligations. Such an approach is unreasonable, may be thought of as having the application of Section 301 in mind, and Japan should not accept such an approach.*

Analysis

The Kodak-Fuji decision is the first Dispute Settlement Panel Report in the post Uruguay Round period to decide a non-violation claim under Article XXIII. It, along with the Australian Subsidy and EEG—Oilseeds cases, is perhaps one of the more significant Article XXIII cases. There have indeed been very few non-violation cases in the history of the GATT, with only 14 of the 250 claims under Article XXIII brought as non-violation claims and the rest as violation claims. Of the fourteen non-violation cases that GATT working parties have considered on the merits, only three have resulted in a finding of nullification or impairment. Only one of these three decisions was not based on the nullification or impairment of tariff concessions made under GATT Article II.

The Kodak-Fuji panel report has prompted significant response from both the academic and practitioner legal communities. A good deal of the commentary has either criticized the U.S. position in the dispute or has argued for a narrow approach to Article XXIII:1(b) interpretation. One commentator has criticized the U.S. position as an attack on local constituency preferences in Japan and as an attack on Japanese culture. A common critical theme is that the United States attempted to bootstrap competition policy into the WTO agreements, when, in fact, the WTO members have not reached an agreement on whether competition policy should be regulated in the WTO regime. Others criticize the U.S. contention regarding vertical restraints in the Japanese economy because vertical restraints, in some circumstances, may be efficient and because ambiguity exists as to whether vertical restraints should be unlawful under competition law.

Augmenting the literature on the Kodak-Fuji case, a significant amount of writing addresses Article XXIII. Most commentators argue for a narrow interpretation of Article XXIII, contending that a broad interpretation would result in "wrong cases" and would contravene the bargains that WTO members make in multilateral trade negotiations. Another common theme is that Article XXIII has diminished in importance because the WTO agreements increasingly restrict nontariff barriers, regulate government measures that occur inside the borders of countries, and constrain the domestic policy autonomy of governments when domestic policy affects international trade.

This Chapter takes a different approach than the mainstream literature on the Kodak-Fuji case specifically, and on Article XXIII generally. The DSB should adopt a "common law" approach to interpreting Article XXIII in WTO dispute settlement cases, which would be best suited to policy evolution and trade liberalisation in the world trading system. This Article makes the case that fears of "opening the floodgates" and the parade of horribles that those seeking narrow interpretations of definitive texts typically assert may be unfounded, given the constraints imposed on the DSB by the rules and institutions of the world trading system. These conclusions are an institutionalist analysis of treaties as well as a doctrinally oriented approach to understanding the meaning of Article XXIII:1(b).

As John Jackson and others have asserted, the WTO is a constitutional regime. The WTO sets forth a constitutional order for international trade relations between countries. There are many ways to theorize about constitutions, but a set of tools that assist in the understanding of WTO dispute settlement and Article XXIII can be found in new institutional economics, political economics, and positive political theory. An institutionalist analysis of treaties focuses on the function of treaty rules and institutions in reducing and affecting transaction costs to facilitate agreement among treaty parties. In this analysis, institutions matter because they "alter the relative costs of transactions." WTO dispute, settlement makes it "cheaper for governments to get together to negotiate agreements." WTO dispute settlement is a coordination mechanism for international trade regulation, which facilitates WTO member bargaining under the shadow of the law and legal institutions.

All constitutional regimes rely, to some extent, on conflicts of interests among institutions to accomplish monitoring functions. This is a dominant theme in all regulatory regimes. The DSU, in conjunction with Article XXIII, has the potential to provide a significant component of such monitoring in the multilateral trading system. Article XXIII has fallen into desuetude in some major respects and has been rarely relied upon in GATT/WTO dispute settlement. It has the potential, however, to serve as a significant principal-agent monitoring device if applied with constraints that provide the DSB with incentives to make decisions that maximise WTO member preferences and enhance global economic welfare.

Institutionalist theories of treaties explain a number of features of international trade agreements. We can analyse treaty formation and implementation using these theories. Because the drafting of a perfect trade agreement is impossible, parties must take into account a number of contingencies in the agreement. Trade agreements tend to be relatively long-term deals. They are characterised by open-ended language and procedures that vest substantial discretion in both the WTO members and in the WTO itself. The style of their drafting is around substantive standards (rather than discrete rules) and procedural mechanisms that provide for monitoring and enforcement.

The transaction costs associated with international trade agreements cause difficulties in the implementation and enforcement of the provisions of the agreements. Effective dispute settlement is necessary to accommodate the institutional weaknesses in any treaty regime in which transaction costs are present. Substantial transaction costs will likely be present in any treaty regime that requires performance of treaty obligations dynamically over time, as do the WTO agreements.

The Legal and Policy Analytical Framework—Article XXIII Principles in the Post-Uruguay Round Period

The concept of nullification or impairment found in Article XXIII:1(b) has been said to originate in the bilateral trade agreements entered into between the United States and other countries in the 1930s and 1940s. Article XXIII has the potential to operate in a manner roughly analogous to judicial review in domestic legal orders. The Australian Subsidy decision has been called the Marbury v. Madison of the pre-Uruguay Round GATT period. The Australian Subsidy case developed a reasonable anticipation or legitimate expectations test to assess non-violation claims. Certainly, Kodak-

Fuji confirms that similar standards of review under Article XXIII will continue to incorporate themselves into the WTO adjudicatory infrastructure. Kodak-Fuji extends the Australian Subsidy analysis by providing concrete guidance on how to assess complex Article XXIII disputes that rely on facts going back into several rounds of multilateral trade negotiations.

As explained above, some have argued that Article XXIII may be of lesser importance in the WTO regime. Actually, the opposite seems to be true. Article XXIII seems to be enjoying a revival in the WTO regime. The Uruguay Round resulted in the inclusion of provisions similar to Article XXIII in several WTO agreements and, despite a modicum of protest, Article XXIII has remained intact even though the GATT framework underwent a major overhaul in the Uruguay Round. With the substantial shift in power from the WTO members to the WTO DSB, however, comes substantially increased power for the DSB in Article XXIII cases.

WTO members can make six different kinds of complaint under Article XXIII:1. Two of these complaints are "violation" complaints requiring that a WTO member violate a provision of an applicable WTO agreement to trigger a violation of Article XXIII. Two complaints are "non-violation" complaints, which do not require a separate violation of other WTO agreements. Finally, two complaints are "situation" complaints, which are very broad complaints that WTO members can raise when "any other situation" leads to a circumvention of WTO obligations.

The language of Article XXIII is the best place to start in analysing these causes of action. Article XXIII:1(a) sets forth the violation complaints. The first violation complaint is as follows:

> *If any contracting party should consider that any benefit accruing to it directly or indirectly under this Agreement is being nullified or impaired.. as the result of ... the failure of another contracting party to carry out its obligations under this Agreement.... the contracting party may, with a view to the satisfactory adjustment of the matter, make written representations or proposals to the other contracting party or parties which it considers to be concerned.*

The second violation complaint is as follows: "If any contracting party should consider ... that the attainment of any objective of the Agreement is being impeded as the result of ... the failure of another contracting party to carry out its obligations under this Agreement." There are two kinds of non-violation complaints, both found in Article XXIII:1(b). The first one is as follows:

> *If any contracting party should consider that any benefit accruing to it directly or indirectly under this Agreement is being nullified or impaired as the result of ... the application by another contracting party of any measure, whether or not it conflicts with the provisions of this Agreement.*

The second one is as follows: "If any contracting party should consider ... that the attainment of any objective of the Agreement is being impeded as the result of ... the application by another contracting party of any measure, whether or not it conflicts with the provisions of this Agreement." Finally, there are two kinds of "situation" complaints, which have their basis in Article XXIII:1(c). The first one provides: "If any contracting party should consider that any benefit accruing to it directly or indirectly under this Agreement is being nullified or impaired ... as the result of... the existence of any other situation." The second one provides: "If any contracting party should consider ... that the attainment of any objective of the Agreement is being impeded as the result of ... the existence of any other situation."

The above provisions show the broad wording of the Article XXIII treaty language. The provision has the potential to give the DSB significant power. When coupled with the need for consensus in the WTO to render a panel report ineffective, and appeal possibilities to the WTO Appellate Body only on points of law, it makes the putative powers of the DSB under Article XXIII formidable. The United States argued Kodak-Fuji case under the first nonviolation complaint identified above—nullification or impairment of tariff concessions made to the United States by Japan in the film and photographic market as a result of the application of measures by the Japanese government. The case could have been argued and decided as a situation complaint. Situation claims, however, are extremely rare. There have been no successful situation claims under the GATT/WTO regime, and some argue that they should fall into disuse.

Alternative Interpretations of Article XXIII:1(b)

Given the breadth and ambiguity of Article XXIII, what standards should the DSB apply when deciding Article XXIII claims? We are concerned here primarily with non-violation claims and perhaps secondarily with situation claims. Kodak-Fuji involved a non-violation claim. We are also concerned here with the third part of the non-violation standard identified in Kodak-Fuji—nullification or impairment of a GATT/WTO benefit. This is the core non-violation complaint.

There are at least six ways to interpret the nullification or impairment provision. They are discussed below.

An "Expectations" Test

One test for non-violation claims is a legitimate expectations test. It is the test used in Kodak-Fuji, although Kodak-Fuji seems to confuse "legitimate expectations" with "reasonable expectations." The WTO Appellate Body's position on appropriate standards, moreover, is unclear at present. The U.S. decision not to appeal Kodak-Fuji suggests that there may have been strategic reasons for a settlement with Japan.

The Kodak-Fuji panel relied on past GATT non-violation cases and found:

> *In all but one of the past GATT cases dealing with Article XXIII:1(b) claims, the claimed benefit has been that of legitimate expectations of improved market-access opportunities arising out of relevant tariff concessions. This same set of GATT precedents suggests that for expectations to be legitimate, they must take into account all measures of the party making the concession that could have been reasonably anticipated at the time of the concession.*

The Kodak-Fuji panel thus merged the concept of "legitimate expectations" with that of "reasonable expectations." Elsewhere, the panel explained that it would examine the "reasonable expectations" of the parties. Based on its review of prior GATT panel reports deciding non-violation claims, the Kodak-Fuji panel concluded that, under Article XXIII:1(b), the United States may only claim impairment of benefits related to improved market access conditions flowing from relevant tariff concessions by Japan to the extent that the United States could not have reasonably anticipated that such benefits would be offset by the subsequent application of a measure by the Government of Japan.

The standard GATT practice in prior cases was to not make a stark distinction between these two tests. The Kodak-Fuji panel report relied on EEC—Oilseeds, a pre-Uruguay Round GATT panel report issued in January 1990, for the legitimate or reasonable expectations concept. The EEC—Oilseeds Panel stated that the rationale for non-violation claims under Article XXIII:1(b) "is that the improved competitive opportunities that can be legitimately expected from a tariff concession can be frustrated not only by measures proscribed by the General Agreement but also by measures consistent with that Agreement." It also stated in several places that the non-violation provisions protected "reasonable." Expectations. The EEC—Oilseeds Panel characterised the main issue for determination to be "whether it was reasonable for the United States to expect" that the European Community would forego subsidy programs "systematically counteracting" the benefits of tariff concessions. Other GATT non-violation cases state substantially similar tests. The Australian Subsidy on Ammonium Sulfate and Germany—Sardines cases both set forth a reasonable expectations test based on the reasonable anticipations of the claimant at the time it negotiated concessions that it alleged the respondent had nullified or impaired. It is unclear how the WTO Appellate Body would have dealt with the Kodak-Fuji panel report had the United States appealed. The rulings and obiter dicta in two Appellate Body decisions, EC—Customs Classification of Certain Computer Equipment and India—Patent Protection for Pharmaceutical and Agricultural Chemical Products, are relevant on the issue of the appropriate legal standards for non-violation claims.

One day after the Kodak-Fuji panel issued its interim panel report, the Appellate Body issued its opinion in the India—Patent Protection case. In that case, the panel found that India had not complied with obligations in the TRIPS Agreement to provide adequate patent protection for pharmaceutical and agricultural chemical products. The Appellate Body upheld most of the findings of the panel but criticized the panel's interpretation of TRIPS obligations based on the "legitimate expectations" of the parties. The panel's use of the legitimate expectations concept to interpret WTO obligations generally was found to be improper. The Appellate Body found:

> *Although the panel states that it is merely applying a "well established GATT principle," the panel's reasoning does not accurately reflect GATT/WTO practice. In developing its interpretative principle, the panel merges, and thereby confuses, two different concepts from previous GATT practice. One is the concept of protecting the expectations of contracting parties as to the competitive relationship between their products and the*

> *products of other contracting parties. This is a concept that was developed in the context of violation complaints ... brought under Article XXIII:1(a) of the GATT. The other is the concept of the protection of the reasonable expectations of contracting parties relating to market access concessions. This is a concept that was developed in the context of non-violation complaints brought under Article XXIII:1(b) of the GATT.*

The Appellate Body further found that "the panel's invocation of the `legitimate expectations' of Members relating to conditions of competition melds the legally distinct bases for `violation' and `non-violation' complaints." The Appellate Body issued the EC—Computer Equipment panel report on June 5, 1998, after the WTO adopted the Kodak-Fuji panel report, on April 22, 1998. In EC—Computer Equipment, the Appellate Body reversed a panel's finding that tariff schedules are to be interpreted in light of the "legitimate expectations" of the parties. The Appellate Body criticized the panel for confusing the concept of "legitimate expectations" with "reasonable expectations" and for conflating the two distinct causes of action of violation and non-violation complaints into one cause of action. Moreover, the Appellate Body disagreed with the panel's finding that the "maintenance of the security and predictability of tariff concessions" permits the interpretation of concessions basis on the "legitimate expectations" of the exporting party. Reliance on legitimate expectations, according to the Appellate Body, leads to an inappropriate examination of the subjective views of WTO members in delimiting the terms of a concession.

The Appellate Body appears to be struggling to restrict the application of the non-violation provisions to a narrow range of cases. It also seems to prefer to avoid a common law approach in WTO dispute settlement cases in which panel members would have substantial discretion to formulate standards for interpreting the WTO agreements. The Appellate Body has engaged in a highly formal style of reasoning in the above recent cases. It is possibly reacting to criticism of the DSB by various domestic and international constituencies.

The lack of clarity in the law on non-violation claims occurs on at least four levels. First, from a positive standpoint, it is unclear whether there is a distinction between "legitimate expectations" and "reasonable expectations." Second, from a normative standpoint, it is unclear whether there should be a distinction between the two verbalizations. The Appellate Body seems to prefer the "reasonable expectations" language for assessment of non-violation claims because the "legitimate expectations" language would permit subjective and unreasonable expectations. Third, it is unclear whether the Appellate Body sees any role at all for a legitimate expectations approach, preferring instead to apply a reasonable expectations test to non-violation claims and no expectations test at all to violation claims. Fourth, one could argue that such open-ended standards should perhaps be abandoned altogether, given their indeterminacy.

Some commentators have argued that Article XXIII:1(b) is analogous to the frustration of purpose doctrine in English contract law or to the principle of clausula rebus sic stantibus, which has been codified in Article 62 of the Vienna Convention of the Law of Treaties. Although there are similarities in the three legal concepts, perhaps most notably in that they do not require a violation of contract or treaty, the differences are substantial. Most importantly, a successful non-violation claim does not excuse or discharge a WTO member from performance of its WTO obligations. To the contrary, the relevant WTO provision continues in force, and the obligations of the offended WTO member are either adjusted or the offending WTO member pays compensation to the offended member.

The concept of legitimate expectations as expressed in both English contract law and English administrative law provides a better analogy. As explained above, a contract or institutionalist theory of treaty relationships can explain WTO rules and institutions. The WTO agreements are essentially long-term bargains subject to renegotiation by members in successive negotiating rounds. In addition, WTO law is regulatory or public in nature. It is different in character from transactional law or private international law, which applies directly to transactions between private persons.

Some legal theorists, notably P.S. Atiyah, maintain that legitimate expectations are the foundation for much of contract law. In contract law, legitimate expectations form the basis for reliance-based theories of contract law. Reliance-based contract doctrine focuses analysis on a person's reaction to a promise; the promise itself is important, but it is not the source of the obligation. Alternatively stated, reliance-based theory focuses on the interaction of contract parties to find contractual obligation. The test for legitimate expectations in reliance based contract theory is whether justifiable or reasonable reliance exists. In administrative law, particularly the English version, the concept of legitimate expectations comes into play when a party justifiably relies on the promise or action of a public official. Legitimate expectation in administrative law is tied intrinsically to concepts of fairness and justice.

Once the fundamental role of legitimate expectations is exposed, the use of a legitimate expectations standard by DSB panel members to determine WTO member obligations seems straightforward. The concept could be said to be a legal foundation for most agreements, private (contractual) or public (administrative and constitutional). The standard tests for legitimate expectations, moreover, typically conflate "legitimate" and "reasonable." In contract law, reliance must be reasonable for it to have legal effect. In administrative law, reliance depends on the credibility of the representations and conduct of public officials. Thus, there is no meaningful distinction to be made between the formulation of "legitimate" and "reasonable" expectations.

A Reciprocity Test

Given the inevitable imprecision of language in Article XXIII and in "judicial" standards for interpreting WTO provisions, an alternative approach to interpreting Article XXIII:1(b) would be an even more explicit focus on the contract or bargain relationships between the parties. Such an approach is based on the concept of reciprocity, "a system of continuous `trades' or `swaps' of measures to liberalise (or restrict) trade."

The reasoning for a reciprocity test would proceed as follows. The real focus of Article XXIII:1(b) analysis should not be on unduly indeterminate language. Any reasonably open-ended formulation will vest substantial discretion in panel members. Non-violation claims should focus on whether measures have upset the competitive relations or balance of concessions among WTO members. Violation claims, on the other hand, should focus on whether there has been an actual violation of a provision in a WTO agreement.

The above Appellate Body decisions, as well as Kodak-Fuji, seem to at least hint at such distinctions, although they do not clearly articulate them. The Appellate Body in India—Patent Protection explained that a WTO member can bring a non-violation complaint when the negotiated balance of concessions between Members is upset by the application of a measure, whether or not this measure is inconsistent with the provisions of the covered agreement. The ultimate goal is not the withdrawal of the measure concerned, but rather achieving a mutually satisfactory adjustment, usually by means of compensation.

The reciprocity approach seems to reflect the way that WTO members actually interact in the world trading system. There are three possible states of affairs for the world trading system. The first state of affairs is one of totally open free trade. This is, of course, a theoretical possibility but not much else. In a world of free trade, "unilateral disarmament" would be the preferred option—removal of all trade restrictions regardless of whether countries have agreed to remove them. There would be no need for institutions such as the WTO or its DSB because governments, through their politicians and bureaucrats, would perceive free trade as the optimal solution. The neo-classical economic theory of comparative advantage reflects this approach. As explained by Paul Krugman, "the economist's case for free trade is essentially a unilateral case: a country serves its own interests by pursuing free trade regardless of what other countries may do." Governments in this state of affairs are interested only in economic efficiency and in maximising the welfare of their populace as a whole. In other words, the sole focus is on the size of the pie, with no consideration of the distribution of the pie. It is clear that the first state of affairs ignores or assumes away the transaction costs of institutions. The second state of affairs its an intermediate position and one that, from an economic point of view, is second best. In this second state, the WTO agreements function as a set of incomplete contracts. The focus of the WTO regime is on pacta sunt servanda, not on welfare maximisation. The second state of affairs represents a Pare to improvement in comparison to the third state of affairs outlined below, but it permits WTO members to take into account the distributional interests of producers to the potential detriment of consumers.

The third state of affairs is ,one of an economy completely closed off from international trade. In terms of strategic interaction, it is a state of affairs that could arise in the event that countries engage in a trade war involving retaliation. This third closed state of affairs is unrealistic for at least two reasons. First, government officials in industrialised countries may receive poor payoffs for substantial across the board restrictions in international trade. The disastrous consequences of the Smoot-Hawley Tariff Act may still loom on the time horizons of many politicians, which make such payoffs foreseeable. Second, economists have more-or-less clearly demonstrated that import substitution leads to substantial welfare losses.

The world trading regime falls within the second state of affairs. The WTO regime, by its very nature and existence, represents a divergence from the neo-classical economic approach. Either the WTO shows that governments are unable to stop intervening and have to negotiate away concessions that they should give anyway, or economics fails to account for the very real consequences of institutions. The second state of affairs is also reflected in the structure of the DSU and in the DSB's Article XXIII:1(b) interpretations. The DSB enforces the WTO bargain of tariff concessions and agreements on non-tariff barriers without regard to economic efficiency. The DSB exists in the nation state system of reciprocity, and it is bound to adhere to an approach resembling the legal doctrine of freedom of contract even when this approach is inconsistent with the maximisation of consumer welfare or economic efficiency. In a reciprocity based system, the DSB focuses on the balance of concessions, the competitive relationships between the WTO members, and similar conceptualisations to either preserve or restate the WTO bargain struck by the WTO members.

An Inefficiency Test

A radical alternative test for non-violation claims that would depart significantly from the language of Article XXIII and from the reciprocity orientation inherent in the WTO agreements would be an inefficiency test. Using an inefficiency test, a panel could interpret reasonable expectations, with economic efficiency as the primary consideration. Claimants would have to demonstrate that the measures of the respondent unambiguously reduce economic welfare below a certain level, agreed to by the WTO members. There are many possible formulations, from a very broad test that makes measures actionable under Article XXIII:1(b) if they substantially decrease the economic welfare of any WTO member or global welfare generally, to a narrow test that resembles the expectations test, which would require claimants to show that the measures in question reduce, stop, or block welfare improvements that were anticipated by the parties in the relevant rounds of trade negotiations. The test could include a Pareto or Kaldor-Hicks efficiency standard. Such a test would accommodate the widely accepted notion that trade liberalisation increases economic welfare. It explicitly recognises at least the avowed purpose for international trade agreements.

An inefficiency test could accommodate the notion that a trade agreement would be subject to efficient breach doctrine in few, if any, instances. Countries are rarely in a position to argue that more trade barriers are more efficient than fewer trade barriers because trade barriers imposed by governments block Pare to efficient exchanges by persons in different countries.

The position of Uruguay in Uruguay Recourse to Article XXIII is helpful in understanding how an inefficiency test would (or would not) work. In 1961, Uruguay complained to the GATT that GATT benefits accruing to it had been nullified or impaired by 562 trade restrictions imposed by fifteen industrialised countries. According to the GATT Panel that considered Uruguay's claim, Uruguay drew to GATT's attention "the trade problems concerning temperate primary producers such as Uruguay, both as regards the limited marketing opportunities available to them and the failure of the prices of their products to be maintained at a satisfactory level." Uruguay essentially made a situation claim. Uruguay did not provide a detailed demonstration of how each trade restriction impaired or nullified a particular GATT benefit. According to the panel, Uruguay: repeatedly referred to the general difficulties created for Uruguay by the prevalence of restrictive measures affecting its exports and to the resulting inequality in the terms on which temperate zone primary producers participate in world trade. The panel noted that is was not charged with the examination of broader issues falling outside the purview of Article XXIII. It also noted that those broader issues are being actively discussed by the Contracting Parties.

In the Uruguay Recourse case, the GATT panel avoided the issue of whether Uruguay's claim was justiciable and instead relied on procedure to decide the case. In this case, GATT established standards for the burdens of proof in nullification or impairment claims. The panel stated:

> *In implementing the compensation provision of Article XXIII:2, the Contracting Parties would ... need to know what benefits accruing under the Agreement, in the view of the country invoking the provisions, had been nullified or impaired, and the reasons for this view. In cases where there is a clear infringement of the provisions of the General Agreement, or in other words, where measures are applied in conflict with the provisions of the GATT and are not permitted under the terms of the relevant protocol under which the GATT is applied by the contracting party, the action would, prima facie, constitute a case of nullification or impairment and would ipso facto require consideration of whether the circumstances are serious enough to justify the authorisation of suspension of concessions or obligations. While it is not precluded that a prima facie case of*

nullification or impairment could arise even if there is no infringement of GATT provisions, it would be in such cases incumbent on the country invoking Article XXIII to demonstrate the grounds and reasons of its invocation. Detailed submissions on the part of that contracting party on these points were therefore essential for a judgment to be made under this Article.

The inefficiency test is subject to at least six objections. First, it conflates a situation complaint with the non-violation complaint. Second, it is not supported by the text of Article XXIII. These objections should not prove fatal to its existence, however, because the tests that panels already use are not explicit in the text of Article XXIII. Third, the inefficiency test could be formulated in a way that is not much different than the expectations test. The major difference in the tests, however, could be on the focus on the source of the claim. The inefficiency test would focus on a very important avowed economic function of trade agreements—economic welfare enhancement. With very few exceptions, economists support trade liberalisation to bring about gains from trade and specialisation, and to increase global welfare through enhanced international trade. Politicians, however, may have other goals in mind, and are often concerned about distribution, although they may use free trade rhetoric to support their positions. A potential advantage of an inefficiency test is that it has the potential to channel political incentives toward the normative policy preference of free or liberalised trade.

Fourth, the test may be viewed as impinging on sovereignty, in that it may prescribe or attack the domestic policy autonomy of municipal institutions of WTO members. It could lead panels to declare, as impermissible under WTO agreements, policy or behaviour that WTO members did not consider to be affected by the WTO regime. Worse, it could provide panels with incentives to be too active and intrusive and to add new substantive obligations to the WTO regime on a case-by-case or judicialized basis in dispute settlement rather than on a codified or legislative basis in WTO negotiating rounds. An overly broad inefficiency test could also lead to violations of DSU Article 3.2, which provides that "recommendations and rulings of the DSB cannot add to or diminish the rights and obligations provided in the covered agreements." The result of an evolutionary legal regime brought about by an inefficiency test could be asymmetrical policy and differing obligations amongst WTO members. On the other hand, it may be more efficient for members that lose dispute panel cases to apply such policies across the board to all WTO members than to have different policies for different members. This could lead to substantial augmentation of WTO obligations via dispute settlement "case law." As demonstrated below, these concerns may be unfounded to the extent that WTO rules and institutions are effective in constraining DSB preferences in a manner that align with the preferences of WTO members.

Fifth, and related to the fourth objection, an inefficiency test vests substantial discretion in members of dispute settlement panels and the Appellate Body. But are these decision makers any worse at making decisions than other WTO decision makers? DSB decision-makers are insulated, to a significant extent, from conflicts-of-interest and, as shown below, they are constrained by decisions made by other WTO institutions. This fifth objection is really part of the fourth objection—it is an objection to the sovereignty impinging nature of the shift of power to the DSB. The objection reflects a recognition that decisions about the nature of multilateral trading obligations are political in nature and that DSB panelists should not make political decisions.

Finally, the inefficiency test presents the DSB with difficult information problems. This, however, could be said about non-violation claims generally, and also about a host of other claims that the DSB is bound to decide. Having said this, an inefficiency test will likely lead to more onerous information problems than the contract-related standards that the DSB currently employs.

A National Treatment Test

A final test to be considered for assessing non-violation claims is the national treatment requirement found in Article II of GATT 1947. This is an approach that has been developed by Trebilcock and Howse in posing alternatives to harmonisation across countries in order to maintain domestic policy autonomy and to obtain the benefits of the existence of competitive governments. As explained by Trebilcock and Howse:

> *The focus of attention on domestic policies that may constitute non-tariff barriers to trade should relate principally to two objectives: first, elaborating on the principles of negative integration that have historically characterised the approach of the GATT to these issues, i.e. the application of the National Treatment principle in Article III of the GATT to domestic policy measures*

of member states (requiring that produces of foreign countries receive no less favourable treatment than that accorded to like produces of national origin), and elaborating the criteria presently contained in Article XX of the GATT that justify exceptions to this basic obligation of non-discrimination and the constraints thereon, in particular constraints on disguised or unjustified forms of discrimination (the sham principle and the least trade-restrictive means or proportionality principle); and second, to structure the ground rules pursuant to which mutually beneficial agreement between member states can be reached over policy harmonisation or convergence that are both non-coercive and non-discriminatory vis-a-vis other trading partners (i.e. respect the Most-Favoured Nation principle.

A subsidiary argument of the United States in Kodak-Fuji was that Japanese distribution countermeasures violated the national treatment obligation set forth in Article II of GATT 1947. The Kodak-Fuji panel found that the Japanese measures did not discriminate, de jure or de facto, against foreign firms. In addition, the panel found that the activities in question—single brand distribution in particular—were becoming standard industry practices without government intervention, even in the United States. As explained above, the Kodak-Fuji panel found few significant distinctions between national treatment and non-violation standards. The main difference between the two provisions was that the non-violation provision requires a comparison of competitive relationships between products both currently and at the time of the relevant concession, while the national treatment provision requires a consideration generally of whether foreign goods are treated no less favourable than domestic goods, with no references to the timing of concessions.

The main drawback of using a national treatment test under Article XXIII is that it could render the non-violation language in Article XXIII ineffective or meaningless. The non-violation claim is designed to deal with situations that do not result in a violation of any WTO obligation, including Article III. A national treatment test, in essence, would turn every non-violation claim into a violation claim. These drawbacks, however, do not refute the proposition that Article III and its substantial jurisprudence provides useful guidance in understanding how to decide non-violation claims and to properly delimit Article XXIII:1(b) coverage.

Summary Critique: Regulating Domestic Policy Externalities

The fundamental problem that Article XXIII has the potential to contend with are "domestic policy externalities." The term "externalities" is used loosely here and not necessarily in the strict economic sense of the term; the term may have more precise meanings in mainstream economic theory. The term is used here to refer to situations in which the laws or policies of one WTO member have a negative effect on the benefits that another WTO member enjoys under a WTO agreement that is subject to Article XXIII:1(b). Moreover, the relevant interest here is negative effects rather than positive effects, because negative effects are more likely to result in nullification or impairment that is actionable under Article XXIII: 1(b).

Scholars have described the problem of domestic policy externalities in different ways. In promoting the idea of harmonisation of competition policy, Ostry describes the problem as one of "system frictions":

> *Competition among firms is also competition among systems and the slow "natural" process of convergence will produce serious discord—system friction—along the way. A globalising world has a low tolerance for system divergence. Continuing instability and growing pressure for new forms of managed trade are the likely outcomes. But a new approach to mitigating system friction is, in fact, to undertake an international policy process to promote the convergence of those government policies which are most relevant to the process of innovation. Most of these policies are domestic: the new international arena beyond the border.*

Jackson, on the other hand, has distinguished between harmonisation, reciprocity, and "interface." Interface "recognises that different economic systems will always exist in the world and tries to create the institutional means to ameliorate international tensions caused by those differences, perhaps through buffering or escape-clause mechanisms." Hard-to-define language such as "globalisation" and "interdependence" are used frequently to describe these sorts of problems. The incentives for states to externalize the costs of their domestic policies are numerous and varied. Competition policy is one of the primary areas of public policy that presents significant opportunities for policy makers to devise domestic legal and political institutions that result in a disguised protectionism. The disguise in competition policy is a very good one because the government in question can hide behind the argument that it is the structure of the economy and the actions of the private sector, not official measures undertaken by the government, that close or restrict markets. Competition policy can form an integral part of a strategic trade policy by changing the strategic interaction of firms to facilitate the shift of wealth (or, in economic terms, surplus) from foreign firms to domestic firms.

The methods by which domestic policy externalities are dealt with in international relations fall into three categories: methods based on bilateral persuasion, methods based on institutionalisation, and unilateral techniques such as extraterritorial application of laws. In the early days of the GATT, when conciliation was the prevalent policy conception underlying GATT dispute settlement, Article XXIII served an important role as a "bilateral persuader." Countries could use Article XXIII to conciliate potential disputes about the respective benefits that they anticipated under the GATT. This was the power-based system that pervaded GATT diplomacy. In the post-Uruguay Round period, there is the institutionalisation of a judicialized based dispute settlement. Countries can now use Article XXIII to litigate disputes that cannot be resolved through conciliation. This is the rule-based system that exists in the WTO system.

Finally, Article XXIII can be posed as an alternative to harmonisation and to extraterritorial application of domestic laws. The relevant question is: should competition policy be the subject of regulation in a WTO code framework, or should the DSB be left alone, at least for the time being, to produce "case law" that would serve the purpose of revealing the preferences of WTO member positions on competition policy? Article XXIII can serve as a "grant of common law jurisdiction" to deal with domestic policy externalities as they arise.

The Positive Political Framework: Conceptualising the Constraints in the WTO System—The WTO Policy Evolution Game

As explained above, a substantial amount of literature on Article XXIII argues that Article XXIII should be interpreted narrowly to avoid "wrong cases" and to avoid the typical parade of horribles or opening of the floodgates. These arguments are made when there is disagreement as to interpretation of a text or when a judicialized decision-maker is viewed as being too active in its approach to adjudication. Positive political theory can be used to understand institutional interaction and to show that these concerns may be unfounded and may result in unneeded limits on the authority of the DSB.

For this analysis, attribute the worst motivations to DSB panel members: assume that they act as any WTO member would with the power to write an obligation into a WTO agreement that maximises their own preferences. No judicialized system of decision making can operate without some degree of discretion vested in the decision-maker. The issue, however, is how that discretion is constrained by rules and institutions, in this context WTO rules and institutions. In the WTO legal system, members of dispute settlement panels and the Appellate Body can be viewed as players in a policy evolution game. Although the WTO constitutional structure does not closely resemble the structure of typical domestic constitutional structures, with legislative, executive, and judicial functions more or less plainly carved out in the domestic constitution, there is a separation of powers within the WTO system. There are also conflicts of interest among institutions within the WTO system that facilitate principal-agent monitoring. Policy is formulated in negotiating rounds, in the Ministerial Conference, in the four Councils, and, to a more limited extent, in Committees. There is no discrete executive as in a domestic legal order, but the WTO Secretariat serves a coordinating and administrative role. The DSB serves a judicial or judicialized role.

If a "decisive coalition" of WTO members disagrees with a panel report or Appellate Body report, they may overrule it in any number of ways. There are at least seven constraints on the DSB:

First, panel reports have no precedential value. As Jackson explains:

> *The ... DSU does not contain anything that would lead to a view that the legal effect ... of a panel report is different from that of the practice under GATT. This suggests that ... neither a stare decisis effect, nor any "definitive interpretation" effect (particularly given that there is an alternative procedure for a definitive interpretation) of a panel report exists. Nevertheless, the panel report remains persuasive, and presumably is part of the "practice" of the parties under the agreement.*

Second, a Ministerial Conference and a General Council have exclusive authority to issue interpretations of the basic WTO treaties and the multilateral trade in goods agreements found in Annex 1 of the Uruguay Round Final Act. These constitute the bulk of the WTO texts. An interpretation requires a three-fourths vote by WTO members. Third, GATT 1994 provides that the WTO may issue "decisions" on the basis of a majority vote if the WTO members cannot reach a consensus. Fourth, the Ministerial Conference may grant waivers of WTO obligations on the basis of a three-fourths favourable vote of WTO members.

Fifth, WTO members may affect DSB panel reports by negotiating new obligations or by changing obligations in successive negotiating rounds of multilateral trade negotiations. Sixth, WTO agreements may be amended. There are complex voting rules for amending a WTO agreement. They range from consensus requirements to actions by a Ministerial Conference without any vote. A two-thirds vote is required to amend most WTO obligations. It has been the GATT/WTO practice, however, to avoid amendments and to instead revise obligations through bargaining, in successive negotiating rounds. Seventh, the Appellate Body serves as an additional constraint on dispute settlement panels. The Appellate Body, a permanent group comprised of a roster of seven experts, has issued very conservative appeals, possibly to preserve their credibility in the early years of the post-Uruguay Round period. Appellate Body members serve for four years, subject to one renewal for another four years.

The DSB is constrained by these WTO institutions—any widely expansive opinion is likely to have limited effect, and indeed could be limited to the particular proceeding—even though the consensus rule has been reversed. Procedures exist to "reverse" decisions prospectively, despite the powers given to the DSB in the Uruguay Round. Judicialized dispute settlement and the institutional constraints in the WTO give WTO members the opportunity to engage in an iterative policy evolution game, which allows for the screening of issues for consideration under future rounds.

A spatial choice model initially conceived by Harold Hotelling and developed by Marks and others can be used to understand the constraints on WTO panels. Assume that policy choices in the WTO system can be represented on a one-dimensional interval, [0, x]. We can define x to be 10 or 1000; it does not matter to the analysis. This one-dimensional interval cart be used to derive a policy evolution game applicable to the WTO. Assume that all of the actors in this policy evolution game have single peaked preferences. This means that each player in the game prefers policies that are closer to their ideal policy, as those policies are mapped out spatially on the one-dimensional interval. Three dispute settlement panel members have ideal points on this interval labelled [x_p1], [x_p2], and [x_p3]. The ideal points of the approximate 135 WTO members are given by [x_m1], ... [x_m135], and the ideal points of the seven members of the Appellate Body are [x_a1], ... [x_a7]. Only three members of the Appellate Body may sit on any given appeal, and in this analysis the decision of the Appellate Body is represented by the median Appellate Body member.

Assume at the beginning of the play of the game that a status quo WTO agreement choice, [x_w], is in place. This may be the result of actions taken during previous plays of the policy evolution game, such as a rule resulting from a ministerial round, an interpretation, or any other decisionmaking process in the WTO. A typical policy evolution game in an Article XXIII context would occur as follows. A WTO member decides to take action possibly nullifying or impairing the benefits of another WTO member, depending on the Article XXIII interpretation to apply to the given situation. The offended WTO member decides to bring a dispute, and the dispute panel decides whether or not to find nullification or impairment. The losing party may appeal if it has a colourable argument for disagreeing with the panel's interpretation of the proper legal standard under Article XXIII, i.e., if it believes that the preferences of the Appellate Body are closer to its own rather than to those of the panel. The Appellate Body then issues its decision. The Appellate Body can only hear appeals on matters of law, not fact. The distinction between "fact" and "law," however, is widely acknowledged to be tenuous, and it is particularly unhelpful in an Article XXIII context because the choice of legal standard—the interpretation of Article XXIII—will, in effect, determine whether there is a new WTO obligation for the WTO member that is a respondent in the proceeding. If WTO members are dissatisfied with the Appellate Body's decision, or with the panel outcome, then they can nullify it or stop it from becoming WTO practice through the various WTO decisionmaking modes outlined above. This last action by the members sets the stage for another round of the game. On the next occasion of the game, a panel may have to make a decision under Article XXIII constrained by the new action or code provided by the members. With numerous iterations along these lines, the long-term "common law" evolution of policy can be studied. WTO members can use this policy evolution to understand, for example, the effects of the lack of a WTO competition policy on international trade.

This may be a troublesome assumption because, clearly, not all decisions are made by majority rule and the preferences of WTO members are heterogeneous. This simplifying assumption is made to keep the model tractable and to avoid the cluttered exposition of mapping every preference of all the WTO members. The model could be made more realistic and incorporate a consensus rule approach, but this would add much more detail with no increase in the usefulness or predictability of the model.

The fundamental issue for consideration is what actions by a dispute settlement panel will trigger a response by either the WTO members or by the Appellate Body. Consider in which there is no Appellate Body; panel members must only be concerned with the preferences of the WTO members. This resembles the situation existing prior to the Uruguay Round. We will assume that the interval [[x_ma], [x_mb]] is an interval of indifference or deadlock for WTO members. It is the interval in which WTO members cannot reach agreement to change policy through the modes of policy change that are available to them. Assume, for purposes of conceptualisation, that as one moves to the left along the entire one-dimensional interval, policy preferences tend to favour an expansive Article XXIII, and as one moves to the right, policy preferences tend to favour a restrictive Article XXIII. If a panel's ideal preference lies to the left of this interval, and there is no Appellate Body, then the best that a panel could do is [x_ma]. Thus, the panel report would be at [X=[x_ma]. This is the policy closest to the panel's ideal that would not trigger a response from the WTO members. Now, add the Appellate Body into the game. Suppose that the Appellate Body's ideal preferences lie to the left of [x_p]. This Appellate Body would prefer an expansive Article XXIII. The best that the Appellate Body could do would be [x_ma]. Thus, if the panel report is at X=[x_ma], then the Appellate Body would uphold the decision at [x_ma]. This is the best it could do, given its preferences and the preferences of the WTO members.

Suppose that [x_a] were inside the interval [[x_ma], [x_mb]]. The Appellate Body could overrule the panel, whose preferences are outside the interval, and choose any interpretation of Article XXIII within the interval. Finally, what if [x_a] is to the right of [x_mb]? This Appellate Body would prefer a restrictive Article XXIII. Any panel report at X=[x_p] would be overruled unless it was at [x_mb], which is the best that the Appellate Body could get, given the preferences of the WTO members.

This analysis provides a method for determining whether Article XXIII decisions by dispute settlement panels are constrained by the rational responses of other actors in the WTO system. Notably, it shows that if effective constraints on DSB decision making exist, concerns about overly broad Article XXIII decisions by the DSB could be misguided.

Unilateral Remedies: An Opting Out of the Policy Evolution Game?

One of the more contentious disagreements in the world trading system is whether states may impose in unilateral remedies against other states. Can a domestic institution in state A (perhaps a political body such as a legislature or some body within the executive of state A) determine, on its own, that state B has violated its WTO obligations or some other international obligation relating to international trade liberalisation, or has acted unfairly in protecting markets located in state B? With the promulgation of the Uruguay Round agreements, the question has been transformed from a normative one to a positive one—can states still undertake unilateral action despite the establishment of the Uruguay Round DSU?

The question is relevant to the policy evolution game described in the preceding section because WTO members that use unilateral remedies (most notably the United States) may have an "out" from the policy evolution game, or may be playing a different game. With the possibility of unilaterally imposed sanctions, the strategies and players of the game would be fundamentally altered. There would be at least one additional player (a domestic decision maker) and additional strategies (the choice of unilateral sanctions outside of the multilateral legal framework). The addition of players and strategies could be detrimental to policy evolution. Parties could play a different game and the development of Article XXIII as a tool for developing WTO jurisprudence could be thwarted. In Kodak-Fuji, the United States used Section 301 to set the agenda for its dispute with Japan and then moved the case into the WTO. U.S. reliance on Section 301 in the initial stages of Kodak-Fuji did not seem to result in the abandonment of the multilateral system to resolve the dispute. In future cases, however, the payoffs may provide the United States with the incentives to take unilateral action outside of the multilateral dispute settlement system.

One of the fundamental problems with the DSU in its current state is that it may not effectively constrain parties from relying on unilateral approaches. Many commentators and government officials quickly conclude that the DSU prohibits all forms of unilateral action. Such a flat prohibition would appear to be an oversimplification. It cannot be stated unequivocally that a unilateral regime is inconsistent with the DSU. DSU Article 23.3(a) states that WTO members "shall not make a determination to the effect that a violation has occurred, that benefits have been nullified or impaired or that attainment of any objective of the covered agreements has been impeded, except through recourse to dispute settlement" under the DSU. Moreover, DSU Article 23.2(c) requires WTO members to follow the procedures set forth in the DSU to determine the level of suspension of concessions or other obligations and obtain DSB authorisation in accordance with those procedures before suspending concessions or other obligations under the covered agreements in response to the failure of the Member concerned to implement [DSB] recommendations and rulings within a reasonable period of time.

These provisions seem to mandate that WTO members resort to the DSU for disputes concerning WTO agreements. They do not explicitly forbid unilateral action, and the provisions could reasonably be interpreted to permit unilateral action to attack measures that are not covered by WTO agreements. The fundamental question is whether the DSU should be interpreted or amended to forbid WTO members from undertaking any unilateral action whatsoever in international trade matters. Such an approach would be necessary to bring about the policy evolution game set forth in the preceding section.

Kodak-Fuji in Context

The above analytical framework can be applied to understand the Kodak-Fuji dispute. Much of the discussion to date on Kodak-Fuji and related policy issues has focused on Japanese "structural" barriers to trade, and on whether the WTO should regulate competition policy or restrictive business practices. These are good questions, but they do not address the core of the problem. Further, these questions do not explain why the economic institutions of two large trading nations such as Japan and the United States are so different.

The Panel Report is evidence of the different approaches of Japan and the United States to the role of law and regulation in the market-oriented economy. These differences have been well documented, prior to and independent of the dispute between the two countries on the openness of markets for film and photographic paper. Much of this literature explains Japanese and American differences on the basis of culture, and asserts that Wesphalian conceptions of nation-state sovereignty should protect culture from external intrusions. In addition to the culture arguments, a host of explanations for Japanese and American differences are based on differing conceptions of the role of industrial policy or trade policy in an economy. Japan, it is argued, has well-established approaches to industrial policy and strategic trade policy that originated in the Meiji era, when Japan rapidly industrialised.

Kodak-Fuji suggests an alternative explanation to the culture explanation. It illustrates the existence of significant domestic policy externalities that cross Japanese and U.S. borders. The case shows how property (or contract) rights exist in different forms in the United States and Japan, and how the differences affect international trade liberalisation. As explained by one Japanese social scientist, Takeo Kikkawa:

> *The problem of the 'closed' Japanese market lies in the existence of a large gray zone within which two—in theory mutually contradictory—principle,;, the market principle and the organisation principle, are mixed together. This gray zone is known as the 'organised market.' The market, in essence, is a place which members can enter and leave freely and where they can freely make exchanges, with price as the most important signal and with maximisation of profits or benefits as the most important motive. The organisation, on the other hand, is a place where a fixed set of members carry out transactions, their behaviour steered ultimately by orders backed up by authority. According to conventional, two-dimensional theory the market and the organisation are incompatible. The problem is that in every sphere of economic activity in Japan we find organised markets which conventional theory has great difficulty in explaining.*

Conceptualising a market-oriented order is a Hayekian notion of the market as spontaneous order. Its apparent roots are in the neoclassical notion of freedom of contract. The Japanese approach, on the other hand, is a combination of Oliver Williamson and James Buchanan—transaction cost economics, captured in the political process. This is what Kikkawa refers to as "organised markets"—the Japanese government involves itself in establishing property rights at the transactional level. The Western approach is based on freedom of contract, where contract rules are designed principally as default terms or ground rules, and it is up to participants in the market to make transaction decisions. In the United States and the West generally, government involvement in transaction structuring is considered a questionable form of government interference, to be used exceptionally to implement public policy designed to deal with market failures, such as information problems in securities offers and monopoly problems in mergers and acquisitions. In Japan, government involvement in transaction structuring is a routine and vital part of government activity. In both systems, the state is involved in the creation of property rights, albeit in different ways. Why do these differences exist?

Though it would be easy to look to the cultural differences for explanations, there is perhaps a rational choice explanation, found in the costs of implementing a legal and regulatory regime, and in the concept of path dependence. Although it is beyond the scope of this Chapter to explore these questions in detail, some tentative generalisations will be provided. Two events designed to facilitate Japan's "catch up" with the West—comprehensive transplantations of Western law and the implementation of assertive industrial policy—affected the costs of Japanese government involvement in the "organised market." In the nineteenth century, the Japanese undertook a substantial reform and "modernisation" of the Japanese legal system, focused on transplanting civilian code-based approaches into the country.

This process occurred relatively recently, with purposeful transplantation of Western law and institutions starting in the Meiji era. Japanese government officials were of the view that common law or evolutionary systems of governance were inefficient and would take too long to develop. The development of the legal system was complemented by industrial policies that sought rapid industrialisation. The two-fold focus on transplanted Western law and assertive industrial policy made it less costly for the Japanese government to be involved at the transactional level in the economy. It is, therefore, less costly for Japan to depart from neoclassical contract-firm paradigms that are entrenched in the West.

This explanation seems to be confirmed by the Kodak-Fuji panel report. Examples from the panel report are set forth here. The 1967 Cabinet Decision on Liberalisation of Inward Direct Investment states the following three policies to direct measures on the regulation of foreign investment in Japan: "(1) prevent disorder that may arise from the advancement of foreign capital; (2) create the foundation to enable our enterprises to compete with foreign enterprises on equal terms; and (3) actively strengthen the quality of domestic enterprises and reorganise the industrial system so that they can fully compete with foreign capital." The 1967 Cabinet Decision also identified the Japanese distribution sector as in need of substantial improvement:

> *Modernisation lags behind most in the distribution sector. Here, the power of resistance against the inroad of foreign capital is weak, and the impact of foreign capital advancing into this sector will also pose significant impact on the production sector. It is necessary, therefore, to implement countermeasures in support of the efforts of industry with the objectives of modernising the distribution structure, fundamentally strengthening the enterprises in this sector, and establishing a mass sales system.*

The Sixth Interim Report of the MITI Industrial Structure Council Distribution Committee, entitled "Distribution Modernisation Outlook and Issues," warned of "a risk that the process of sales expansion by foreign capital affiliated distribution enterprises will aggravate excessive competition and hinder the smooth implementation of distribution modernisation plans, and the established order of trade will be disrupted." The Report also identified "a risk that the manufacturing sector will be dominated by controlling the sales routes, bringing about the international subcontracting o f Japanese industry. The Seventh Interim Report of the MITI Industrial Structure Council Distribution Committee, entitled "Systemisation of Distribution Activities," proposed the following four ideas to "systematise" the distribution system: "(i) establishing a Distribution Systemisation Council; (ii) presenting guide posts and promoting standardisation; (iii) establishing a system for providing distribution-related information; and (iv) providing incentives in areas such as financing and taxation."

In 1968, MITI asked the Institute for Distribution Research to survey transaction terms in several industries. The purpose of the survey included the dissemination of "rational trade practices." In March 1969, the Institute submitted its report on the film industry, which examined the terms and conditions of contracts. The Report included the following findings:

> *There is a view and an impression that the industry of general use photographic film, based on an oligopoly of two domestic manufacturers [Fuji and Konica], is superficially in a stable and normal state in which*

contract formation and documentation of transactions are progressing. Consider, however, one postulate:

(1) If the oligopoly of the two domestic manufacturers is broken up by a foreign company; and

(2) If a new distribution route emerges to compete against the route of photographic material dealers, which is the core existing route in the distribution market. There may be very few observers who have a sense of crisis regarding (1) and (2) as realistic issues; however, they should now be considered as the most concrete and realistic problems.

The Report recommended the following: "Given this situation, it is necessary to formulate measures before hand in order to minimise the anticipated disorder in the distribution market. This is why it is significant to rationalise and standardise transaction terms and to create an ... order of distribution." In 1968, MITI also established a Transaction Terms Standardisation Committee, to examine the issue of standardisation of contract terms in industry. In 1970, the Committee published "Guidelines for Rationalising Terms of Trade for Photographic Film."

On July 28, 1971, MITI's Distribution Systemisation Council published a "Basic Plan for the Systemisation of Distribution." The plan essentially promoted the "systematisation" and "rationalisation" of the distribution sector. In accordance with the above 1971 Basic Plan, the Distribution Systemisation Development Centre was formed in 1972, the purpose of which was to facilitate the work of the Distribution Systemisation Council. The Centre was tasked with working with industry to produce industry-specific "Systemisation Manuals." In March 1975, the Distribution Systematisation Centre published the "Manual for Systemisation of Distribution by Industry: Camera and Film." The 1975 Manual was prepared by the Centre in collaboration with industry and with a MITI official as an observer.

The Japanese Diet passed a Large Stores Law on October 1, 1973, which became effective on March 1, 1974. The law as amended set forth a mixture of notification and regulatory requirements that stores in excess of a certain size were required to follow. The law required advance notification prior to a store's building or opening. The relevant government authority could recommend a reduction in size of the store, a delay in its opening, and could direct opening times and store holidays. The Large Stores Law has been repealed. It has been argued that its appeal was part of a set of concessions that Japan gave to the United States as part of structural impediment negotiations. Despite its repeal, the law, and its continued existence and evolution over the course of many years, illustrates the limited point being made here, that legal rights are structured differently in Japan than in the United States.

The Japanese Fair Trade Commission established a Distribution Sector Office with the approval of the Japanese Cabinet. Its purpose is to "administer duties pertaining to unfair trade practice designations related to distribution." In December 1981, the Office made findings and recommendations to "camera, photographic materials, colour photo laboratories and related industries" in an article entitled "The Status of Distribution of Cameras." In this chapter, the Office advised the industry to deal with "problems" that were the result of the dispatching of employees by manufacturers to large retail stores. Further examples from the panel report that seem to show government sanctioned transaction structuring include the establishment of the Japanese Fair Trade Promotion Council and the issuance of Self-Regulating Rules Concerning Fairness in Trade with Business in 1982. The Self-Regulating Measures regulate, among other things, the dispatch of employees for sales promotion and other marketing activities and financial standards for promotions. The Fair Trade Promotion Council, established by industry, is involved in the policing of "fairness" in transactions and the implementation of the Self-Regulating Measures.

The panel report refused to find many of the above items to be "measures" under Article XXIII:1(b), but they are nevertheless illustrative of the differing ways of establishing rights in Japan and the United States. There was some government involvement in establishing all of these policies. The focus here is not so much on what Article XXIII:1(b) actually means (or on what a panel report says it means), but on what it should mean. It is now well understood that Japan promulgates norms through non-binding administrative guidance; the Kodak-Fuji panel ruled that such guidance could indeed constitute measures under Article XXIII:1(b). One of the principal issues examined here is whether Article XXIII:1(b) standards may require reinterpretation or modification.

The issue confronted in the WTO is how to deal with domestic policy externalities when they have international trade implications—when they negatively affect WTO obligations among WTO members. It is highly unlikely that any WTO agreement in the foreseeable future will explicitly deal with the problems addressed in this Chapter. Various future WTO agreements may touch upon specific areas that

WTO members can agree upon as part of progressive liberalisation, such as a competition policy. In some instances, these new agreements will deal with symptoms rather than causes. What the WTO members can develop to promote deeper liberalisation is a norm-based system that relies on the DSB as an active player in a policy evolution game. WTO members can thus develop norms that can be amended in future negotiating rounds and in the WTO policy evolution process generally.

This Chapter has attempted a comprehensive examination of the non-violation provision of Article XXIII:1(b). It has examined the provision in the context of a major decision interpreting its terms. There are no easy answers to the question of what the proper scope of Article XXIII:1(b) or the role of WTO dispute settlement should be. An interdisciplinary approach that focuses on the analytical social sciences, including political economics and positive political theory, can provide tentative answers. The social sciences can serve in a complementary role to a traditional legal or policy analysis. This Chapter is an attempt to synthesize teachings from various disciplines into a coherent whole to understand the role that WTO dispute settlement might take in the future. This Chapter was being completed as the Seattle Ministerial Conference was coming to a close. That Conference furnishes a stark reminder: politics matter. WTO policy will be shaped in response to politics, perhaps more than any other factor. The analysis set forth in this Chapter, and the recommendations it makes, may be impracticable from a political or practical point of view. The politicians and public officials of the WTO members may not be in a position to provide additional power to the DSB for a long time and, indeed, in response to widespread popular misunderstandings and distrust of the role of the WTO, they may be required to promote a conservative agenda for the WTO. The purpose of this Chapter is not to engage the populist politics that currently surround the WTO in controversy, but to examine the potential of the WTO in the evolution of norms that promote global welfare.

When this Chapter was in the final stages of completion, the WTO issued the panel report, United States—Sections 301-310 of the Trade Act of 1974, The panel ruled that sections of the trade Act of 1974 were not inconsistent with DSU Article 23.2 or any relevant GATT 1994 provisions. The DSB adopted the panel report on January 27, 2000. It is unknown whether the complainant will appeal. The findings of the panel report may have important implications for those parts of the Article dealing with the effect of unilateral remedial regimes on the functioning of the DSU.

Chapter 6

Independent Judicial Review of Post-WTO China

"Can the Confucian person be transformed into a legal person, and can the Confucian society support it?" The accession to the World Trade Organisation (WTO) of the People's Republic of China (China) on December 11, 2001, triggered an eclipsing interest in the nomenclature of rule of law. On the brink of modernity, China faces the task of major legal reforms in the hopes of transforming itself into a modern economy and establishing itself as an effective participating member of a global economy where open markets and free trade reign. China's major legislative goals are expressed three fold: "Continuing to revise laws that are not in conformity with China's obligations under the WTO rules; revising laws that are not conducive to enhancing the competitive power of Chinese enterprises in the international market; and improving laws offering protection to domestic enterprises and ensuring industrial safety." At the forefront of China's on-going legal reforms is a tacit globalisation imperative of implementing the rule of law.

Despite staggering numbers in trade and affiliate sales, the market access of transnational corporations (TNCs) to Mainland China's consumer market remains a problem and an elemental motivation of TNCs. A problem of TNCs entrance into China's market is that they must employ "barrier-jumping" investments to overcome tariffs and other measures effectively discriminating against foreign traders. It is here that we begin to see the need for the rule of law in China as outlined by the WTO and General Agreement on Tariffs and Trade (GATT). It is a prescription for broad, systemic reforms in the areas of transparency, independent judicial review, and fairness.

China's commitment to the rule of law derives from its acceptance of a key provision in the Protocol on Accession. A WTO Appellate Body Report confirms that a WTO member must establish sound legal mechanisms for implementing its obligations under the WTO Agreement. The implementation of the rule of law is an imperative necessity to both legal reform and economic development. China itself recognises its obligation and its need to reform its legal system. For China, a well-established, socialist-market economic system requires a well-established, socialist-market legal system. The view of China from a Western perspective is grounded in Western taxonomies and is in a constant struggle with Sinicism in its insistence to westernize Sinicism. The West must lend more understanding to the jurisprudence that has driven China's legal system over the centuries. The jurisprudence of a nation-state influences the rule of law and mirrors its general culture. Jurisprudence provides an invaluable tool for establishing and evaluating a legal system.

Chinese jurisprudence is a foundational philosophy grounded in antiquity, with Confucianism and Legalism vying for dominance. An on-going and ageless struggle of competing Chinese philosophical thought persist in modern China, with their influence offering an often neglected dimension to understanding China's legal system. A China in antiquity presents a reality of traditional Chinese philosophy forged into modern Chinese nationalism. Although there are many traditions of Chinese philosophy—Confucianism, Neo-Confucianism, Legalism, Taoism, Ying Yang school, Logicians, Buddhism, and even New Confucians, or third-wave New Confucians —for purposes of this chapter, a predominating Confucianism is representative of all traditional schools of Chinese philosophical thought. Although differing from each other, the major Asian religions and philosophies share similar concepts about the origins and purpose of power.

Arguably, a China in antiquity reinvents itself as a modern China with Asian values. Modern phraseology indicates an East Asian policy of putting economic reform before the rights of individual citizens. Some argue that these Asian values are the new face of authoritarianism; others argue that these Asian values represent no more than a cliche or exercise in political rhetoric, rather than theory in practice. Assuming the applicability of the rule of law, the question becomes what influence Chinese jurisprudence plays in the construct of a positive discursive model for judicial review. It is a question of whether a legal system rooted in 5,000 or more years of Chinese philosophy, culture, and history can truly embrace the rule of law and positive discursive model for judicial review. This is dependent upon the question "Can the Confucian person be transformed into a legal person, and can the Confucian society support it?"

Confucianism, Asian Values, and Particularism

The Method and Need to Study Chinese Jurisprudence On traditional Confucianism Sang-Jin Han writes: For East Asians living in "the Confucian cultural sphere" ... where the influence of Confucianism has been relatively great—the burning question today is the reconciliation of various "Western" values with traditional Confucian ones in both the public and the private realms of existence.... We need to investigate under which conditions the East and the West, despite the many differences between them, can be engaged in an equal and dignified dialogue.

To accomplish this sort of dialogue, the West must commit more resources to the study of Chinese jurisprudence. Lack of resources, training, and translation typically hinder the West in its understanding of Chinese philosophy. Additionally, Arif Dirlik notes a proclivity of the West to explore Sinicism, or study Sinology, in terms of its own history and thought. The approach of the West is shrouded in Western ideology, social generalisations, and an unconscious bias—perhaps romantically induced—engendering a persistent proclivity to assimilate a preconceived subordinate Sinic culture. Barry M. Hager writes: "The tendency in the West too often is to pay little tribute to the existence of other legal traditions, largely because the other legal traditions do not have the hallmarks of the Rule of Law approach that developed in the West." Western jurisprudence is based more on Roman law, than Greek law, because Roman law placed limitations on the arbitrary and discretionary acts of government.

The rule of law partly evolved from the influences of the Roman era, but its greatest influence came from intellectual European sixteenth century philosophers—Hobbes, Locke, Rousseau, Montesquieu, and other Enlightenment thinkers. During the Age of Reason (1660-1798), these philosophers expressed the core ideas of the Enlightenment, which posited a focus of ethics directed at the search for a universal principle of law that would be binding for circumstances. (30 all individuals regardless of their particular circumstances. Thomas Hobbes in Leviathan (1651) and Jean-Jacques Rousseau's formulation of the social contract offer prime examples of the philosophical thought that gave birth to the Western rule of law. Hobbes provided a modern foundational basis for Western jurisprudence by asserting the rationality of absolute power, which evolved into the ideal of a democratic share of power. This ideal arguably serves as the foundational ethos for democracy, constitutionalism, the rule of law, and positive discursive models for judicial review. It is a foundational ethos, or constitutional value, reflective of Western culture and values, which is essential to constitutionalism and rule of law.

The role of philosophical thought taken in conjunction with the role of historical accident forges the Western rule of law, which in turn, forges positive discursive models for judicial review. How Chinese jurisprudence influences the implementation of the rule of law remains unanswered. A study of Chinese jurisprudence should lend understanding to China's journey toward the rule of law.

Stephen C. Angle urges the best approach to the study of Confucianism should start from a historical perspective, rather than an ahistorical perspective. First, Angle argues that a historical consciousness in Confucianism may help us to understand why we have not achieved a moral consensus, and where and how to best reach such a consensus. Second, he argues that we will see that "the Chinese rights tradition has rich resources," which will broaden the range of available Chinese perspectives on rights. Third, he argues that reviewing a Chinese history of rights discourse will give us an appreciation for the wisdom of seeing moral traditions as contingent and rooted in historical particularity.

The previously mentioned arguments for studying Confucianism from a historical perspective are applicable to the study of Chinese jurisprudence. The study of Chinese jurisprudence from a historical perspective may assist the West in understanding the judicial problems now confronting China and in reaching a mutual accord on the problem of implementing the rule of law. Western universalising cosmopolitanism brings preconceived ideals and taxonomies that impede the sort of Sino-West dialogue envisioned by Sang-Jin Han.

Ethos of Confucianism and Legalism

Traditional Chinese jurisprudence deals with various philosophies of proper social behaviour and law from about 500 B.C. until significant Western influences in the nineteenth and twentieth centuries. It is from the latter representative period that scholars extract traditional Chinese jurisprudence from a larger general philosophical literature representing the various schools of ancient Chinese philosophy.

The writings on law of Confucianists and Legalists are legal philosophies. Notwithstanding other schools of traditional Chinese philosophy, such as Taoists, Ying Yang school, Logicians, Chinese Buddhists, the many of the Sung dynasty (960-1279), the many of the Ming dynasty (1368-1644 A.D.), and even Neo-Confucianist, the dominate legal philosophies appear to be Confucianism and Legalism.

Although Neo-Confucianism influences general philosophers who directly discuss law, Neo-Confucians have actually little to say about law. An on-going debate between Confucianism and Legalism is a discourse directed to the clash between rule by man and rule by law. Confucianism infuses law with moral qualities, while Legalism, as an antithesis, is a harbour for positive law.

Han Fei Tzu (c. 298-238 B.C.) is a renowned propagator of Legalism, which embodies a radical reliance on centralised power and characterises Machiavellian principles in controlling and maximising power. Legalism is mostly distinguishable from Confucianism because of its reliance on law rather than rules of proper behaviour, and for controlling a subject people and centralising power in a ruler. Legalism relies on harsh laws, at least initially, to promote correct behaviour. Traditional Chinese legal philosophy begins with Confucius (551-479 B.C.). The Analects of Confucius are the principle source of Confucianism. The gist of Confucianism, "the orthodoxy of the traditional Chinese state," is the notion that human society expresses itself through a finite number of hierarchical relationships. These relationships impose certain duties on, and grant certain rights to, the individuals in such relationships. These pre-determined relationships evolve into reciprocal, if not mutual, relationships. Categorising individuals into such relationships brings about respective assignments to related duties, because the relationships define duties. Confucianism, in essence, teaches that properly defined relationships result in desired behaviour on the part of both the individual and society.

Traditional Chinese philosophy continues to exert its influence on modern China. Xuezhi George Guo best describes the transformation of Chinese philosophy to the practical realities of modern China, and writes:

> *Traditional Chinese political thought fuses idealistic altruist pursuit with functional practicability, which is based on a combination of the values and ethics of Confucian, Daoist, and Legalist traditions. Contemporary Chinese political figures are still influenced by those traditions, even though communist ideology plays an important role in shaping their worldview and guiding their revolutionary practice. The ultimate goal of Chinese politics is to search for not only power and influence but also legitimacy of political rule that requires political leaders to behave correctly*

according to a moralistic ideology and rule based on benevolence.

In China, Confucianism is persistent and systemic. On Confucianism Sang-Jin Han writes: "More controversial still is the third topic of the role of Confucianism on culture and morality. The existence and importance of positive cultural-moral, ethical, and aesthetic-resources of action deeply imbedded in East Asian traditions, which may differ significantly from the Western paradigm of rationality cannot be denied." A China bound to Confucianism, which also has evolved its society and class system, necessitates that the West search for a more thorough understanding of modern Chinese jurisprudence in light of Chinese antiquity. It is a question of whether Confucianism is present in modern China, and if so, whether there is a definable link between Confucianism and modern Chinese nationalism. Lastly, if there is a causal relationship between Confucianism and modern Chinese nationalism, there remains the question of how such a nexus influences the rule of law and positive discursive model for judicial review.

If remnants of antiquity foster vestiges of an authoritarian, bureaucratic version of Confucianism, the analysis takes a turn for the worst. In such instance, the rule of law offers no more than an invasion of Chinese culture and morals. Confucianism is not reflexively authoritarian or statist, however. The pages of Chinese history hail from a variety of resources and periods, from dynastic to post-Mao. Utsa Patnaik aptly describes the world's image of China. He writes:

> *Successive images and events flash through the mind: the humiliation of the Triple Intervention by the Western imperialist powers, Beijing students in the May 19 Movement, the 21 demands made by the Japanese, the seizure of Manchuria, the peasant movement in Hunan, the Canton uprising, Chiang Kaishek's annihilation campaigns against the Communists, the incredible Long March by a band of ill-clad and ill-equipped revolutionary soldiers with only handfuls of millet to sustain them physically but fired by the resolve to survive and wrest victory from retreat, the long guerilla war, land reforms in the liberated areas, and final victory over the Japanese and the Kuomintang, enabling the initiation of the historic second experiment in the world of an autonomous strategy of building socialism. The consternation in the advanced capitalist world at that*

> *time when China "went Communist" and the joy of the majority of the populations in the Third World at the victory can now only be imagined.*

Albeit a history predominated by Confucianism, China's history is one of struggle, civil strife, revolution, isolationism, xenophobia, and proto-nationalism, which arguably justify particularism and historical occurrences of authoritarian, bureaucratic versions of Confucianism. On the infusion of Western ideas with Eastern culture, Sang-Jin Han refers to the words of Samuel P. Huntington, who writes:

> *Western ideas of individualism, liberalism, constitutionalism, human rights, equality, liberty, the rule of law, democracy, free markets, the separation of church and state, often have little resonance in Islamic, Confucian, Japanese, Hindu, Buddhist or Orthodox cultures. Western efforts to propagate such ideas produce instead a reaction against "human rights imperialism" and a reaffirmation of indigenous values, as can be seen in the support for religious fundamentalism by the younger generation in non-Western cultures. The very notion that there could be a "universal civilization" is a Western idea, directly at odds with the particularism of most Asian societies and their emphasis on what distinguishes one people from another.*

In modern world reality, globalisation and the end of the Cold War caused a shift in the nature of nation-state conflicts from ideological to cultural. Cultural determinism offers a predictor for cultural values: "Cultural determinism is the conviction that the accumulated knowledge, the organised beliefs, and the way of life prescribed by a culture determines not only all other aspects of human cognition and social behaviour but also the dynamics of the culture itself. Such a conviction sees culture as an autonomous cultural system." Cultural determinism plays an important role in understanding our changing world and its wealth in diversity. Cultural determinism posits that cultural values condition all modes of cultural relationships, for example, socioeconomic, political, and legal modes.

China's particularity is a by-product of Chinese philosophy, culture, and history. Confucian values predict foundational ethos or morals, and as a result, institutions in China are reflexive of Confucian values. China's particularity serves as a point of intersection for traditional Confucianism and modern Chinese nationalism. According to Diane Ravitch, particularism in this context is a matter of particularistic multiculturalism, which holds that "no common culture is possible or desirable." In harmony with the history of China and as a certain harbinger of its future, Confucianism serves as a foundational Chinese ethos for culture, morals, and jurisprudence, and prophesies of a future of particularistic multiculturalism.

Moreover, a prognostication for China is not one necessarily identifying Confucianism or communitarianism with authoritarianism. The contention of William de Bary and others, even as early as Chen Huanzhang (1888-1931), that communitarianism is not identifiable with authoritarianism remains a difficult contention to refute. Contrarily, Randall Peerenboom antithetically interprets Confucianism as being identifiable with statism. In extending the same argument, he postulates that if there is the rule of law in China, it is a statist rule of law serving as an instrument of the state. This arguably appears as an extension of a biased Western taxonomy foreordaining an interpretation of statist Confucianism. As Michael W. Dowdle notes, "everyone agrees that there is no rule of law in China," but everyone has a difficult time explaining why.

Admittedly, one witnesses periods of authoritarianism when opportunists—be they private actors, public actors, or governmental entities employ Confucianism for non-Confucian ends. The reality of an actor or polity employing a rhetorical political Confucianism in pursuit of statist ends is not the same as validly identifying Confucianism with either authoritarianism or statism. As de Bary notes, statism originates with the Han dynasty, when Legalists modified a Confucian model to fit the Han State structure so that public interest coincided with the state interest. Further, de Bary notes that Confucianism is not identifiable with statism, because a Confucian point of view looks for a balance between self and society, and Confucianism persists in acting on behalf of the way to reform an imperfect society.

Additionally, the late eminent scholar Qian Mu (1895-1990) found that despite the contributions of the Qin dynasty (221-207 B.C.) in establishing a central administration for the empire, it was during the Han dynasty (206 B.C. to 220 A.D.) that new forms of government achieved permanence and stability. It is for this reason that Han institutions best illustrate patterns of traditional government in China. Moreover, an interpretation of the basic thesis of Qian Mu concerning his views on traditional dynastic government describes traditional government as generally avoiding rule by autocracy and absolutism until the Northern Sun dynasty (960-1127). This latter governmental avoidance of rule by autocracy and absolutism is attributable to Confucianism except when government is under the influence of an overbearing Emperor or powerful court coterie.

There are means to an end, but an end does not always define its means, especially in the case of non-Confucian ends. Confucianism bears no causal relation to authoritarianism or statism because Confucianism is not innately reflexive of either. A China in antiquity provides a fundamental ethos, which is reflexive of a persistent and systemic Confucianism, by virtue of cultural determinism and the nature of Confucianism. Further, Confucianism and particularistic multiculturalism find expression in Chinese nationalism, a by-product of a recovered sovereignty after nearly a century of neo-colonialism and exploitation, and perhaps even in the reality or rhetoric of Asian values.

Asian Values: Reality or Rhetoric

Confucianism is a strongly entrenched ethnocentric social fact in China. Confucianism transcends political and economic models and serves as substitute for political and economic models, at least rhetorically. In East Asiatic countries, arguably, particularistic multiculturalism serves as a governmental policy finding its expression through rhetorical political Confucianism. In international affairs, there is on-going debate over human rights. In China, a polity under the guise of Confucianism espouses the language of socioeconomic rights, as opposed to civil-political rights, in response to requests for human rights inspections. China defends its prioritisation of socioeconomic rights over civil-political rights as a matter of traditional or Asian values.

The debate over a trade-off between economic development and democracy serves as an example of the nexus between Confucianism and particularistic multiculturalism. Some Asian leaders argue that Confucianism is a justification for the successful economic development in East Asian nation-states. The success of the Asian "Tigers" engenders debate about Asian values as a justification for economic success. Prominent leaders of East Asian countries tout Asian values to justify their successes while espousing the superiority of Eastern social and political forms to Western ones. Deepak Lal writes:

> *Rather than succumb to Western classical liberal values, which have produced decadence amongst prosperity in*

> *the West, the East, they argue, should stick by its familial and authoritarian cultural and political values as embodied in Confucianism and neo-Confucianism. Thus, in a neat reversal of Max Weber's famous thesis on the role of Protestantism in the rise of Western capitalism, we now have an Eastern 'religion' being touted as the source of East Asia's success.*

The birth of the phrase "Asian values" is attributable to several possible sources. One source is a 1995 article in The Economist, which reads, "the rise of Japan and the East Asian tigers has caused many people to reinterpret the economic impact of Confucianism." Many East Asiatic governmental leaders generally recognise, if not articulate rhetoric for, a role of Confucianism in economic development and refer to Confucianism in the new phraseology of Asian values. Use of the phrase is also attributable to Lee Kuan Yew, senior minister of Singapore; although he now exhibits trepidation, if not denial, in reference to such assertion. Dr. Mahathir Mohamad, prime minister of Malaysia, is another alleged source of the phrase. On Asian values, Alice Erh-Soon Tay writes:

> *For these leaders, the term embodies a system of values which places economic development first and above all else. It asserts the primacy of economic development for their country and implies that such development would be followed by improved standards of living for all; it follows that civil and political rights could be properly postponed until economic development has been achieved, and indeed that the denial of civil and political rights was a necessary measure to ensure economic progress and the benefits that flow from it.*

There are also divergent opinions on whether Confucianism helps or hinders economic development. Statistical studies conflict on the question of whether a link between democracy and economic development exists. Some cross-sectional statistical studies find such a relationship. A statistical study by Lal and Hla Myint concludes there is no relationship between the form of government and economic performance. However, Lal does note that the Chinese family serves as the engine of growth in the Sinic world, which he attributes to successes in Hong Kong, Taiwan, and the growth of family-based enterprise in China's non-state sector. Further, Lal contends that it is possible to modernise without Westernizing. Nevertheless, there is a causal relationship between Confucianism and modern Chinese nationalism, or China's particularistic multiculturalism. Such a nexus makes the rule of law and positive discursive model for judicial review contingent upon a Chinese jurisprudence that is representative of a persistent and systemic Confucianism.

China and Independent Judicial Review

The Constitution of the People's Republic of China

In 1982, China adopted its present constitution, the Constitution of the People's Republic of China (1982 Constitution). The 1982 Constitution has undergone legal reform, specifically four constitutional amendments—mostly economic in nature on April 12, 1988, March 29, 1993, March 15, 1999, and March 14, 2004. China's amendments mostly address economic reform, the fourth amendment includes a general provision that addresses human rights and a rule addressing compensation in cases of property expropriation. XIANFA amend. IV, arts. 33(3), 10(3), 13(3) (2004). Relevant portions of the fourth amendment follow:

1. "... along the road of building socialism with Chinese characteristics ..." and "... under the guidance of Marxism-Leninism, Mao Zedong Thought and Dang Xiaoping Theory ..." Revised to: "... along the road of Chinese-style socialism..." and "... under the guidance of Marxism-Leninism, Mao Zedong Thought, Deng Xiaoping Theory and the important thought of Three Represents' ..."
2. Seventh paragraph of the Preamble: After "... to modernise the industry, agriculture, national defence and science and technology step by step ..." Is added: "... promote the coordinated development of the material, political and spiritual civilizations..."
3. The second sentence of the 10th paragraph of the Preamble: "In the long years of revolution and construction, there has been formed under the leadership of the Communist Party of China a broad patriotic united front that is composed of the democratic parties and people's organisations and embraces all socialist working people, all patriots who support socialism, and all patriots who stand for the reunification of the motherland. This united front will continue to be consolidated and developed." After "... a broad patriotic united front that is composed of the democratic parties and people's organisations

and embraces all socialist working people ..." is added "... all builders of socialism ..."

4. Third paragraph of Article 10: "The State may, in the public interest, requisition land for its use in accordance with the law." Revised to: "The State may, in the public interest and in accordance with the provisions of law, expropriate or requisition land for its use and shall make compensation for the land expropriated or requisitioned."
5. Second paragraph of Article 11: "The State protects the lawful rights and interests of the individual and private sectors of the economy, and exercises guidance, supervision and control over individual and the private sectors of the economy." Revised to: "The State protects the lawful rights and interests of the nonpublic sectors of the economy such as the individual and private sectors of the economy. The State encourages, supports and guides the development of the non-public sectors of the economy and, in accordance with law, exercises supervision and control over the non-public sectors of the economy."
6. Article 13: "The State protects the right of citizens to own lawfully earned income, savings, houses and other lawful property", and "The State protects according to law the right of citizens to inherit private property." Revised to: "Citizens' lawful private property is inviolable" and "The State, in accordance with law, protects the rights of citizens to private property and to its inheritance" and "The State may, in the public interest and in accordance with law, expropriate or requisition private property for its use and shall make compensation for the private property expropriated or requisitioned."

In considering the amendments, the March 15, 1999 amendment is most noteworthy. Article 13 is a prescription for the rule of law, and adds the following words to Article 5: "the People's Republic of China governs the country according to law and makes it a socialist country ruled by law." Additionally, there is an amendment to the preamble, which adds Deng Xiaoping's theory and the words "developing a socialist market economy," thereby bestowing constitutional import upon both the theory and words. It has been proposed that Deng Xiaoping's Four Cardinal Principles require that "China must be made a true rule by law country." The National

People's Congress (NPC) of China is the highest organ of state power. It is the national legislature and the supreme organ of state power. The NPC's standing body is the Standing Committee of the National People's Congress (SCNPC). The NPC exercises typical legislative functions such as enacting and amending basic laws, electing Procurator-General, planning for national economy and social development, declaring war, and other powers. However, the powers of the NPC are distinguishable in two respects. The NPC has the power to enforce the Constitution and, through the SCNPC, has the power of judicial review. The NPC meets once a year, which results in its State Councilors and Ministers in charge of ministries or commissions—such as the Ministry of Commerce (MOC)—retaining more powers than expressly delegated to them in the 1982 Constitution.

Comparatively, notwithstanding the legislative hierarchy of the government, the Standing Committee of the State Council wields its power as the executive hierarchy of government; however, in actual practice, the Standing Committee is often subordinated to the Central Finance and Economic Leading Group of the Chinese Communist Party. The Central Finance and Economic Leading Group is compromised of a few party members in charge of all crucial economic issues who exercise their executive authority through a Joint Commission of the Politibureau and State Council. This alignment of power is best described as a governmental agency relationship, with the party—representing the polity—as principal, and government-the NPC and its appointed delegates of power—as agent.

The 1982 Constitution marginalises the power of the judiciary. One must read Articles 5, 67(1), 67(4), and 127 in conjunction with the previously discussed constitutional division of governmental power to understand how the judiciary is rendered constitutionally weak and marginalised. The preamble of the 1982 Constitution reads:

> *This Constitution, in legal form ... is the fundamental law of the state and has supreme legal authority. The people of all nationalities, all state organs, the armed forces, all political parties and public organisations and all enterprises and institutions in the country must take the Constitution as the basic standard of conduct, and they have the duty to uphold the dignity of the Constitution and ensure its implementation.*

Further, amended Article 5 reads: "The People's Republic of China governs the country according to law and makes it a socialist country ruled by law." Article 127 of the 1982 Constitution reads: "The Supreme People's Court is the highest judicial organ." Articles 67(1) and (4) are the greatest possible source of violation to the principles of constitutionalism, in that they vest the SCNPC with the power "to interpret the Constitution and supervise its enforcement" and the power "to interpret laws." A measure of a constitution is constitutionalism because there is a great deal of difference between a constitution—the written article itself—and the principles of constitutionalism. It is a matter of general rules of interpretation that "constitutional values contribute to proper understanding of constitutional provisions." Confucian values arguably provide the needed constitutional value, or fundamental ethos, for constitutionalism. Peerenboom describes Chinese philosophy as possessing a pragmatic, anti-foundational character. He writes "any rights theory justifiable on Chinese terms will almost assuredly be a contingent one" because legal rights in China will necessarily be contingent upon Chinese culture, traditions, and historical and economic conditions. Moreover, the previously mentioned contingencies also share a foundation in Confucianism.

Rule of law is also reflexive of Chinese culture, tradition, historical and economic conditions. In an argument by analogy, Confucianism provides a foundational ethos requisite for constitutionalism, the rule of law, and judicial review. Although a foundational ethos for constitutionalism may arguably flow from Confucian values, the problem of implementing constitutionalism remains. A constitutive process is two fold: it involves the constitutional decisionmaking process and the implementation of constitutionalism. A core problem for China—and Chinese constitutionalism—is the lack of positive discursive machinery for judicial review.

The 1982 Constitution does not vest the judicial organ of its government with the judicial independence shared by courts in the United States, but neither do the constitutions of some Western countries. In Western countries, the responsibility of constitutional interpretation will generally vest with the judicial bodies of its respective countries. In the West, models for constitutional review, or constitutional courts, are models of either a centralised or a decentralised constitutional review. The 1982 Constitution reveals a lack of any real semblance of constitutional authority in its judiciary. Its judicial model subscribes to neither a decentralised nor a centralised constitutional review. Initially, China's governmental structure bears resemblance to a parliamentary form of government, such as Great

Britain. The NPC serves a similar role of legislative supremacy for China. In terms of political, as opposed to legal, control mechanisms for the protection of fundamental rights—Britain, not unlike China—arguably focuses on political, rather than legal, accountability.

There are dissimilarities, however. An electorate determines the legal sovereignty of Parliament, or at least its composition. In the protection of rights, "because 'Parliament is supreme,' there exist in the British constitution 'no guaranteed or absolute rights.'" An enactment is beyond the control of its judiciary, but the courts assume Parliament legislates for a European, liberal democracy founded on common law principles and approaches such legislation under a presumption that Parliament intends to legislate consistent with such principles.

These interpretive means allow Britain's judiciary to protect a range of fundamental norms, such as access to justice, judicial review, and rights of due process. The courts of Great Britain cannot strike down legislation, but they can, by interpretative means, bring legislation that appears to offend fundamental rights into line. Individual rights in Great Britain, under legislative supremacy, receive protection from both political and legal factions of government. In this context, a modified ultra vires doctrine serves as the juridical basis of judicial review. The pivotal role of courts—their interpretative means—and popular sovereignty are contrasting features.

In terms of democracy, judicial review, and constitutionalism, one must also evaluate the role of the Central Committee of the Chinese Communist Party (CCP) in structuring polity and constitutionalism. The CCP represents that it is "an integral body organised under its program and constitution, on the principles of democratic centralism." John Wong predicts that reforms will result in a weakening of the power base of the polity, the CCP, and eventually culminate in a new constitution that removes the special privileges of the CCP. The result of this would be that "political and institutional changes will hasten the emerging of some kind of democracy in China." Assuming the latter is true, one can reasonably prognosticate a Chinese variant of Western democracy.

The Third Plenary Session of the Eleventh Central Committee (November 1978-November 1980) (Third Plenum) was the watershed event of the post-Mao era. For the purpose of moving toward a socialist democracy, the Third Plenum mandated direct, popular voting for local electorates to a county-level people's congress by enactment of the Organic Law of Village Committees of China (Organic Law). Although Wong may have contrary intentions, he nonetheless predicts an eventual fulfillment of a recent interpretation of Deng Xiaoping's Four Cardinal Principles, namely that "China must be made a true rule by law country." In contrast—and as evidence of the problems in China with popular sovereignty and constitutionalism—although direct elections are in progress in local villages, the practice of indirect election of deputies to the NPC persists.

Upon further examination of the 1982 Constitution, the weaknesses of the judiciary become more obvious. The sole power to interpret the constitution and laws of China—or legislative interpretive power—is vested with the SCNPC. Further, on March 2000, there was a promulgation of new legislative procedural laws that seek to better define the roles and the procedures of lawmakers and attempt to establish legal hierarchy between the constitution, laws, administrative regulations, and orders at both national and local levels. The State Council has administrative interpretative power, which is the constitutional power to interpret all administrative regulations. Additionally, Ministries and Commissions have administrative interpretative power over departmental rules and regulations.

The constitutional alignment of governmental power places the NPC in greater power over both the Supreme People's Court and State Council Ministries and Commissions. Although the State Council—the highest executive organ—is not subordinate to the NPC in actual practice or power, the Supreme People's Court—the highest judicial organ—is, in constitutional text, practice, and power, subordinate to both the NPC and State Council in judicial interpretative powers. The Supreme People's Court has judicial interpretative power, but it is a limited, delegated power to interpret laws and regulations of China arising from actual cases, which is not the same power constitutionally vested with the SCNPC to interpret the constitution and laws of China. The distinction between interpreting laws arising from actual cases, as opposed to interpreting a constitution, is a fine one. Two Letters of Reply (Reply) from the Supreme People's Court show this fine line of demarcation. In a 1955 Reply, the Supreme People's Court wrote that it is not appropriate to cite the constitution as a basis for a decision. Further, in a 1986 Reply, the Supreme People's Court writes that courts should not cite opinions or Replies.

The judiciary has marginalised powers. In its supervisory role over lower judicial bodies, the Supreme People's Court assumes—with origins of constitutional vestige being debatable and tenuous—a power to render general interpretations of laws that are binding on lower judicial bodies in limited circumstances. First, the Supreme People's Court is responsible to both the NPC and the SCNPC. Second, the Supreme People's Court interprets its responsibility, in part pursuant to the constitution and statutes, as "giving judicial explanations of the specific utilisation of laws in the judicial process that must be carried out nationwide." The natural meaning of the words "judicial explanation" is self-limiting in the sense of judicial interpretation and is likewise difficult to elevate to the level of judicial review—the "power of courts to review decisions of another department or level of government." Further, the words "judicial explanation" fall short of being judicial power, which is "the authority exercised by that department of government which is charged with declaration of what law is and its construction," because the constitution charges the SCNPC with the power to interpret the constitution and laws of China.

Although not using the words "judicial explanation," Zhai Jianxong contends that China has a history of judicial interpretation dating back to 1954. In support of this claim, Zhai cites the SCNPC 1955 Decision on Interpretation of Law, which provides "that those questions connected with specific application of laws and decrees should be interpreted by the Supreme People's Court." He contends that this Decision resulted in a power of enacting judicial interpretation, which the legislature confirmed by enactment of the 1979 Organic Law of People's Court of the People's Republic of China. Finally, Zhai concludes that a resolution adopted by the SCNPC of the fifth NPC at its nineteenth session supports such contention. The resolution reads:

> *Where an interpretation of questions involving the specific application of laws and decrees in court trials shall be provided by the Supreme People's Court and; where an interpretation of problems concerning the concrete application of laws and decrees in procuratorial practices shall be prescribed by the Supreme People's Procuratorate. If there is any difference in principle between them, it should be delivered to the Standing Committee of NPC for interpretation or decision.*

An antithetical argument comes from Zhai's own words when he contends that judicial interpretation refers to interpretations "made by the national supreme judicial authorities on questions relating to specific application of laws in their judicial practices according to the authorisation of the NPC." His statement is a "negative pregnant" in that the words themselves, according to the authorisation of the NPC, deny a meaningful power of judicial review. The words "according to the authorisation of the NPC" speak to the continuing power of the SCNPC to interpret the constitution and laws of China and are antithetical to a claim of historical judicial interpretation. The limited powers of judicial interpretation bear little semblance to the judicial activism of courts in the West, especially the United States. Hallmarks of judicial activism are judicial decisions, or interpretations, calling for social engineering, which also occasionally represent intrusions into legislative and executive matters.

The right of abode cases, such as Ng Siu Tung vs. Director of Immigrations, provide further insight into judicial activism in China. The Court of Final Appeal (CFA) in Hong Kong attempted to exercise an assumed power of independent judicial review, but on June 26, 1999, succumbed to another superior authority—the SCNPC in Beijing. A background of the case follows:

> *Many of Hong Kong's first constitutional test cases have revolved around the question as to who has the right of abode (permanent residency) in Hong Kong under the Basic Law after reunification on July 1, 1997.*

These cases resulted in two Court of Final Appeal (CFA) decisions delivered on January 29, 1999. These decisions set in motion a number of other legal challenges on the issue. The January 1999 decisions gave the right of abode to two categories of people whose right of abode claims had not previously been recognised. Significantly, that CFA judgment also held that all claimants who arrived in Hong Kong after July 10, 1997, had to make their Right of Abode applications from the Mainland and could be removed from Hong Kong if they entered or remained before their applications had been processed and their status confirmed.

The government requested the State Council to seek an interpretation from the Standing Committee of the National People's Congress (NPCSC) on the true legislative intent of the Basic Law articles in question. Under the Basic Law, the CFA has the power of final adjudication while the NPCSC has the power of final interpretation of the Basic Law. In keeping with common law tradition and Basic Law provisions, the government did not seek to overturn the effect of the January 29 ruling on the parties to that case. On June 26, 1999, the NPCSC issued an interpretation of the relevant Basic Law provisions. This interpretation has since been followed by the courts in other cases dealing with the right of abode matter.

The NPCSC's interpretation stated that only children whose parents were Hong Kong permanent residents at the time of their birth were entitled to the right of abode. This is in keeping with international practice. Few countries, if any, allow immigrants to pass on their right of abode to children born elsewhere before they themselves have acquired that right.

The government's decision to seek an interpretation was not without controversy, prompting some to comment that the CFA's authority had been undermined. But in a subsequent right of abode ruling in December 1999, the CFA confirmed that the NPCSC interpretation was both lawful and constitutional. The rule of law and the independence of the judiciary had not been undermined.

In Hong Kong, under the Basic Law—a sort of mini-constitution—the CFA has the power of final adjudication, while the SCNPC has the power of final interpretation of the Basic Law. Despite a provision at Article 84 of the Basic Law allowing the Hong Kong Special Administration Region (HKSAR) to refer to precedents of other common law jurisdictions, the SCNPC and its power of judicial interpretation prevails. In November 2002, China and its SCNPC reiterated and buttressed its position by a decision on the handling of the existing law of Hong Kong.

Moreover, on 6 April 2004, in one of the most important historical events since China resumed sovereignty over Hong Kong, on 1 July 1997, the SCNPC again exercised its political, constitutional and interpretational powers over Hong Kong, by adopting, "Interpretations of Clause 7 of Annex I and Clause 3 of Annex II to the Basic Law of the Hong Kong Special Administrative Region of the People's Republic of China by the Standing Committee of the National People's Congress."

Wu Bangguo, chairman of the SCNPC and a member of the Standing Committee of the Political Bureau of the Communist Party of China (CPC) Central Committee, at the closing session of the Eighth Meeting of the Tenth NPC Standing Committee, indicated that :

> *"the development of the constitutional system in Hong Kong has a bearing on the implementation of the principle of 'one country, two systems' and the Basic Law, relations between the Central Authorities and the Hong Kong SAR, the interests of all Hong Kong people, and the long-term prosperity and stability of Hong Kong."*

In noting that "The Central Government has always given top priority to the development of a constitutional system in Hong Kong," Wu also announced that according to the Constitution and the Basic Law, "the right to interpret the Basic Law belongs to the NPC Standing Committee." Wu indicated that the current interpretations "have the same power as the Basic Law" and are "necessary and timely ... to ensure the healthy development of Hong Kong's constitutional system in line with the Basic Law." Generally, the two clauses interpreted, at Clause 7 of Annex I and Clause 3 of Annex II, respectively, relate to the selection of the Chief Executive of the Hong Kong Special Administration Region (SAR), formation of the Legislative Council, and procedures for voting on bills and motions after 2007. Finally, China condemned the responses of the United States and Great Britain to these interpretations as interfering with Hong Kong's internal affairs.

Additionally, the right of abode cases move one to question the role of case law or legal precedent in China's legal system. If the SCNPC has the power of constitutional interpretation, what becomes of the legal renderings of the People's Supreme Court? In China, court renderings routinely officially appear in the Gazette of the Supreme People's Court of the People's Republic of China (Gazette), as well as other non-official publications. Nanping Liu provides insight into the past and present reporting of legal renderings and states, as an elemental contention, "that decisions reported in the Gazette may actually carry force as precedents, depending on the comments the Court makes as well as on the sensitivity of the issues involved."

Liu traces the history of precedents in light of three periods: before 1912, 1912 to 1949, and after 1949 (during the Maoist era). He contends that before 1949, China had a long history of using decided cases as legal precedent. From 1912 to 1949, during the period of the Republic of China, one finds a Western style of legal precedence. Comparatively, Liu opines that the Gazette has a deliberately vague mandate for guidance. He notes the conclusion of scholars on the new publication of law that "these published decisions do not carry ... the force of precedent. They will be used only as models to help less experienced judges learn methods of legal reasoning." The earlier observations of Liu may still hold true. He writes:

> *Publication of the Gazette signals a development and a change in the way the Chinese judicial hierarchy is administered.... But it should be recognised that the purposes and underlying rationales for following judicial*

> *precedents in the Chinese context and the effects such practice may have on the general power structure within and without the written Constitution have not fully unfolded and need to be further explored.*

Nonetheless, a discontinuance of the practice of non-transparency and a history of legal precedence offer hope for the rule of law in China. The laws enacted pursuant to legal reforms also contribute to a weak judiciary. First, only in matters pertaining to commercial and financial laws does China borrow from the principles of Anglo-American common law. In this sense, the Chinese legal system characterises a bifurcated system of foreign and domestic laws with divergent treatment. Legal reform in China thus far entails an adoption of principles of civil law, common law, and international law—all of which only adds to confusion.

Second, the polity has a problem of laws that operate inconsistently on national and local levels. An illustration of this problem is the implementation of the Organic Law by local polity, creating electoral processes violative of the Basic Law; for example sea elections, two-ticket systems, preliminary voting, three-time selections, and group election systems. The Organic Law provides, "candidates are to be nominated directly by the villagers who have the right to vote in that village"—being sea election. The result is formalisation of the electorate processes by non-approved methods. Stanley Lubman writes: "As localities increase their control over their own economic resources, their power to broaden their own jurisdiction becomes increasingly problematic for the central government." This further adds to the problem of implementing a stronger judiciary with constitutional decisionmaking authority.

The Chinese judiciary remains intact as the weakest organ of government. The People's Supreme Court and its present realm of judicial power—with or without the 1982 Constitution—lacks the power of genuine substantive social discourse in the sense of constitutionalism. Nevertheless, the reality or rhetoric of Asian values can serve as a plausible justification for the constitutional mandate of a weak and marginalised judiciary. Despite the admonitions of some, China is a non-market economy transitioning to a socialist-market economy. In recent times, economic development often surfaces as a justification for prioritising socioeconomic rights over civil-political rights.

China and other East Asian nation-states, under the umbrella of traditional or Asian values, often place greater significance on socioeconomic rights. In the context of issues concerning human rights, economic development, or independent judicial review in a Confucian society—which is in transition and undergoing major legal reforms and economic development—it is a plausible argument that China's particularism warrants the patience, understanding, and assistance of the West in effecting both the rule of law and a positive discursive model for judicial review. The crisis in constitutionalism warrants a multilateral approach from the West, as opposed to a unilateral or a hegemonic approach. It is also arguable that present socioeconomic conditions in China, amidst gradual legal reform and economic development, justify extra-constitutionalism as there would not be a shock to China's infrastructure by invocation of a liberal constitutional political economy and its coercive proclivities.

Rule of Law in China

There are divergent opinions on the status of the rule of law in China, mostly subscribing to one of several theories that proclaim that the rule of law does not exist in China. Michael W. Dowdle approaches the subject of the rule of law by asking the question, "should there be rule of law in China as we currently conceive of that concept?" Dowdle evaluates the various arguments advancing that there is no real rule of law in China, and resolves that whatever problems attend the rule of law in China, "they are not due to any of the factors rule-of-law analyses like to point to." He contends that "everyone agrees that there is no rule of law in China," but everyone has a difficult time explaining why. Dowdle cites Alford, Hintzen and Peerenboom as representatives of the pool of theorists.

Dowdle rightly concludes that these theorists may expect too much because the problem does not lie with the legal system per se, but with the state of China's social and constitutional development. Instead of requiring that China immediately adopt a mature legal system, he posits that rule-of-law theories need to lend more consideration to the conditions and needs of a developing society.

Dowdle does not intend to suggest that there is rule of law in China. His contention is merely that while most theorists agree that there is no rule of law in China, their justifications or theories advanced in support of their arguments have many fallacies. A problem with the present legal paradigm of China is that it appears to be at the outer periphery of the rule of law. Notwithstanding vast legal reforms in China, it is still intimated that the goal of the government of China is to achieve rule by law, as opposed to rule of law.

Although the theories on the rule of law in China are many, the writings of Eric W. Orts and Peerenboom are representative of the dominant theorists. Orts makes a distinction between rule by law (as a descriptive, positive, and instrumental view of the relationship) and rule of law (as a prescriptive, normative, and political view of what the relationship should be). In this context, rule by law implies that the law serves as an instrument of government, or as a mere instrument of policy. In constrast to the comparisons offered by Orts, Peerenboom distinguishes between thin and thick theories of rule of law, arguing that "as thick and thin theories serve different purposes, I do not want to privilege thin theories over thick theories by declaring the thin version to be 'the rule of law.'"

In this context, if China's legal system finds itself on the periphery of a thin rule of law, Peerenboom will not declare such a system to be under the rule of law. In the Peerenboom analysis, the thin rule of law possesses the characteristics of a rule-of-law model where the predominate and overriding purpose is to have law serve as a mere instrument of governmental policy—what Orts termed a policy-driven model of rule by law. Regardless of the paradigm employed in assessing rule of law in China, there appears to be a consensus that China and its rule of law remain at the outer periphery of Western rule of law.

In answer to Dowdle's question, there is rule of law in China, but not in the way the West perceives rule of law. The conclusions of Dowdle well address the issues and problems surrounding the many theories advanced regarding the rule of law in China. However, Dowdle in his conclusion omits one important factor—the interplay between economic development and legal reform. The West assumes that the protection of certain values requires a modern legal system—a paradigm that the West itself has invented.

What is amiss in Dowdle's conclusion is the role of economic development in securing these values cherished in Western jurisprudence. For developing countries, the prioritisation of socioeconomic rights over civil-political rights is arguably justifiable because the citizens will neither enjoy the benefits of the rule of law nor civil-political rights without economic development. Prompting China to expediently implement a modern legal system and immediately place civil-political rights on an equal footing with socioeconomic rights is arguably asking China to put the proverbial cart before the horse. William Kovacic writes: "There is no assurance that this attempted transformation will succeed in all or most cases, as economic and political turmoil today besets many countries seeking to rely more extensively on market systems." Kovacic is speaking in terms of communist or socialist nations, not unlike China, that have, since the mid 1970s, undertaken market-oriented reform.

In 1960, the Asian Development Bank commissioned a thirty-five-year study examining the role that legal systems played in six Asian economies: China, India, Japan, Republic of Korea, Malaysia, and Taipei. The study concludes:

> *A key finding of this research project therefore is that law and legal institutions should not be viewed as technical tools that once adopted will produce the desired outcome.... This finding cautions against the blind transplantation without due consideration for the relevant economic framework within which they shall operate. It also suggests that law reform projects should be assessed not in isolation, but within a broader context of economicpohcles."*

Before accession to the WTO, China made substantial advances toward modernisation that included legal reforms. Since initiating economic reform and an open-door policy some twenty-five years ago, the Chinese economy has experienced high rates of growth. Economic barometres show an average annual growth rate of 9.5% from 1978 to 1995, and double-digit rates for four consecutive years, from 1992 to 1995. Presently, projections from China indicate that China's economy will grow at the rate of 8% in 2004 and Foreign Direct Investment will continue to rapidly grow. "In its latest report on foreign trade, the ministry said China's gross domestic product (GDP) for next year will be 7 per cent higher than 2003, thanks to efficient domestic policies and the rebound of other major economies around the world." The West now stands in critical judgment of China's progress toward the rule of law, especially the lack of a positive discursive model for judicial review.

It is a pre-judgment tainted by Western bias and taxonomies, however. Some critiques ignore the dangers to China's fragile infrastructure—polity, socioeconomic, and legal—that must be carefully guarded lest China suffer setbacks in its legal reforms and economic development. A need for stability results in a steady yet gradual approach to modernity, which often finds its expression through espousal of Asian values. The rhetoric or reality of Asian values justifies a higher priority for socioeconomic rights instead of civil-political rights during this transitory period.

For China, legal reforms and economic development confront real life dilemmas. They necessitate realpolitik, and the expansion-contraction cycle, which is political tightening and political loosening as needed, rather than blind adherence to Western taxonomies and Western prescription for the rule of law. As previously mentioned, Wong intimates that democracy will follow legal reforms. Given the success of reforms to date, it is a reasonable contention that the rule of law and democracy, albeit a Chinese variant, are gaining a foothold in China. Further, Wong writes, "such drastic political transformation as full democratization for a big and diverse country like China is plainly unrealistic at the present stage: it will simply bring more chaos to China, if the democracy experiments in several Asian countries can serve as a guide." There is rule of law in China-perhaps at the outer periphery of Western ideal rule of law—but nonetheless it is rule of law. In modern China, 5,000 or more years of Chinese philosophy (particularly Confucianism), culture, and history educed a distinctive legal culture that prophesizes both a distinctive Chinese rule of law and judicial review. There is rule of law in China, but it is a Chinese variant of Western rule of law that continues to evolve.

China and the History of Judicial Review in the West

Judicial independence presents itself as the noblest concept of Western jurisprudence, which is logical given its Western origins—Roman philosophers, Enlightenment Thinkers during the Age of Reason, The Case of the College Physicians, commonly known as Dr. Bonham's Case, and Marbury v. Madison. The historicity of Western judicial independence emanates from both philosophical ideals and a fear of oppressive government. The U.S. Constitution bore its roots in the fear of a monarch and the need to limit the exercise of popular democracy, which paralleled a fear of Nazi rule under the Weimar Republic when writers drafted a post-World War II German Constitution.

The historical contingent of England's "Glorious" Revolution of 1688 resulted in the divergence between the American notion of constitutional supremacy and England's doctrine of parliamentary sovereignty. In England, the principle of Dr. Bonham's Case fell from grace, while it continued to flourish in the American colonies. The famous words of Lord Coke read:

> *And it appears in our books, that in many cases the common law will control Acts of Parliament and sometimes adjudge them to be utterly void: for when an*

act of parliament is against common right and reason, or repugnant or impossible to be performed, the common law will control it and adjudge such act to be void.

Although not necessarily by grand design, the rule of law established itself as the dominant legal system in America and culminated in the landmark decision of Marbury v. Madison. China's journey to judicial independence ignores the historicity of judicial review in the West. China's journey is fraught with disappointment and misjudgments in timing and strategy. The right of abode cases in Hong Kong are representative of failing efforts to establish judicial independence, especially when such efforts predicate themselves upon the case of Marbury—a symbolic threshold for China's bar. China's attempt to emulate this historical decision has been carried out in a void divorced from the reality of a distinctive historicity of Western jurisprudence and in disregard of its own historicity of jurisprudence.

China's Road to Judicial Review

The road to judicial independence is inevitable because China proclaims that it is a democratic government. The preamble to the 1982 Constitution states the goal is "to turn China into a socialist country with a high level of culture and democracy." While speaking highly of China's rapid economic growth, the United Nations' Human Development Report 2002 released on July 24 in Manila said Chinese people have been given greater voice in formulating national reform policies and programs." With local elections, China is building toward a more representative, democratic government. It is difficult to refute that since Deng Xiaoping's reforms of the 1980s, China has presented itself as a socialist-political polity with a capitalist-economic policy.

A Justiciable China Constitution

The July 24, 2001 Reply is arguably an implicit adoption by the Supreme People's Court of the principles of constitutionalism embodied in Marbury. The English translation of this Reply reads:

Announcement of the Supreme People's Court. The reply of the Supreme People's Court Concerning Whether Civil Liability Arises When the Constitutionally-Protected Fundamental Right of Citizens to Receive Education Is Violated by Means of Violating Rights in a Person's Name was adopted at the 1,183rd Session of the Judicial Committee of the Supreme People's Court on June 28, 2001. It is hereby promulgated. It shall come into effect as from August 13, 2001. July 24, 2001.

The Reply of the Supreme People's Court Concerning Whether Civil Liability Arises When the Constitutionally-Protected Fundamental Right of Citizens to Receive Education Is Violated by Means of Violating Rights in a Person's Name, To the Shandong Provincial Higher People's Court: We have received your court's Request for Instructions Concerning the Dispute Involving Rights in a Person's Name Between Qi Yuling and Chen Xiaoqi, Chen Kezheng, the Jining Municipality School of Commerce of Shandong Province, the Tengzhou Municipality No. 8 High School of Shandong Province and the Tengzhou Municipal Education Commission of Shandong Province. After study, we hold, on the basis of the facts in this case, that Chen Xiaoqi and others have violated the fundamental right to receive education enjoyed by Qi Yuling in accordance with the provisions of the Constitution by means of violating rights in a person's name. This has produced the result of actual damages. Commensurate civil liability arises. Reply is hereby given.

The 2001 Reply and its reliance on the constitution are antithetical to the court's long practice of refusing to rely on the constitution, and it is here the controversy begins. Although the language seems innocuous, its subsequent interpretation caused a stir. The genesis of the controversy is an article written by Huang Songyou, Chief Judge of the First Civil Division of the Supreme People's Court, entitled "Making the Constitution Justiciable and its Significance." Judge Huang analyses the reasons the Supreme People's Court will not cite directly to the Constitution. A 1955 Reply states that it is not appropriate to cite the Constitution as a basis for decision. A 1986 Reply of the Supreme People's Court also provides that courts should not cite opinions and replies. An interpretation given to the Replies forbids a direct citing of the Constitution. Judge Huang does however note that the 1955 Reply and 1986 Reply are equally subject to an interpretation as recommendations rather than mandates and further distinguishes them on other grounds.

Judge Huang argues that the Reply establishes a precedent for the justiciability of the constitution since the constitution may now enter judicial proceedings just as with any other law or regulation and may serve as a legal basis for judgment. He sees far-reaching implications arising from this Reply. First, the Reply establishes a precedent for court protection of fundamental rights of citizens stipulated in the Constitution. It is in this distinction that Judge Huang argues that the Reply creates a landmark decision in China's legal system. The fundamental rights of citizens, if stipulated in the

Constitution, are now subject to protection irrespective of a conversion of such rights under ordinary legal norms. He is addressing the judicial norm of converting fundamental rights into ordinary laws and regulations. Second, Judge Huang argues that the Reply implicitly creates a precedent for justiciability of the Constitution. Third, the Court uses a civil method to redress violations of fundamental rights as opposed to criminal or administrative law remedies.

However, Judge Huang does not contend that this Reply is an express, or even implicit, grant of the power of constitutional review. In this respect, the Reply falls short of the full constitutional measure of Marbury v. Madison. Nevertheless, the effort of the China bar in the right of abode cases, taken in conjunction with the previously mentioned Reply of July 24, 2001, prophesizes an optimistic future for judicial independence. Although Judge Huang does not explicitly assert a power of constitutional review emanating from this Reply, he does rightly hail the protection of fundamental rights of citizens as the most salient point. In this context, the Reply is of the stature of landmark constitutionalism because the judiciary is arguably flexing its power of interpretation into the realm of constitutionalising fundamental rights. Given this Reply, one can draw a correlative argument similar to parliamentary supremacy, when one collimates the interpretative means of courts in Great Britain with an anticipation of similar interpretative means for China's judiciary.

Constitutional Ethos and Marbury v. Madison

China's road to judicial independence evidences a marked proclivity toward reliance on Marbury. If judicial independence is to become a reality in China, it must necessarily bear its own distinctive characteristics. Its judiciary must view constitutionalism "not just as a formal state structure, but also as a dynamic process" that is "the crossroads of law and society, culture and history, economics and politics." Lurking somewhere in China's journey to judicial review and the proclivity to emulate Marbury is a subconscious notion that constitutionalism is contingent upon Western values and culture. Constitutionalism is subject to many forms and structures. Barry Hager writes: "It becomes an unfair tautology that the absence of a Rule of Law heritage suggests an absence of any legal system at all."

China's judiciary must look to its own jurisprudential historicity, rather than Western jurisprudence. Modern China enjoys its own unique historicity and attendant historical accidents, all of which justify a China shrouded in a particularism reflective of Confucian values. The answer to China's journey to judicial review lies not in the theories of the Enlightenment Thinkers. Rather, it lies in the philosophical underpinnings of its own great thinkers who contributed to the creation of a culture where Confucianism is persistent and systemic. There has always been a historical dimension to Western jurisprudence. The historicity of Western jurisprudence dates back to the twelfth century, while the historicity of Chinese jurisprudence dates back 5,000 years or more. As Harold J. Berman writes:

> *Ever since the early formation of discrete modern Western legal systems in the twelfth century, it had been taken for granted that a legal system has an ongoing character, a capacity for growth over generations and centuries. This was a uniquely Western belief: that a body of law, a system of law, contains, and should contain, a built-in mechanism for organic change and that it survives, and should survive, by development, by growth.... The law was thought to be not merely ongoing; it had a history; it constituted a tradition.*

The same holds true for China. A Chinese jurisprudence in antiquity continues to evolve. In modern China, a historical debate between Confucianism and Legalism and an on-going debate between rule by man and rule by law continues to evolve and constitutes a tradition. Further, constitutionalism is not necessarily contingent upon democracy. Mark Tushnet contends that liberty in the United States would not be less without the Supreme Court having the power of judicial review. On the question of introducing Western democracy to China at its present stage of development, Wong writes:

> *Liberal detractors would hastily jump to the conclusion that for political reform China must necessarily call for a Western style of democracy. This is clearly unwarranted in the East Asian tradition, which has followed instead the sequence of "development first, democratisation later." Furthermore, such drastic political transformation as full democratisation for a big and diverse country like China is plainly unrealistic at the present stage: it will simply bring more chaos (luan) to China, if the democracy experiments in several Asian countries can serve as a guide. Nor will political democracy necessarily facilitate China's present economic growth and social progress. It is to be remembered that South Korea's industrial take-off took place under a military*

> *dictatorship, Taiwan's under martial law, and Hong Kong's under a colonial rule.*

Moreover, Orts makes an all-important, yet controversial, claim "that developing the rule of law in China in the normative and political sense may be divorced from a theory of democracy." The Western terms of "democracy, the rule of law, fundamental human rights, markets, economic development, and civil society" are presumed social goods that warrant reconsideration in the promotion of foreign policy. This presumed social goods argument recognises the difficulty of applying rule of law to distinctively different non-Western cultures and implicitly implores the West to employ a less Hobbesian approach to multilateralism. China's particularity warrants the understanding and assistance of the West in effectuating both the rule of law and a positive discursive model for judicial review. It must however be an understanding that recognises Chinese jurisprudence in antiquity as being persistent and systemic, as it continues to evolve in modern China amidst gradual legal reforms and economic development.

Chinese philosophy (particularly Confucianism), culture, history, particularism, and nationalism educe a distinctive legal culture that prophesizes both a distinctive Chinese legal system and judicial review. There is rule of law in China, but it is a Chinese variant of rule of law evolving amidst gradual legal reforms and economic development. At some point, the West must develop its viewpoint from a China-centred perspective, which will enable an emic understanding of the rule of law in terms of Asian ethos instead of Western culture and morals. In answer to the question "Can the Confucian person be transformed into a legal person and can the Confucian society support it?" —the Confucian person is a legal person and the Confucian society supports it.

Chapter 7

Unilateralism under the Multilateral Trading System

Since the U.S. Trade Act of 1974 (Act) was enacted, the Act's Sections 301-310 have been the principal statutory means for addressing allegedly unfair trade practices by foreign governments that adversely affect exports of U.S. goods and services. Prior to the Uruguay Round (UR) negotiations, the United States frequently relied on Section 301 to unilaterally open foreign markets to resolve its trade deficit. A major U.S. justification for the unilateral use of Section 301 before the birth of the World Trade Organisation (WTO) was the lack of an effective dispute settlement mechanism under the General Agreement on Tariffs and Trade (GATT) 1947.

During the UR, however, U.S. trading partners sought to constrain its "aggressive unilateralism" within the ambit of WTO disciplines, and the UR negotiating parties adopted a new agreement on dispute settlement, the Understanding on the Rules and Procedures Governing the Settlement of Disputes (DSU). The DSU was intended to strengthen the dispute settlement mechanism of the multilateral trading system. In particular, Article 23 of the DSU (Article 23), entitled "Strengthening of the Multilateral System," requires that the WTO's Members resolve all trade disputes falling under the scope of the WTO Agreements through the process set out in the DSU, and requires disputing parties to abide by the rules and procedures of the DSU.

After the conclusion of the UR negotiations, particularly after agreement was reached on the DSU, major trading partners of the United States expressed the view that Section 301 was "no longer viable" under the WTO. It was generally understood that one of the most important reasons why U.S. trading partners agreed to improve the WTO dispute settlement process and to make it more judicial was to impose restrictions on the use of Section 301. To the contrary, United States' officials declared on several occasions that Section 301, far from being weakened, became more "effective" with the DSU. As if to reaffirm the viability of Section 301 after the birth of the WTO System in the spring of 1995, the United States pursued a then pending Section 301 investigation against alleged unfair trade practices within the Japanese auto parts markets. In May 1995, based on an affirmative determination under Section 301, the United States Trade Representative (USTR) formally published a retaliation list targeting luxury type motor vehicles from Japan. Right after the publication of the retaliation list, Japan challenged the publication of the retaliation list in its request for consultations with the United States, as well as the proposed sanctions under Section 301 procedures. After a series of bilateral negotiations, however, the United States and Japan settled their dispute on June 28, 1995, the eve of the effective date for the proposed sanctions.

As anticipated, however, the controversy over Section 301 resurfaced when the European Communities (EC) challenged the United States. In October 1998, the United States invoked the Section 301 procedure against the EC, claiming that the EC had failed to implement the recommendations made by the WTO Dispute Settlement Body (DSB) in the famous case: EC—Regime for the Importation, Sale and Distribution of Bananas (Banana III). Subsequently, the USTR published a retaliation list and announced its intention to adopt retaliatory measures against the EC. Eventually, in April 1999, the DSB authorised the United States' request for retaliation against the EC up to the level that was decided by arbitrators pursuant to Article 22.6 of the DSU (Article 22.6).

While this dispute was underway, the EC challenged the consistency of Sections 301-310 with WTO obligations in a separate procedure, and requested the establishment of a panel (United States—Section 301 Panel or Panel) on February 2, 1999. This panel proceeding captured the attention of all the Members of the WTO. The Panel circulated its final report (the United States—Section 301 Panel Report) on December 22, 1999. According to the Panel, the statutory language of Sections 304, 305 and 306 allows the USTR to exercise its discretion contrary to U.S. obligations under Article 23 of the DSU (Article 23), and this discretionary element constitutes a prima facie violation of Article 23. Nonetheless, in light of the non-statutory elements of Sections 301-310, such as the Statement of Administrative Actions (SAA) and statements by the United States to the Panel, the Panel concluded that Sections 301-310 were not inconsistent with the United States' obligations under the WTO.

In reaching this conclusion, the Panel noted that the U.S. Administration had pledged in the SAA, and before the Panel, that it would not exercise its discretion contrary to its obligations under Article 23. The Panel took the view that these undertakings effectively and legally curtailed the offending discretionary element, and therefore removed the prima facie WTO inconsistencies created by the statutory language of Sections 301-310. However, the Panel emphasized that should these U.S. undertakings be repudiated in the future, this finding of conformity would no longer be warranted. On a legally different matter, the EC challenged before the WTO the United States' decision on March 3, 1999, to withhold customs liquidation for the targeted EC goods prior to the DSB authorisation to suspend concessions.

While the United States—Section 301 Panel Report is politically astute, its legal underpinnings are flawed in some respects and its policy implications for the future of the WTO Dispute Settlement Body (DSB) generate serious concerns. Moreover, the Panel ruling explicitly left many important legal questions unresolved, including consistency with the WTO obligations of specific actions taken by the USTR under Section 301 procedures. This chapter examines how specific U.S. actions taken under the Japan—Auto and the EC—Banana disputes constitute violations of U.S. obligations under the WTO. This legal examination is important because the United States persistently argued in the United States—Section 301 Panel proceedings that specific actions taken in the Auto and Banana cases did not constitute a violation of WTO obligations, and the Panel took the view that the EC could not submit sufficient evidence to rebut U.S. claims of a complete compliance record. Accordingly, the U.S. is expected to repeat the same practices that may violate its WTO obligations. A thorough analysis of the consistency of specific U.S. actions with the WTO in individual cases will lead to a recommendation that the U.S. Administration not repeat such practices and will thereby avoid future legal challenges by other Members of the WTO.

In particular, this chapter examines the WTO consistency of the following: (1) the U.S. decision to use Sections 301 procedures rather than resort to the DSU rules and procedures in the Auto case; (2) the U.S. affirmative determination under Section 301(b) that Japanese measures in the Auto case were "unreasonable and discriminatory"; (3) the U.S. affirmative determination under Section 306(b) in the Banana dispute that the EC failed to implement the DSB's recommendations, prior to the completion of compliance panel proceedings under Article 21.5 of the DSU (Article 21.5); and, most importantly, (4) the U.S. threats of unilateral action—retaliation. For example, the early publication of a retaliation list and the suspension of customs liquidation for targeted goods, in both the Auto and Banana cases. This examination of the WTO consistency of specific U.S. actions in individual cases will also demonstrate the weakness and incompleteness of the legal reasoning of the United States—Section 301 Panel Report.

An examination of the WTO consistency of a threat of retaliation, in particular, is critical. Experience has shown that the power of Section 301 lies in the threat of a trade sanction, rather than sanction itself. In fact, in only fifteen of the 119 Section 301 investigations made and disposed before August 9, 1999, were trade sanctions actually imposed. The threat of retaliatory measures alone has been powerful enough to persuade U.S. trading partners, particularly smaller developing countries, to voluntarily open their markets or enter into bilateral agreements to resolve their trade disputes. However, U.S. officials take the view that a mere threat of retaliation is not contestable in the DSU procedures unless the threat is formally materialized by a retaliatory measure.

If this U.S. view were legally acceptable, the United States would be free to rely on the threat of trade sanctions under Section 301 in order to achieve its goal of opening foreign markets without the risk of facing legal challenges before the WTO. A serious problem would exist if the United States could effectively and routinely bypass the DSU procedures on WTO matters by using the mere threat of retaliation under Section 301 to negotiate bilateral agreements and successfully resolve disputes. This is precisely what occurred in the Japan—Auto dispute. Even if the United States followed the procedures under Article 22 of the DSU (Article 22) and obtained the DSB's authorisation to retaliate, in the end the threat problem would still remain. A threat to retaliate can also alter the market for targeted goods long before DSB authorisation, as demonstrated by the Banana dispute. This Chapter attempts to analyse why a threat of retaliation could constitute a violation of WTO obligations. To the best of the author's knowledge, no legal scholar has seriously examined this important legal issue.

Section 301 and its Battlefields

The 1995 United States—Japan Auto Dispute

The automobile dispute between the United States and Japan did not materialize overnight. Even before the United States initiated a

Section 302 investigation into the Japanese automobile market in October 1994, the United States had conducted a series of bilateral negotiations with Japan for several years. During these negotiations, the United States consistently criticized the closed Japanese automobile market. The United States wanted Japan to open its automobile market by:

(i) changing its "genuine parts" certification rules, which favoured local producers and virtually forced Japanese-certified garages to purchase Japanese-made auto parts for replacement;

(ii) enabling Japanese distributors using a keiretsu relationship with Japanese automobile manufacturing firms to carry U.S. automobiles as well; and,

(iii) implementing the Japanese automobile manufacturers' voluntary plan to expand the purchase of U.S. automobiles.

Following a failure to reach a bilateral agreement by September 30, 1994, the USTR initiated a Section 302 investigation into the Japanese aftermarket for auto parts. Between October 1994 and early May 1995, bilateral talks broke down three times. On May 10, 1995, the USTR officially determined under Sections 301 and 304 that certain acts, policies and practices of Japan with respect to the aftermarket for auto parts were "unreasonable and discriminatory and burdened or restricted U.S. commerce." Japan refused to meet with the United States under this threat of retaliation and made clear its intention to refer the case to the WTO. On May 16, 1995, the United States formally published a retaliation list and indicated its intention to withhold the liquidation of customs entries with respect to sixteen different types of Japanese luxury-model automobiles entered on and after May 20, 1995.

The proposed retaliation was to levy 100% retaliatory ad valorem duties on these Japanese automobiles beginning on June 28, applying the duties retroactively to the Japanese automobiles entered on and after May 20, 1995. On May 17, 1995, Japan requested consultation with the United States pursuant to Article 4 of the DSU and Article XXII:1 of the GATT 1994 with respect to these measures. The representatives of the United States and Japan met twice in Geneva for formal consultations. The USTR held a public hearing as required under Section 301 in June 1995 on the proposed sanctions. A series of high-level negotiations, including meetings between USTR Kantor and Japanese Trade Minister Hashimoto, were conducted from mid-June right up to the June 28, 1995, deadline for implementing the proposed sanctions when they dramatically settled their dispute by entering into a bilateral agreement. As a result, the proposed retaliatory duties were never imposed, and Japan never requested the establishment of a panel to resolve the matter. Accordingly, the question of whether a threat of retaliation under Section 301 was inconsistent with the WTO Agreement remained untested under the WTO dispute settlement procedure.

Prior to settlement, Japan invoked both a violation complaint and a non-violation complaint in its request for consultations under Article 4 of the DSU and Article XX:1 of the GATT. Interestingly, Japan challenged the threat of retaliation rather than the actual retaliatory measures. The threat of retaliation included all of the measures implemented before the imposition of the retaliatory tariff, such as (1) affirmative determinations under Sections 301 and 304 made on May 10, 1995; (2) the publication of a retaliation list made on May 16, 1995; and, (3) the withholding of customs liquidation from May 20, 1995. Of course, Japan also claimed that the proposed retaliatory measure, if implemented, would have been a violation of the WTO Agreement. There is no doubt that the actual imposition of the retaliatory duties without obtaining an authorisation from the DSB would have violated Articles I and II of the GATT 1994.

The 1999 EC—Banana Dispute

This infamous dispute originates from a WTO case, Banana III. The United States, Ecuador, Guatemala, Honduras and Mexico jointly requested the establishment of a panel to examine the legality of the EC's banana import regime. In May 1997, the panel found that the EC's banana regime was inconsistent with its WTO obligations, and the EC appealed nineteen points of the panel report. On September 9, 1997, the Appellate Body issued a report that confirmed almost all of the panel findings and recommended that the EC bring the impugned measures into conformity with the obligations of the EC under GATT 1994 and the General Agreement on Trade in Services (GATS). The panel and Appellate Body's reports were adopted by the DSB on September 25, 1997. On January 7, 1998, the arbitrator appointed in accordance with Article 21.3 of the DSU (Article 21.3) determined that the EC had until January 1, 1999, approximately fifteen months, to implement the DSB's recommendations. During that period, on July 20, 1998, the EC repealed the contested measure, Regulation Number 404/93, and enacted a new regulation, Regulation Number 1637/98. It entered into force on July 31, 1998, and became applicable on

January 1,1999, the end of the "reasonable period of time" allowed for the implementation of the DSB's recommendations. The EC notified the DSB that it had partially implemented the DSB's recommendations and that implementation would be completed by January 1, 1999. The United States, with the support of the other Banana III complainants, disagreed. The United States also officially expressed its belief at several DSB meetings that the newly enacted regulation was inconsistent with WTO obligations.

From June through September 1998, during the early stages of the dispute regarding the EC's new regulations, the United States resorted to Article 21.5 in order to ask for the original panel's expeditious review of whether the EC's new legislation complied with the WTO. The EC, however, refused to accept the U.S. proposal to reconvene the original panel for such a review, arguing that a panel could not be established to examine the proposed EC regulation because it had not yet been finalised. The EC added that it would not object to establishing a panel to review its final measures, arguing that the original panel should be reconvened only after the new regulation's effective date, which corresponded with the expiration of the reasonable period of time. The EC also disagreed with the United States on the length of time for the Article 21.5 review process and revealed its intention to appeal if necessary.

In October 1998, the United States initiated proceedings under sections 305 and 306 to seek authorisation for retaliation from the DSB pursuant to Article 22 of the DSU (Article 22). Under Article 22, a Member may request authorisation from the DSB to retaliate against a Member that has failed to comply with a DSB recommendation within the "reasonable period of time" allowed under Article 21.3. Before the United States requested authorisation from the DSB on January 14, 1999, the USTR had already made a determination that the EC had failed to implement the DSB's recommendations and had already published a retaliation list in November and December 1998. The trade sanction, in the form of a prohibitive 100 percent ad valorem duty, was to be applied against selected items imported from the EC as early as February 1, 1999, but in no case later than March 3, 1999.

Article 22.6 of the DSU (Article 22.6) requires the DSB to grant authorisation to retaliate within thirty days of the expiration of the reasonable period of time. However, if the subject of the retaliation objects to the level of retaliation the matter is referred to arbitration, which must be concluded within sixty days after the expiration of the reasonable period of time. Retaliatory measures must not be taken during the arbitration. The specific dates of February 1, 1999, and March 3, 1999, appear to have been chosen in order to comply with the time limits under Article 22.6. In response to these U.S. actions, the EC argued that the United States is required to follow Article 21.5 before requesting authorisation from the DSB to retaliate under Article 22. The United States, of course, disagreed.

While the debate on the relationship between Articles 21.5 and 22 was still unsettled, the United States, arguably, pursued Section 301 proceedings in preparation for the commencement of proceedings under Article 22. In response, the EC requested consultations with the United States with regard to Sections 301-310 on November 25, 1998, pursuant to Article 4 of the DSU (Article 4) and Article XXII:1 of the GATT 1994. The consultations held on December 17, 1998, did not result in a mutually agreeable solution, and on January 26, 1999, the EC requested the establishment of a panel on this matter. Essentially, the EC claimed that the strict time limits under Sections 301-310 required the USTR to make unilateral determinations and take actions before the DSB had authorised the United States to do so.

Additionally, the EC requested consultations with the United States under Article XXII:1 of the GATT 1994 regarding the specific determinations made and actions taken by the United States pursuant to Section 301 in the course of the EC—Banana dispute. This consultation request targeted the threat of retaliatory trade sanctions under Section 301. For whatever reason, however, the EC did not request the establishment of a panel to examine specific U.S. determinations and actions. Therefore, this matter fell outside the terms of reference for the United States—Section 301 Panel.

On December 18, 1998, Ecuador requested the DSB to reconvene the original panel in accordance with Article 21.5 to examine the EC's implementation of the DSB's recommendations made at the original dispute. Shortly thereafter, despite criticism from many WTO Members, the United States requested that the DSB authorise its proposed retaliation pursuant to Article 22.6 on January 14, 1999. The United States proposed the suspension of tariff concessions and related obligations under GATT 1994 covering trade in an amount of US $520 million to the EC and its member States. Not surprisingly, at the DSB meeting held on January 29, 1999, the EC objected to the suspension proposed by the United States and, pursuant to Article 22.6, requested that the original panel arbitrate the level of the suspension.

As it turned out, the members of the panel for the review-proceedings commenced by Ecuador under Article 21.5 were identical to the arbitrators appointed under Article 22.6. Thus, the original panel was assigned two important tasks at the same time: examining whether the EC's new banana importing regime was consistent with the WTO, and assessing the level of suspension of concessions. The original panel announced that it would not be able to issue a decision by March 3, 1999, the time limit set forth by Article 22.6.

The next day, the United States announced that the U.S. Customs Service would immediately begin withholding liquidation and reviewing the sufficiency of bonds on imports of selected European trade products in the amount of US$520 million. The EC requested consultations with the United States on the same day. The DSB established a panel on this matter on June 16, 1999, and the panel was constituted on October 8, 1999. It was recently reported that this panel issued a final ruling on April 19, 2000, upholding the European Commission's complaints.

On April 6, 1999, the original panel issued a panel report and an arbitration decision. In the Article 21.5 proceedings, the panel decided that the EC's new banana importing regime was inconsistent with Articles I:1 and XIII:1 and 2 of GATT 1994, and Articles II and XVII of GATS.

In its arbitration decision, the panel ruled that the EC's revised banana importing regime was inconsistent with the GATT 1994 and GATS and determined that the United States was impaired US$191.4 million per year as a result of the EC's non-compliance. Thus, this amount was set as the amount of concessions that the United States could suspend. The United States received DSB authorisation to suspend the concessions, finally, on April 19, 1999. The report of the panel requested by Ecuador under Article 21.5 was ultimately adopted by the DSB on May 6, 1999.

The United States appears to have won this dispute, but the issue is not entirely over. Although the EC lost on the consistency of its new banana-importing regime with the WTO Agreement, the EC pursued panel proceedings with respect to Sections 301-310 and the United States' withholding of goods before receiving DSB authorisation. The Panel rendered its final report on the former action on December 22, 1999, and it was adopted by DSB on January 27, 2000. The latter is still pending. The next section reviews the United States—Section 301 Panel Report.

The WTO Consistency of Section 301

The WTO Panel Ruling on U.S. Section 301

Claims of the Parties : In this case the EC challenged certain aspects of Sections 301-310. In essence, the EC claimed that Sections 301-310 mandate unilateral action by the United States, thereby breaching Article 23 and several provisions of the WTO Agreement. In its panel request, the EC claimed that:

> *"by imposing specific, strict time limits within which unilateral determinations must be made that other WTO Members have failed to comply with their WTO obligations and trade sanctions must be taken against such WTO Members, this legislation does not allow the United States to comply with the rules of the DSU and the obligations of GATT 1994 in situations where the Dispute Settlement Body (DSB) has, by the end of those time limits, not made a prior determination that the WTO Member concerned has failed to comply with its WTO obligations and has not authorised the suspension of concessions or other obligations on that basis."*

Specifically, the EC claimed that:

(a) inconsistently with Article 23.2(a) of the DSU (Article 23.2(a)): Section 304(a)(2)(A) requires the U.S. Trade Representative ("USTR") to determine whether another Member denies U.S. rights or benefits under a WTO agreement irrespective of whether the DSB adopted a panel or Appellate Body finding on the matter; and Section 306(b) requires the USTR to determine whether a recommendation of the DSB has been implemented irrespective of whether proceedings on this issue under Article 21.5 of the DSU have been completed;

(b) inconsistently with Article 23.2(c) of the DSU: Section 306(b) requires the USTR to determine what further action to take under Section 301 in case of a failure to implement DSB recommendations; and Section 305(a) requires the USTR to implement that action, and that in both instances, irrespective of whether the procedures set forth in Articles 21.5 and 22 of the DSU have been completed; and

(c) Section 306(b) is inconsistent with Articles I, II, III, VIII and XI of GATT 1994 because, in the case of disputes involving trade in goods, it requires the USTR to impose duties, fees or restrictions that violate one or more of these provisions.

In addition, the EC argued that even if the above-cited provisions of Sections 301-310 could be interpreted to permit the USTR to avoid determinations and actions inconsistent with the WTO, they create legal uncertainty as to the USTR's conformity with the WTO. The EC alleged that this undermines the "security and predictability" of the multilateral trading system, and thus constitutes a violation of Article XVI:4 of the WTO Charter. For these reasons, the EC requested that the panel:

(a) rule that the U.S., by failing to bring the Trade Act of 1974 into conformity with the requirements of Article 23 of the DSU and Articles I, II, III, VIII, and XI of the GATT 1994, acted inconsistently with its obligations under those provisions and under Article XVI:4 of the WTO Agreement and thereby nullifies or impairs benefits accruing to the EC under the DSU, GATT 1994 and the WTO Agreement; and

(b) recommend that the DSB request the U.S. to bring its Trade Act of 1974 into conformity with its obligations under the DSU, GATT 1994 and the WTO Agreement.

The United States responded that Sections 301-310 are discretionary in the sense that they permit the United States to comply with the WTO Agreement in every case, including DSU rules and procedures. "Section 304 permits the USTR to base his or her determinations on adopted panel and Appellate Body findings in every case; and Sections 305 and 306 permit the USTR, in every case, to request and receive DSB authorisation to suspend concessions in accordance with Article 22 of the DSU." Accordingly, the United States argued that Sections 301-310 are fully consistent with its WTO obligations.

The Scope of the Panel's Ruling and the Measure in Question **:** The Panel was not requested to make an overall assessment of Sections 301-310 conformity with the WTO Agreement. The Panel's mandate, as expressed in its terms of reference, was limited to the EC's specific claims. Therefore, it did not examine the U.S. actions taken under Sections 301-310 in individual cases, such as the Japan—Auto and EC—Banana cases. Additionally, the Panel did not address the WTO compatibility of the U.S. initial deferral decision—a determination as to whether or not a matter falls outside the scope of the WTO agreements.

In assessing the consistency of Sections 301-310 with the WTO Agreement as outlined in the terms of reference, the Panel not only included the statute within the scope of the measure which was to be examined by the Panel, but it also included other institutional and administrative elements, such as the SAA and other statements made by the United States before this Panel.

The EC Claim that Section 304 is Inconsistent with Article 23.2(a) Of The DSU

Claims and Arguments of the Parties

Section 304(a)(2)(A) provides in relevant part:

The Trade representative shall determine whether the rights to which the United States is entitled under any trade agreement are being denied in the case of an investigation involving a trade agreement on or before ...the earlier of

(i) the date that is 30 days after the date on which the dispute settlement procedure is concluded, or

(ii) the date that is 18 months after the date on which the investigation is initiated.

In the EC's view, a period of nineteen-and-a-half months is necessary for the normal operation of a given dispute settlement procedure under the DSU procedures. The strict time limit under section 304(a)(2)(A), the EC argued, requires the USTR to make a unilateral determination as to whether another WTO Member has violated U.S. rights under the WTO within the eighteen-month deadline. According to the EC, this determination under Section 304 is required even if the DSB has not yet adopted a report with findings on the matter, contrary to Article 23.2(a). Article 23.2(a) of the DSU provides: Members shall: (a) not make a determination to the effect that a violation has occurred, that benefits have been nullified or impaired or that the attainment of any objective of the covered agreements has been impeded, except through recourse to dispute settlement in accordance with the rules and procedures of this Understanding, and shall make any such determination consistent with the findings contained in the panel or Appellate Body report adopted by the DSB or an arbitration award rendered under this Understanding.

In response, the United States argued that Section 304 does not always compel the USTR to make a specific determination that U.S.

rights have been denied without regard to the availability of the findings of the panel and Appellate Body. Furthermore, the United States argued that under Section 304, a determination that U.S. rights have been denied before the adoption of DSB finding is precluded. According to the United States, Section 304 only requires the USTR to determine whether—not to determine that—U.S, rights have been denied. In addition, the United States argued that the EC's calculation of the time period was simply wrong, and the correct time period is sixteen months and twenty days.

Preliminary Panel Findings and Legal Issues in Question

With regard to the statutory language of Section 304 in relation to the relevant provision of the WTO, the Panel made the following findings:

(a) First, as a matter of fact, we find that under the statutory language of Section 304(a)(2), the USTR is mandated, i.e. obligated in law, to make a determination on whether U.S. rights are being denied within 18 months after the request for consultations. This is a mandatory feature of Section 304 in which the Legislature left no discretion to the Executive Branch.

(b) Second, as a matter of law, since most of the time-limits in the DSU are either minimum time-limits without ceilings or maximum time-limits that are, nonetheless, indicative only, DSU proceedings—from the request for consultations to the adoption of findings by the DSB—may take longer than 18 months and have in practice often led to time-frames beyond 18 months. As a result, the USTR could be obligated in certain cases brought by the U.S.—and indeed in certain cases has already been so obligated—to make a unilateral determination as to whether U.S. rights are being denied before the completion of multilateral DSU proceedings.

(c) Third, as a matter of fact, we find that even though the USTR is obligated to make a determination within the 18 months time-frame, under the broad discretion allowed under Section 304 there are no circumstances which would compel him or her to make a determination to the effect that U.S. rights under the WTO Agreement have been denied—hereafter referred to as a "determination of inconsistency" —before the exhaustion of DSU proceedings.

Section 304(a) requires the USTR to determine whether U.S. rights are being denied within eighteen months. It does not require the USTR to determine that U.S. rights are being denied at the eighteen months deadline. The criteria referred to in Section 304(a) on which the USTR has to base its determination—"the investigation initiated under section 302 ... and the consultations (and the proceedings, if applicable) under section 303"—allow the USTR to exercise wide discretion in all cases concerning the actual content of the determination he or she has to make. As will be seen below, however, this discretion does not necessarily absolve Section 304 from a breach of the DSU.

(d) Fourth, as a matter of fact, we find that even though the USTR is not obligated, under any circumstance, to make a Section 304 determination of inconsistency prior to exhaustion of DSU proceedings, it is not precluded by the statutory language of Section 304 itself from making such a determination. We find that the broad discretion given to the USTR allows him or her to do exactly what the statutory language suggests: to determine whether U.S. rights have been denied, i.e. to determine that they have not been denied but also to determine that they have been denied.

In sum:

The statutory language of Section 304 mandates the USTR in certain cases to make a unilateral determination on whether U.S. rights have been denied even before the adoption by the DSB of its findings on the matter. However, the statutory language of Section 304 neither mandates the USTR to make a determination of inconsistency nor precludes him or her from making such a determination.

Based on this finding, the Panel examined the legal issue of whether Section 304 is inconsistent with Article 23.2(a), "given, on the one hand, the duty in some cases to make a unilateral determination prior to exhaustion of multilateral proceedings and, on the other hand, the full discretion as to the content of that determination." Therefore, the Panel turned to the interpretation of Article 23. After examining the language of Article 23.1 of the DSU, the Panel took the view that a violation of the explicit provisions of Article 23 can be caused not only "by an ad hoc, specific action in a given dispute, mobilise but also by measures of general applicability, e.g., legislation or regulations." The Panel then addressed the general question of what kind of legislation, in abstract, can violate the WTO obligations. Not surprisingly, the United States strongly argued that only mandatory legislation—legislation mandating noncompliance with the WTO or precluding WTO compliance—could violate WTO obligations. In contrast, the EC argued that certain types of legislation allowing conduct inconsistent with the WTO Agreement could violate WTO provisions. In the EC's view, Section 304 falls under that category.

The Panel did not take the risk of resolving this dispute. Considering this abstract question not germane to the resolution of the claims before them, the Panel noted that the issue before the Panel was about the interpretation of Article 23. Therefore, it needed to examine closely the precise obligations contained in Article 23 rather than adopt "the legal logic that there has to be one fast and hard rule covering all domestic legislation." The Panel reasoned that the specific obligations in Article 23 may prohibit legislation having certain discretionary elements, and the existence of such discretion in the statutory language of Section 304 could, in effect, preclude consistency with the WTO. Consequently, the Panel interpreted the statutory language of Article 23 in accordance with the general rule of interpretation set out in Article 31 of the Vienna Convention on the Law of Treaties (Vienna Convention). The primary part of Article 31 of the Vienna Convention provides: "A treaty shall be interpreted in good faith in accordance with the ordinary meaning to be given to the terms of the treaty in their context and in the light of its object and purpose." In the Panel's view, the ordinary meaning of the provisions of Article 23 in light of the DSU's and the WTO's object and purpose supports the position that the certain aspects of Section 304, as preliminary found above, constitute a prima facie violation of Article 23 of the DSU.

Article 23.2(a) Interpreted in Accordance with the Vienna Convention—The Ordinary Meaning of the Terms of the Treaty

The text of Article 23.1 generally obliges Members to seek recourse through and abide by DSU rules and procedures. Among these rules and procedures, Article 23.2(a) specifically prohibits making a unilateral determination of the WTO compliance before exhaustion of DSU proceedings. In the Panel's view, the ordinary meaning of Members' obligations under Article 23 could be violated if statutory language allows a determination of inconsistency prior to exhaustion of DSU proceedings. The Panel concluded that the very discretion granted under Section 304 constitutes a presumptive violation because this discretion precludes the United States from abiding by its obligations under the WTO.

Interpreted in Good Faith

The Panel believed that the good faith requirement in the Vienna Convention suggests that Article 23 should restrain Members from adopting national laws, which threaten prohibited conduct. According to the panel, Section 304 is equivalent to erecting a large sign by a farmer on the contested boundary: "No Trespassing. Trespassers may be shot on sight."

The Treaty's Object and Purpose

The most relevant objects and purposes of the DSU and the WTO generally, in the Panel's view, are "those which relate to the creation of market conditions conducive to individual economic activity in national and global markets and to the provision of a secure and predictable multilateral trading system." Because individual economic operators are a major component of the multilateral trading system, legislation reserving the right for a unilateral determination of inconsistency contrary to DSU procedures may constitute an ongoing threat and produce a "chilling effect" that causes serious damage to individuals and market-place. From the perspective of the individual economic operators, there is little difference between a law mandating unilateral determinations and a law that threatens unilateral determinations but does not actually mandate them—as is the case here. For this reason, the Panel concluded that the objectives and purposes of the DSU and the WTO support its position, which conforms to a plain reading of the terms of Article 23. Additionally, a systematic consideration of the context of Article 23 and the DSU in the overall WTO system confirms the textual interpretation of Article 23.2(a).

Pursuant to the examination of text, context and object-and-purpose of Article 23.2(a), the Panel found that the statutory language of Section 304 precludes compliance with Article 23.2(a), and therefore, constitutes a prima facie violation of that provision.

The Non-statutory Elements of Section 304

Although the Panel found grounds for a prima facie violation, it did not confirm the violation. Since the measure in question includes statutory language as well as other institutional and administrative elements, the Panel examined all of these elements to evaluate its overall WTO conformity. The Panel took the view that the prima facie violation created by statutory language can be removed if the offending discretionary feature has been "lawfully curtailed" by other institutional and administrative elements. The Panel concluded that the prima facie violation in this case had been legally removed.

First, the Panel noted that the wide discretion given to the U.S. Administration under Section 304 should be interpreted to include the power of the U.S. Administration to adopt an administrative action limiting the USTR's discretion in a manner consistent with the U.S. obligations under the WTO. In the Panel's view, such limitation on the USTR's discretion under Section 304 was contained in the SAA. In the SAA, the U.S. Administration indicated its interpretation of Sections 301-310, as well as the manner in which it intends to use its discretion under Sections 301-310:

Although it will enhance the effectiveness of section 301, the DSU does not require any significant change in section 301 for investigations that involve an alleged violation of a Uruguay Round agreement or the impairment of U.S. benefits under such an agreement. In such cases, the Trade Representative will:

- invoke DSU dispute settlement procedures, as required under current law;
- base any section 301 determination that there has been a violation or denial of U.S. rights under the relevant agreement on the panel or Appellate Body findings adopted by the DSB;
- following adoption of a favourable panel or Appellate Body report, allow the defending party a reasonable period of time to implement the report's recommendations; and
- if the matter cannot be resolved during that period, seek authority from the DSB to retaliate.

Noting the second point in the above list in particular, the Panel found that the offending discretionary element in the statutory language of Section 304 had effectively been curtailed by this official statement in the SAA. The Panel admitted that there are some other statements in the SAA that appear to contradict the above-cited statement, but noted that this tension should be resolved following U.S. constitutional law principles in favour of a construction upholding compliance with international legal obligations. The Panel also found that the United States confirmed, before the Panel, the commitment expressed in the SAA that the USTR would "base any section 301 determination that there has been a violation or denial of U.S. rights under the relevant agreement on the panel or Appellate Body findings adopted by the DSB." The Panel relied on this U.S. commitment because it viewed the U.S. statements as a reflection of official U.S. policy, "made with the intention not only that the panel relies on them but also that the EC and the third parties to the dispute as well as all Members of the DSB—effectively all WTO Members—place such reliance on them."

The Panel concluded that the aggregate effect of the SAA and the U.S. statements made to the Panel removed the offending discretionary element of Section 304, and, therefore, removed the prima facie WTO inconsistency created by the statutory language of Section 304. Significantly, however, the Panel made it clear that should the undertakings made in the SAA and before it be repudiated or in any other way removed by the U.S. Administration or another branch of the U.S. Government, this finding of conformity would no longer be warranted, and Section 304 would become inconsistent with U.S. obligations under Article 23.

Finally, the Panel examined the practice of the USTR in specific cases relating to Sections 301-310, such as the Japan—Auto and the EG—Banana cases, "as a means of shedding light on the meaning of Sections 301-310." This last statement was made despite the fact that the Panel explicitly acknowledged that it was not their task to examine the consistency of specific U.S. conduct with the WTO in individual cases. While not making a conclusive finding in relation to any of these cases, the Panel simply considered that the evidence presented by the EC and third parties before them was not sufficient to overturn their conclusions regarding Section 304.

The EC Claim That Section 306 Is Inconsistent With Article 23.2(a)—Claims of the EC and the United States

Section 306 provides procedures for the United States to obtain DSB authorisation for retaliation under Article 22 when it considers that another Member has failed to implement the DSB recommendation. In particular, Section 306(b)(2) provides: "If ... the Trade Representative considers that the foreign country has failed to implement a recommendation by the DSB, the Trade Representative shall determine what further action to take under [Section 301(a)] ... no later than 30 days after the expiration of the reasonable period of time...."

The EC claimed that Section 306(b) requires the USTR to "consider" whether a WTO Member has implemented the DSB's recommendations and, in the event of non-implementation, to determine what further action should be taken within thirty days after the expiration of the reasonable period of time granted to the losing party. This consideration constitutes a determination under Article 23.2(a), according to the EC. In the EC's view, any dispute concerning the implementation of the DSB's recommendations must be settled under Article 21.5, which allows for a decision ninety days from the date of referral. Since such referral normally is made at the end or after the expiration of the reasonable period of time, Section 306(b) does not allow the USTR to await the result of an Article 21.5 proceeding before making a unilateral determination. Thus, according to the EC, Section 306(b) requires the USTR to violate Article 23.2(a).

The United States contended that Section 306(b) does not require the USTR to make a unilateral determination contrary to DSU 23.2(a). Furthermore, Articles 22.2 and 22.6 presuppose that, by the thirtieth day following the expiration of the reasonable period of time, a complaining party wishing to suspend concessions would already have indicated its intentions. In other words, WTO Members wishing to exercise their WTO rights under Articles 22.2 and 22.6 must necessarily come to some judgment as to whether other Members are acting consistently with their obligations before turning to the procedures under those Articles. Otherwise, in the U.S. view, they lose the right to obtain such authorisation by negative consensus. The thirty-day deadline has been transposed into Section 306(b), and is therefore, as the United States argues, consistent with Article 23.2(a). On the relationship between Articles 21.5 and 22, the United States argued that recourse to and completion of Article 21.5 proceedings is not a prerequisite for a request for DSB authorisation under Article 22.6 whenever there is an implementation dispute.

Preliminary Panel Findings with Respect to the Statutory Language of Section 306

The Panel interpreted Section 306(b) in two phases. The first deals with a "consideration" by the USTR that another Member has failed to implement the DSB's recommendations. The second addresses the "determination" by the USTR as to what further action should be taken under Section 301. Since the determination is mandatory, ipso facto, the first phase must occur within the thirty-day deadline. The Panel found, therefore, as a matter of fact, that Section 306 mandates such a consideration within thirty days. In certain circumstances this consideration must take place before completion of the Article 21.5 proceeding, because Article 21.5 can be invoked later than sixty days before the expiration of the reasonable period of time.

The Panel further examined whether the first phase of Section 306 meets the four elements that constitute a violation of Article 23.2(a). The four elements are as follows:

(1) the act is taken "in such cases" (chapeau of Article 23.2), i.e. in a situation where a Member "seeks the redress of a violation of obligations or other nullification or impairment of benefits under the covered agreements or an impediment to the attainment of any objective of the covered agreements", as referred to in Article 23.1;

(2) the act constitutes a "determination";

(3) the "determination" is one "to the effect that a violation has occurred, that benefits have been nullified or impaired or that the attainment of any objective of the covered agreements has been impeded";

(4) the "determination" is either not made "through recourse to dispute settlement in accordance with the rules and procedures of the DSU" or not made "consistent with the findings contained in the panel or Appellate Body report adopted by the DSB or an arbitration award rendered under the DSU." The two elements of this requirement are cumulative in nature. Determinations are only allowed when made through recourse to the DSU and consistent with findings adopted by the DSB or an arbitration award under the DSU.

From the first element, it is obvious that Section 306(b) is designed to redress violations of the WTO Member's obligation to implement the DSB's recommendation. Regarding the second element, the Panel states that given its ordinary meaning, an Article 23.2(a) determination "implies a high degree of firmness or immutability, i.e. a more or less final decision by a Member in respect of the WTO consistency of a measure taken by another Member."

According to the Panel, USTR considerations under the first phase of Section 306 can constitute determinations under Article 23.2(a) since the former meets "the threshold of firmness and immutability."

The determination under Section 306 that a losing Member has failed to implement the DSB's recommendations means that such a Member's implementing measures are still inconsistent with the WTO Agreements. Therefore, the Section 306 determination implicitly contains the third element as well. As expected, the Panel had difficulty dealing with the fourth element, which involves a sensitive relationship between Articles 21.5 and 22.6. The Panel addressed this question in a separate section. On the other hand, the Panel found that, notwithstanding the strict thirty-day time limit, the USTR is given wide discretion as to the content of this determination. Under no circumstances does the statutory language of Section 306 compel the USTR to "determine that implementation has failed to make a determination of inconsistency, while Article 21.5 procedures are still pending." However, as in the case of Section 304, the USTR's discretion under Section 306 does not preclude it from making such a determination. The Panel, nevertheless, noted that this issue is different from that of Section 304 in that the determination under Section 306 is only a preliminary step to seek DSB authorisation to suspend concessions under Article 22.6. In other words, this determination is not aimed at retaliation without DSB authorisation.

The Fourth Element of an Article 23.2(a) Violation

The Panel cautiously noted that the fourth element was "highly contentious and far from clear," since this issue involves a question on the relationship between the Articles 21.5 and 22.6. The Panel decided to avoid resolving the dispute by determining what should be the correct interpretation of Articles 21.5 and 22 and the relationship between them, the subject of negotiations in the DSU review context. Instead, the Panel first examined the fourth element of Article 23.2(a) on the assumption that the U.S. interpretation of Articles 21.5 and 22 is correct, and second, on the alternative assumption that the EC interpretation in this respect is correct.

Assuming the U.S. View is Correct

The two criteria of the fourth element of Article 23.2(a) are cumulative in nature. Determinations are only allowed when made through recourse to the DSU and when they are consistent with findings adopted by the DSB or an arbitration award under the DSU. As noted, the United States took the view that Article 22 mandates a USTR determination that implementation has failed as a prelude to requesting authorisation to suspend concessions even prior to the completion of Article 21.5 proceedings. Assuming this view is correct, a USTR determination under Section 306 would be consistent with Article 23.2(a), since it would be made through recourse to the DSU, particularly Article 22. The remaining question is whether the determination under Section 306 is also made "consistent with the findings contained in the panel or Appellate Body report adopted by the DSB or an arbitration award rendered under the DSU." Given the assumption that the U.S. view is correct, the Panel considered that the "findings" in this context should mean only the finding of the original panel or Appellate Body report, rather than the Panel examining implementation in the pending Article 21.5 proceedings. If so, the answer to the remaining question is affirmative. Therefore, a USTR determination, in a specific case, that another Member has failed to implement the DSB's recommendations as a prelude to a request for the DSB's authorisation to retaliate, could not be inconsistent with Article 23.2(a). Therefore, the legislation authorising such a determination would not constitute a violation.

Assuming the EC View is Correct

As noted, the EC believed Article 22 could only be invoked once Article 21.5 proceedings had been completed. Assuming this is true, a Section 306 determination that a specific case is inconsistent with the WTO would not be made through recourse to dispute settlement in accordance with the rules and procedures of the DSU, since it would be a determination contrary to Articles 21.5 and 22. Accordingly, and for the same reason given in the Section 304 context, the statutory language of Section 306, which reserves the United States' right to make this determination, would constitute a prima facie violation of Article 23.2(a). The Panel, however, found that the cumulative effect of U.S. undertakings made in the SAA and before the Panel effectively and lawfully curtailed the offending discretionary element under Section 306, and therefore removed the prima facie violation.

Refraining from further examining the contentious issue on the relationship between Articles 21.5 and 22, the Panel found that Section 306, in the circumstances referred to in the EC's claim, is not inconsistent with Article 23.2(a) of the DSU. Again, the Panel made it clear that the same caveats made in the findings in the context of Section 304 also apply here.

The EC Claim That Sections 305 and 306 Are Inconsistent With Article 23.2(c)

If the USTR considers that the Member concerned failed to implement the DSB's recommendations, Section 306(b) provides that the USTR shall determine what further action to take under Section 301 no later than thirty days after the expiration of the reasonable period of time.

Section 305 regulates the timing of the implementation of the announced action. According to Section 305(a)(1), with some exceptions, the USTR is required to implement the announced action "by no later than the date that is 30 days after the date on which such determination is made."

The EC Claim with Respect to Determination of an Action under Section 306(b)

The second phase of Section 306 requires a "determination" of what action to take within thirty days time frame. The EC claimed that this is inconsistent with Article 23.2(c) of the DSU since it does not "follow the procedures set forth in Article 22 to determine the level of concessions or other obligations." The Panel admitted that this determination under the second phase of Section 306(b) might be mandated even before the completion of Article 21.5 proceedings, if the USTR has "considered" that implementation failed. Again, the Panel examined the conformity of Section 306(b) with Article 23.2(c) on alternative assumptions as to both parties' views on Articles 21.5 and 22.

If the U.S. view were correct, the United States would effectively be authorised under Article 22 to make a determination on what action to take within the thirty-day time limit. If not, it would lose the right to obtain DSB authorisation by negative consensus. In that sense, the second phase determination under Section 306(b) would be construed to "follow the procedures set forth in Article 22 to determine the level of concessions or other obligations," and would therefore be consistent with Article 23.2(c).

If the EC view were correct, the prima facie WTO inconsistency of the first phase of Section 306(b) would spill over to the second phase determination as well. However, the Panel was again persuaded that the cumulative effect of the U.S. undertakings in the SAA and before the Panel legally curtailed the USTR's discretion to make the second phase determination prior to the exhaustion of Article 21.5 proceedings. Thus, the risk of a potential violation of Article 23.2(c) had been eliminated. For these reasons, the Panel found that Section 306 is not inconsistent with Article 23.2(c). The same caveats made in the panel findings in the context of Section 304 also apply here.

The EC Claim with Respect to Implementation Action under Section 305

Section 305 requires the USTR to implement retaliatory action within sixty days after the expiration of the reasonable period of time when it made a second phase determination under Section 306(b). The Panel agreed with the EC that Article 21.5 and even Article 22.6 arbitration procedures may not be over within this sixty-day period. As a consequence, the statutory language of Section 305 may, in certain circumstances, mandate the implementation action prior to receiving DSB authorisation. However, the Panel also found that Section 305(a)(2) allows the USTR to delay the implementing action by as much as 180 days, if it determines, for example, that a delay would be necessary or desirable to obtain U.S. rights under Article 22.6, which provides authorisation to retaliate. Furthermore, the implementation of retaliatory action under Section 305 is also subject to "the specific direction, if any, of the President regarding any such action."

For the same reasons articulated concerning Section 304, the Panel took the view that this discretionary element of Section 305 may constitute a prima facie violation of the U.S. obligation under Article 23.2(c) to "obtain DSB authorisation in accordance with Article 22, procedures before suspending concessions or other obligations." Nonetheless, the Panel once again considered that the U.S. undertakings in the SAA and before the Panel had lawfully curtailed the USTR's discretion in this regard. For these reasons, the Panel found that the aforementioned aspect of Section 305 is not inconsistent with Article 23.2(c). Again, the same caveats made in the context of Section 304 apply here.

The panel stated in its concluding remarks:

> *In the light of the statutory and non-statutory elements of Sections 301-310, in particular the U.S. undertakings articulated in the Statement of Administrative Action approved by the U.S. Congress at the time it implemented the Uruguay Round agreements and confirmed and amplified in the statements by the U.S. to this Panel, we conclude that those aspects of Sections 301-310 of the U.S. Trade Act brought before U.S. in this dispute are not inconsistent with U.S. obligations under the WTO.... Significantly, all these conclusions are based in full or in part on the U.S. Administration's undertakings*

> *mentioned above. It thus follows that should they be repudiated or in any other way removed by the U.S. Administration or another branch of the U.S. Government, the findings of conformity contained in these conclusions would no longer be warranted.*

A Critique After the final panel report was circulated among Members of the WTO on December 22, 1999, both parties to the case expressed their satisfaction with the outcome. The EU Trade Commissioner, Pascal Lamy stated:

> *This is a fair result, a balanced outcome to a difficult case, but overall, it is a victory for the multilateral system.... Neither side can claim triumph, because while the Section 301 legislation can stay on the books, the Panel has clarified that it can be used against other WTO Members only as long as it strictly follows WTO rules. I am glad the U.S. has given the necessary commitments to this effects.*

The USTR announced on December 22, 1999, that "a dispute settlement panel of the World Trade Organisation has rejected a complaint by the European Union, upholding the WTO-consistency of Section 301 of the Trade Act of 1974." Following this reaction from both parties, neither party appealed the Panel's ruling, and it was adopted by the DSB on January 27, 2000. In this sense, the panel decision seems to be a fair "political" decision that pleased both parties, or at least enabled them to save face. However, this panel decision is legally weak, even though it is not entirely wrong. The Panel found that the statutory language of Section 304, 305 and 306, under the circumstances the EC referred to for its claims, constitutes a prima facie violation of Article 23.

In this respect, the Panel purported not to add anything to the generaldebate concerning the "mandatory legislation" theory, and conducted instead, in accordance with Article 31 of the Vienna Convention, an articulated textual analysis of Article 23. In effect, however, the panel's reasoning generally leads to the conclusion that discretionary legislation can be challenged even if the discretion is not exercised. The panel ruling addressed the possibility of noncompliance with procedural rules, such as Article 23. There is no doubt that the possibility of noncompliance with substantive rules, such as GATT 1994 and other substantive WTO Agreements, is also a (or even more serious) problem. In this sense, the Panel's reasoning would be an influential precedent for the future WTO panels that will examine the consistency of discretionary legislation with both substantive and procedural obligations under the WTO.

Nonetheless, the Panel concluded that the prima facie violation in this case had been eliminated, since the offending discretionary element of these Sections has been "effectively and legally curtailed" by the non-statutory elements, such as the U.S. Administration's undertakings in the SAA and before the Panel. In spite of excellent analysis in finding the prima facie violation, the Panel made the following errors in its reasoning for the above conclusion.

Statement of Administrative Action

Highlighting four bullet points in pages 365-66 of the SAA, the panel took the view that the U.S. Administration legitimately made a commitment not to exercise the discretionary power given to it under Section 301 in a manner that violates Article 23. The Panel, however, admitted that some of the language in the SAA appears ambivalent, while noting the following paragraphs in the SAA:

> *There is no basis for concern that the Uruguay Round agreements in general, or the DSU in particular, will make future Administrations more reluctant to apply section 301 sanctions that may be inconsistent with U.S. trade obligations because such sanctions could engender DSU-authorised counter-retaliation. Although in specific cases the United States has expressed its intention to address an unfair foreign practice by taking action under section 301 that has not been authorised by the GATT, the United States has done so infrequently. In certain cases the United States has taken such action because the foreign government has blocked adoption of a GATT panel report against it.*

Just as the Unites States may now choose to take section 301 actions that are not GATT-authorised, governments that are the subject of such actions may choose to respond in kind. That situation will not change under the Uruguay Round agreements.

In fact, it is well known that the U.S. Administration took an ambivalent position on the impact of the DSU on Section 301 when it was waiting for the congressional approval of a bill containing the Uruguay Round Agreement Act of 1994 ("URAA"). In addition to the above paragraphs, the U.S. Administration, in the SAA, asserted that the United States took pains to ensure that Section 301 would remain fully effective. Also, the U.S. Administration repeatedly expressed the views that the existence of the DSU will not change the way the United States conducts Section 301 investigations involving unfair foreign trade barriers that violate U.S. rights or deny benefits to the United States under the WTO Agreements. For instance, Ambassador Mickey Kantor, in his testimony before the Senate, claimed that Section 301 had been preserved ... in its entirety." In particular, Ambassador Kantor confirmed the U.S. Administration's position expressed in the SAA cited above:

> *The U.S. Government can decide that the matter at issue is important enough to take action that is inconsistent with a WTO Agreement. In that case, the other government can go to dispute settlement and object to the action that the United States chose to take. As to why the United States would choose to take action inconsistent with a WTO Agreement, it is a question of the importance of the issue needing resolution and the steps necessary to induce a solution to a significant problem.*

Testifying on a different occasion, Ambassador Kantor simply rejected the EC's claim that the DSU places new restrictions on the use of Section 301. He stated that "just because the European Community puts out a piece of paper indicating they do not think 301 is viable under the new trade agreement does not make it so. Frankly, they are just wrong, and they know they are wrong, and we discussed it in our negotiations." Nevertheless, while noting only the above-cited paragraphs in the SAA, the panel took the view that, following U.S. constitutional law, cases of ambiguity in the construction of legal instruments should, where possible, always be resolved in a manner consistent with U.S. international obligations. The Panel found that it was possible to do so in this case.

Whether it is appropriate to follow the U.S. constitutional principle in this context, it should be noted that the Panel applied a method of interpretation here that is totally different from the one applied to the interpretation of the statutory language of Section 301. In interpreting the statutory language of Section 301, the Panel strongly expressed the view that the discretionary element of Section 301 creates "uncertainty" and "threats" for economic operators that rely on U.S. compliance with Article 23, and is inconsistent with the most relevant objectives and purposes of the DSU. Such blameworthy uncertainty and threats were no less visibly created by this U.S. Administration's ambivalent position than by the statutory language of Section 301. In this sense, the U.S. Administration's ambivalent position, as expressed in the statements in the SAA and before Congress, has contributed to increasing the level of threats to enforce Section 301 in a manner inconsistent with Article 23.

From a WTO policy perspective, it seems undesirable for the WTO panel to follow U.S. constitutional law principles in favour of a construction upholding compliance with international obligations in cases of ambiguity. First, this could give unfair advantage to particular WTO Members, such as the United States, over other WTO Members lacking such established constitutional law principles. Second, except for flagrant violations of WTO obligations in rare cases, most WTO disputes as to the WTO consistency of legislation tend to be cases of ambiguity. Were this panel's view followed by future panels, it would generate incentives for WTO Members to design their legislation to be intentionally ambiguous with regard to its WTO consistency. This is clearly contrary to the objectives and purpose of the WTO. An application of the U.S. constitutional law principles in the domestic courts could promote U.S. compliance with the WTO obligations. In contrast, however, a WTO panel's use of a similar method in assessing the WTO consistency of a Member's legislation may serve against the Member's compliance with WTO obligations.

For these reasons, the Panel should not have found that the statements in the SAA contributed to removing a prima facie violation of statutory language of Section 301.

U.S. Statements before the Panel

The Panel also took the view that official U.S. statements before it confirmed the U.S. Administration's view as expressed in the four bullet points in the SAA. Determining the international legal status of the U.S. representatives' statements before the Panel is not an easy question, and the correctness of the panel's interpretation of their international legal relevance is outside the scope of this chapter. From a policy perspective, however, the Panel's reliance on the U.S. undertakings to it sets a bad precedent for future WTO panels in assessing the WTO conformity of discretionary legislation. If a responding parties' undertakings in panel proceedings could preserve contested discretionary legislation, all the responding parties would prefer to do so in the proceedings. Again, it would create an incentive for WTO Members to create or maintain offending discretionary elements in their legislation. Even after the legislation has been challenged before the panel proceedings, a WTO Member could successfully defend its legislation if it agreed before the panel not to exercise its discretion contrary to WTO obligations in the future.

Of course, the United States—Section 301 Panel found that "the aggregate effect of the SAA and the U.S. statements made to the panel," rather than the U.S. undertakings before the panel alone, adequately curtailed the offending discretionary element of Section 301. Nonetheless, as noted above, the SAA itself is ambiguous and there is not much in the SAA that can be aggregated with the U.S. commitments to the panel so as to remove a prima facie violation of the statutory language.

EC Claims on the Basis of Article XVI:4 of the WTO Charter

One of EC's vital claims was based on Article XVI:4 of the WTO Charter, which provides that "Each Member shall ensure the conformity of its laws, regulations and administrative procedures with its obligations as provided in the annexed Agreements." The EC's panel request explicitly claimed that Sections 301-310 are inconsistent with, among others, Article XVI:4 of the WTO Charter. In essence, the EC submitted that: "Even if Sections 301-310 could be interpreted to provide the USTR with a legal basis for the implementation of U.S. obligations under the WTO, they could not be considered to be in conformity with WTO law within the meaning of Article XVI:4 of the WTO Agreement." Whether Sections 301-310 are inconsistent with Article XVI:4 of the WTO Charter was intensely debated in the panel proceedings between both parties, and most third parties expressed their view on this issue. However, the Panel did not make a separate finding on this important claim, even after it found that Sections 301-310 were not inconsistent with Article 23. Of course, the EC's claim under Article XVI:4 in its First Submission could have been contingent on a panel finding that Sections 301 and 310 are inconsistent with Article 23 and other provisions of GATT 1994. Nevertheless, the EC argued its claim solely on the basis of Article XVI:4, and both parties sufficiently exchanged their views on this issue.

For this reason, the Panel should have resolved this debate. Article XVI:4 of the WTO Charter is also a treaty, no different than Article 23. The Panel should have conducted the textual analysis of the former as rigorously as it conducted its textual analysis of the latter. If the Panel had found that the measure in question was inconsistent with a more specific provision, Article 23, it would not have been required to address the Article XVI:4 issue, perhaps due to judicial economy. But, to the contrary, the Panel found in the end that the measure in question was not inconsistent with Article 23. Therefore, the Panel neglected its duty to examine an important element of the matter at issue, which fell within the Panel's terms of reference.

Section 301 Applications in Individual Cases

As noted above, the consistency of specific U.S. conduct with the WTO Agreements in individual cases was not within the terms of reference for the Panel. Nevertheless, the Panel should have examined the USTR's actions in individual cases since the WTO's inception. This seems necessary in light of the fact that the Panel found that Sections 301-310 were consistent with United States' WTO obligations on the basis of the U.S. Administration's undertakings in spite of a prima facie violation of its statutory language. If in individual cases the USTR had acted in a manner contrary to its undertakings, it would possibly be regarded as an action repudiating at least the undertakings in the SAA. As a result, the United States strongly argued that: "The record shows that the Trade Representative has never once made a Section 304(a)(1) determination that U.S. GATT or WTO agreement rights have been denied which was not based on the results of GATT and WTO dispute settlement proceedings. Not once." While agreeing that this examination of the WTO consistency of specific USTR actions in individual cases was outside the terms of reference for the panel, both parties intensely debated this issue. For this purpose, the EC presented, among others, the Japan—Auto and the EC—Banana cases in order to demonstrate that certain actions and determinations by the USTR under Section 301 procedures were inconsistent with the WTO Agreements, particularly Article 23. Japan, as a third party, also joined the EC to support the argument that the United States breached its obligations under the WTO in the Japan—Auto case.

The Panel again made it clear that it did not make a conclusive finding in relation to any of these cases. However, the Panel found that, on the record before it, the evidence submitted in this proceeding was not sufficient to overturn the U.S. claim of a consistent record of compliance of Section 304 with Article 23.2(a). This panel finding is the result of the application of the burden-of-proof rule. This panel finding did not affirmatively confirm that the United States never breached its obligation under Article 23.2(a) of the DSU in individual cases. Instead, the Panel found that the opposing parties did not submit sufficient evidence. Further, this panel finding was made only with respect to U.S. obligations specifically under Article 23.2(a). The Panel did not formally examine whether the United States breached other WTO obligations, such as its obligations under other elements of Article 23 and GATT 1994.

As shown below, a close examination of certain actions and determinations by the United States in the Japan—Auto and EG—Banana cases led to the conclusion that those actions were inconsistent with U.S. obligations under Article 23 and GATT 1994. Assuming that the United States breached its WTO obligations in the Auto and Banana cases after the entry into force of the WTO, one can forcefully argue that the U.S. undertakings made in the SAA were repudiated by the U.S. Administration's subsequent actions inconsistent with the prior undertakings. Furthermore, given the strong U.S. position on the WTO compliance records of specific actions in individual cases, the United States may logically be expected to repeat the same types of determinations and actions in the future Section 301 procedures, as it did in the Japan—Auto and EC—Banana cases. Such future actions and determinations, if any, would repudiate the recent U.S. undertakings made before the panel proceedings in the United States—Section 301 case, and, if so, the panel's "finding of conformity would no longer be warranted." For this reason, it is very important to examine closely whether specific actions and determinations by the United States in the Auto and Banana cases were inconsistent with WTO obligations. The following Sections examine this question.

The Consistency of Specific U.S. Actions with Article 23

This Section examines whether specific determinations and actions by the United States taken under Section 301 procedures in the Japan—Auto and EC—Banana disputes were inconsistent with Article 23.

The Japan—Auto Case—Violation of Article 23.1

Article 23.1 of the DSU provides, "When Members seek the redress of a violation of obligations or other nullification or impairment of benefits under the covered agreements or an impediment to the attainment of any objective of the covered agreements, they shall have recourse to, and abide by, the rules and procedures of this Understanding." This means that if any WTO Member seeks a remedy in relation to any matter that falls under the coverage of the WTO Agreements, it is required to pursue a WTO claim in accordance with the procedures set out in the DSU. Obviously, the United States did not "have recourse to" the DSU rules and procedures in the Auto case. It is therefore necessary to examine whether the U.S. Section 301 procedures used in the Japan—Auto case (i) "sought the redress" of WTO inconsistencies, and (ii) dealt with "WTO subject matters"—a WTO violation, the nullification of WTO benefits, or an impediment to the WTO objective.

Regarding the second element—WTO subject matters—the subject matter of the U.S. Section 302 investigation in the Auto case included the following Japanese government measures:

> *Certain acts, policies, and practices of the Government of Japan that restrict or deny U.S. auto parts suppliers' access to the auto parts replacement and accessories market ("after-market") in Japan ... In particular, excessively burdensome inspection requirements for imported vehicles, discriminatory access to vehicle registration data and maintaining an unreasonably complex system of motor vehicle inspection and repair regulations.*

A denial or restriction of product market access is a typical violation of obligations under the GATT 1994. More specifically, these matters arguably fall under the coverage of Article III:4 (National Treatment) of the GATT 1994, and the WTO Agreement on Technical Barriers on Trade (TBT Agreement). Article III:4 of the GATT 1994 provides:

> *The products of the territory of any contracting party imported into the territory of any other contracting party shall be accorded treatment no less favourable than that accorded to like products of national origin in respect of all laws, regulations, requirements affecting their internal sale, offering for sale, purchase, transportation, distribution or use.*

The TBT agreement itself is an anti-discrimination agreement. One of its objectives is to elaborate the National Treatment principle in respect of "technical regulations and standards." For instance, Article 2.2 of the TBT Agreement states:

> *Members shall ensure that technical regulations are not prepared, adopted or applied with a view to or with the effect of creating unnecessary obstacles to international trade. For this purpose, technical regulations shall not*

> *be more trade-restrictive than necessary to fulfill a legitimate objective ... Such legitimate objectives are, inter alia: ... protection of human health or safety, animal or plant life or health, or the environment.*

In the middle of the Auto dispute, even the U.S. seemed to concede that the matters in the Auto case fell within the ambit of the WTO Agreements, particularly the TBT Agreement. In a letter dated May 10, 1995, from USTR Kantor to WTO Director-General Ruggiero, Kantor stated that the Japanese regulations that the United States was complaining about were "far beyond what was necessary" for safety purposes or for protecting the environment. He went on to say, "the Japanese regulations ... are applied with the effect of creating unnecessary obstacles to international trade." The language in this letter clearly reflects the language of Article 2.2 of the TBT Agreement. USTR Kantor further expressed his willingness to file an action before the WTO. Apparently he thought that the Japanese measures in question were under the coverage of the WTO Agreements, particularly the TBT Agreement. For these reasons, it can be safely concluded that the Japan—Auto case satisfied the second element of Article 23.1. Regarding the first element—seeking the redress of WTO inconsistencies—USTR Kantor notified Director-General Ruggiero that the U.S. intended to seek a remedy under the WTO dispute settlement system. He said:

> *I am writing you today to give pre-filing notification of the intention of the United States to invoke the dispute settlement mechanism of the WTO to challenge the discrimination against the United States and other competitive foreign products in the market for automobiles and automotive parts in Japan.*

He also added that he has already asked the USTR officials to prepare for the WTO filings. In light of this factual information, it can be implied that the United States "sought the redress of WTO inconsistencies" in the Japan—Auto case. For these reasons, the United States in Japan—Auto clearly violated an obligation under Article 23.1 by pursuing Section 301 proceedings rather than following the DSU rules and procedures. One can imagine some possible U.S. counter-arguments. First, the United States could argue that a WTO Member has the authority to make a self-determination as to whether a matter in dispute falls within the ambit of the WTO Agreements. This argument is simply wrong. This interpretation would seriously undermine the multilateralism embodied in the WTO dispute settlement system. In particular, Article 1 of the DSU explains: "the rules and procedures of this Understanding shall also apply to consultations and the settlement of disputes between Members concerning their rights and obligations under the provisions of ... this Understanding taken in isolation or in combination with any other covered agreement." Under this provision, whether or not a matter in dispute between WTO Members is covered by the WTO Agreements is a matter that must be referred to the DSU procedures. A dispute as to the initial-referral decision itself is a dispute between Members concerning their rights and obligations under the DSU, such as Article 23.1. Therefore, this matter must be referred to the DSU procedures in order that the rules and procedures of the DSU shall also apply to the settlement of such a dispute, according to Article 1 of the DSU.

The United States could also argue that even if non-referral to the DSU procedures is inconsistent with Article 23.1, there is no nullification or impairment of benefits under the WTO Agreements. This argument is also unsustainable. First, under Article 3.8 of the DSU, any violation of a WTO agreement is presumed prima facie to nullify or impair a benefit to a WTO Member available under the agreement. The United States would have to rebut this presumption if it wished to sustain this argument. In light of GATT/WTO dispute settlement history, this is virtually an impossible task. More fundamentally, under the WTO dispute settlement system, "benefits" accruing to a Member under any WTO Agreement should be protected against nullification or impairment, regardless of whether the nature of the benefit is procedural or substantive. Japan, as a Member of the WTO, had a legitimate expectation that it would benefit from the multilateral dispute settlement system, that is, the DSU rules and procedures. A violation of Article 23.1 would certainly nullify or impair Japan's entitlement to, or expectation of, these "procedural benefits" under the DSU.

Another possible U.S. counter-argument is that this dispute was a so-called "hybrid" case—a case involving both WTO and non-WTO matters. In this type of case, the United States may pursue the Section 301 procedure in relation to the non-WTO matters, whether the United States files a claim before the WTO with respect to the WTO matters or not. While theoretically sound, this argument cannot be sustained in relation to the Japan—Auto case. It is clear that the United States investigated WTO matters as well as non-WTO matters as part of the proceedings under Section 301. The USTR Notice initiating the Section 301 procedure stated that:

> *The barriers subject to the Section 301, investigation include Japanese Government regulations such as the so-called "critical parts" and "alteration regulations and the certification system for garages and mechanics. These regulations ... support and work in combination with market restrictive practices by Japanese auto companies and parts distributors substantially to limit foreign access to the Japanese auto parts after market.*

In fact, the primary focus of the Section 301 investigation appears to be the allegedly discriminatory government regulation covered by the TBT Agreement, rather than the market restrictive practices of industry participants, arguably a non-WTO matter. Accordingly, the United States would be wrong if it argued that it pursued a Section 301 investigation in the Auto case only in respect to non-WTO matters.

Violation of Article 23.2

Article 23.2(a) prohibits a Member from making a unilateral determination to the effect that a violation of the WTO agreements has occurred or that benefits under those agreements have been nullified or impaired, or that the attainment of any objective of those agreements has been impeded. Such complaints must be pursued through the rules and procedures of the DSU. On May 10, 1995, the USTR made a determination that "certain acts, policies and practices of Japan that restrict or deny suppliers of U.S. auto parts access to the auto parts replacement and accessories market ("after-market") in Japan are unreasonable and discriminatory and burden or restrict U.S. commerce." As correctly pointed out by the Panel, four elements must be satisfied for a specific act in a particular dispute to breach Article 23.2(a):

(a) the act is taken "in such cases" (chapeau of Article 23.2), i.e. in a case a Member "seeks redress" of WTO inconsistencies, as referred to in Article 23.1;

(b) the act constitutes a "determination";

(c) the "determination" is one "to the effect that a violation has occurred, that benefits have been nullified or impaired or that the attainment of any objective of the covered agreements has been impeded";

(d) the "determination" is either not made "through recourse to dispute settlement in accordance with the rules and procedures of the DSU" or not made "consistent with the findings contained in the panel or Appellate Body report adopted by the DSB or an arbitration award rendered under the DSU.

As discussed, the first element was satisfied in Japan—Auto. In addition, the USTR's determination was made without recourse to the DSB in accordance with the DSU, thereby satisfying the fourth element. That determination can easily satisfy the second element as well. A critical question at issue here is the third element, namely, whether the determination is a determination of WTO inconsistencies. At first glance, this determination does not seem to involve a determination as to the WTO consistency of the Japanese measures. This determination was formally made under Section 301(b) rather than Section 301(a). Section 301(a) authorises the USTR to take action if the rights of the United States under any trade agreement have been denied or if a practice or policy of a foreign country violates or is inconsistent with the provisions of a trade agreement. If the United States had made an affirmative determination under Section 301(a) that Japan violated, for instance, the TBT Agreement, the United States would have clearly violated Article 23.2(a). The TBT Agreement is obviously a "trade agreement" under Section 301(a). Whether intentional or not, however, the United States did not make a determination under Section 301(a), but instead relied on Section 301(b). Under that section, the USTR may take action if it determines that "an act, policy, or practice of a foreign country is unreasonable or discriminatory and burdens or restricts United States commerce."

The question then is whether the USTR's determination under Section 301(b) that certain acts, policies and practices of Japan were unreasonable and discriminatory is contrary to Article 23(a). Section 301(d)(5) defines the term discriminatory as follows: "Acts, policies, and practices that are discriminatory include, when appropriate, any act, policy, or practice which denies national or most-favoured-nation treatment to United States goods, or services, or investments." National and MFN Treatment are basic principles of the GATT/WTO Agreements and those principles are codified in several of the agreements such as the GATT, GATS and the Agreement on Trade-Related Aspects of Intellectual Property Rights (TRIPs). As noted earlier, the TBT Agreement was designed to function as an anti-discrimination agreement with respect to "technical regulations and standards." Article 2.1 of the TBT Agreement provides, "Members shall ensure that in respect of technical regulations, products imported from the territory of any Member shall be accorded treatment no less favourable than that accorded to like products of national origin and to like products originating in any other country." This is simply a reiteration of the National Treatment and MFN principles embodied in the GATT and WTO. As even the United States appears to concede, the contested Japanese measures constitute technical regulations under the TBT Agreement. It follows that the determination made by the USTR pursuant to Section 301(b) in the Auto case could be construed to involve a "determination to the effect" that the contested Japanese measures—the regulations and the certification system—denied National or MFN treatment and, particularly in this case, constituted a violation of the TBT Agreement. For these reasons, the USTR's May 10, 1995 determination in the Japan—Auto case constitutes a violation of Article 23.2(a).

It could be argued that the "National or MFN treatment" under Section 301(d)(5) deals with only non-WTO matters outside the coverage of the WTO agreements, because violations of the National or MFN treatment obligations under the WTO agreements, such as the TBT Agreement, would be exclusively addressed by Section 301(a). However, there is no reasonable basis to interpret Section 301(d)(5) so narrowly. Such an interpretation might also be left open to abuse as the United States might then be able to circumvent Article 23.2(a) in many cases by simply invoking Section 301(b), rather than Section 301(a), even when issues of National or MFN Treatment under the WTO are involved. Since there is no difference between Section 301(a) and Section 301(b) in terms of their unilateral nature, such an interpretation could seriously undermine the objective and purpose of Article 23.2(a) and should therefore be rejected. In addition, as shown in the Japan—Film dispute, the USTR can invoke the WTO dispute settlement to seek redress of WTO inconsistencies even when the USTR's affirmative determination was made under Section 301(b) rather than 301(a). The USTR can do this because Section 303(a), which requires the USTR to request proceedings on the matter under the formal dispute settlement procedures under a trade agreement, refers to Section 302 which, in turn, refers to Section 301 in its entirety, rather than specifically to Section 301(a). This strongly indicates that a Section 301(b) determination of "unreasonableness or discrimination" in effect can involve a determination of inconsistency with the WTO.

In conclusion, the determination of the USTR under Section 301(b) in the Auto case made on May 10, 1995, constitutes a violation of Article 23.2(a). In this sense, it is difficult to agree with the U.S. claim made in the United States—Section 301 Panel proceedings that the USTR has never once made a Section 304(a)(1) determination in breach of Article 23.2(a). A Section 304(a)(1) determination obviously includes the USTR's affirmative determination under Section 301(b). This strongly implies that the USTR, at least once, exercised its discretion to make a determination under Section 304, contrary to the Panel's finding as to the U.S. compliance record.

The EC-Banana Case—A Determination under Section 306 and Article 23.2(a).

In the EC—Banana case, the United States made a "determination" under Section 306 that the EC had failed to implement the DSB's recommendations made in the original dispute (Banana III). Then, pursuant to Article 22, the United States requested that the DSB authorise the suspension of concessions against targeted EC goods. The most controversial question in this dispute was whether Such a specific determination was inconsistent with Article 23.2(a) of the DSU. The Panel left this question open but indirectly expressed its view by stating: "The fact that the USTR did make a determination of non-implementation before the completion of Article 21.5 procedures in Banana III, even if it turns out eventually that this was illegal, is not in our view, an act of bad faith."

In order to assess the WTO consistency of the USTR Section 306 determination in the EC—Banana case, it is necessary as a factual matter to confirm when such a determination was made in the middle of this dispute. In response to the Panel's question of when a Section 306 consideration was actually taken, the United States responded that the consideration that the EC failed to implement reflects no more than a belief on the part of the USTR, and, as such, is not taken. Further, the United States argued that the first formal written record that the USTR considered that the EC had failed to implement was the January 14, 1999 request for DSB's authorisation under Article 22. The United States in its request under Article 22 stated:

> *these new regulations perpetuate discriminatory aspects of the EC banana regime that were identified in the DSB's recommendations and rulings as inconsistent with WTO agreements. Therefore, these amendments fail to bring the EC's banana regime into conformity with the EC's WTO obligations within the reasonable period of time, as required by the DSB recommendations and rulings, thus perpetuating the nullification or impairment of benefits accruing to the United States, directly and indirectly, under the GATT and the GATS,*

> *that was found by the panel and the Appellate Body in this dispute. The United States is entitled to redress under Article 22 of the DSU.*

In fact, the USTR had not formally published its determination under Section 306 before its request for DSB authorisation to retaliate. Nonetheless, the USTR formally announced on several occasions that it must have made its determination no later than thirty days after the expiration of a reasonable period of time for implementation-January 31, 1999. Furthermore, the announcement was accompanied by the publication of a retaliation list initially proposed by the USTR. Accordingly, for the sake of analysis, it can be assumed that the USTR's Section 306 determination was made by January 14, 1999, at the latest. As noted, in order to determine the inconsistency of a specific act with Article 23.2(a), four elements must be satisfied. In the EC—Banana dispute, the United States was obviously seeking redress of WTO inconsistencies in the EC's implementation measures. Thus, the first element is easily satisfied.

The Panel's finding that a specific consideration made under Section 306 is a determination in the sense of the second element under Article 23.2(a). is also correct. In this case the USTR interpreted the distinction between "consider" and "determine" interchangeably, and stated that "the USTR must make the determination required by the first phase of section 306(b) no later than January 31, 1999." Therefore, the Section 306 consideration in this particular case met the second test as well. The third element can also be satisfied in the EC—Banana dispute because the United States determination that the EC failed to implement the DSB's recommendations, as illustrated in its January 14, 1999 request, involved a determination of the WTO inconsistencies of the EC's implementation measures. An examination of the fourth element in the EC—Banana dispute is the most challenging task since this issue involves a question on the relationship between the Articles 21.5 and 22.6. As noted, the Panel did not resolve this dispute.

According to Article 22.6, if the Member concerned fails to implement the DSB's recommendations within the reasonable period of time, the DSB must, upon request, grant authorisation to retaliate within thirty days of the expiration of the reasonable period of time. In order to follow this procedure, the original complaining party needs to make some internal judgment as to whether the original defending party failed to implement the DSB's recommendation. Section 306(b)(2) appears to have been drafted to follow Article 22.6. However, consistently with Article 23, Article 21.5 was intended to provide a forum to carry out a multilateral determination of whether a measure taken in order to comply with the DSB's recommendations is consistent with the WTO.

The problem is that there is an irreconcilable inconsistency between the time limits in Article 21.5 and in Article 22. The Panel also shared this view. If an Article 21.5 procedure is to be fully respected as a prerequisite to an Article 22 procedure, it could delay a Member's right to retaliate under Article 22. And, a failure to make a determination under Section 306(b) within the thirty-day time limit would result in losing a complainant's right obtainable by reverse-consensus rule under Article 22.6. If the time limit under Article 22 is to be fully respected, the complaining party in the original dispute—seeking DSB authorisation to retaliate—should not have to use the Article 21.5 procedure first. The time limit in Article 22, consistent with the objective of the DSU, appears to have been designed to provide the aggrieved party—in this case, the United States—with a speedy remedy without delay. Interpreting the Article 21.5 procedure and the possibility of appellate review following it as prerequisites to the request for DSB authorisation to suspend concessions under Article 22.6 could significantly delay the entire implementation process. It would also deeply undermine a major objective of the WTO dispute settlement system: the prompt settlement of disputes.

On the other hand, saying that the review procedure under Article 21.5 is not a prerequisite for an Article 22 request for DSB authorisation to retaliate would make the Article 21.5 procedure meaningless or redundant in most cases and would deny the defending party its procedural right. Article 21.5 clearly provides that "such dispute shall be decided through recourse to DSU dispute settlement procedures." Article 21.5 is a specifically designed procedure under which the WTO Members can achieve one of the goals set out in Article 23: multilateralism at the stage of implementation. Bypassing an Article 21.5 procedure in most cases would seriously undermine the multilateral trading system. In addition to being contrary to Article 23, this result also disregards a general objective of the WTO: "to develop an integrated, more viable and durable multilateral trading system."

For these reasons, it is best to reserve any conclusion on whether the U.S. determination of the WTO consistency of the EC implementation measure prior to the Article 21.5 panel ruling was inconsistent with Article 23.2(a). Moreover, it is not appropriate to resolve this question in panel or Appellate Body review proceedings through an interpretation of the contradictory provisions in the DSU. In this sense, the Panel's avoidance of resolving this issue seems to be very wise, regardless of the substantive merits of its alternative approach. The best way to resolve the conflict between Articles 21.5 and 22 is through amendment of either or both of those provisions. In fact, the DSU Review, conducted in 1999, produced an important DSU amendment proposal that was submitted to the Seattle Ministerial Conference for consideration. Unfortunately, the Ministers at the Seattle Conference did not make any decisions on this matter. Considering this issue's importance to maintaining a viable dispute settlement system, WTO Members should strongly pursue this issue in future WTO fora.

Other U.S. Actions in the EC—Banana Dispute

Unlike the Japan—Auto dispute, the United States in the EC—Banana dispute obviously pursued DSU procedures, particularly Article 22 procedures. For this reason, except for some controversy surrounding the U.S. determination under Section 306 and its consistency with Article 23.2(a), other U.S. actions taken in the EC—Banana case do not appear to constitute a violation of the other obligations under Articles 23. As noted, however, the threats of trade sanctions made by the United States in the EC—Banana dispute need to be closely examined in order to determine their WTO consistency. The next Part undertakes this task.

Threats of Retaliation and the GATT 1994

The power of Section 301 lies in its threat of trade sanctions rather than sanctions themselves. The consistency of the threat with the WTO Agreement is still an open question. This Part discusses whether threats of retaliation specifically taken under Section 301 in the Japan—Auto and the EC—Banana cases are inconsistent with U.S. obligations under the WTO, particularly Article I of the GATT 1994. This Part will show when threat of retaliation in individual cases can constitute a violation of WTO obligations.

Threats of retaliation can take various forms. Even the initiation of a Section 301 investigation and the determinations that can be made at early stages of Section 301 proceedings could be labelled threats of retaliation, at least from the perspective of those who are the subject of the Section 301 proceedings. This Part, however, focuses on only two forms of retaliatory threats: (1) the publication of a retaliation list, and (2) the suspension of liquidation of customs entries for the targeted merchandise, which are usually implemented several weeks before the actual implementation of retaliatory measures.

Legal Basis of Threats of Retaliation—Publication of a Retaliation List

Section 304(c) requires the USTR to publish in the Federal Register "any determination made under subsection (a)(1)." Such a determination includes a determination of the actions the USTR proposes to take in retaliation against a foreign country's denial of U.S. rights under a trade agreement. Unless expeditious action is required, Section 304(b) mandates that the USTR provide an opportunity for comments by interested persons before making that determination, followed by no less than thirty days prior notice. If expeditious action is required, the USTR must comply with this requirement after making that determination. The same procedural requirement applies to the USTR's determinations under Section 306(b). The exception for expeditious action is not provided for under Section 306. It follows that, once the USTR has made a determination under Section 304(a)(1)(B) or 306(b), the USTR is always required to publish a retaliation list before the actual implementation of proposed trade sanctions, at least in order to meet a prior notice requirement. As a result, the scope and content of the retaliatory measures to be implemented are known well in advance, normally several weeks before a proposed retaliation date.

In Japan—Auto, the USTR published a retaliation list in the Federal Register on May 16, 1995. The measures contained in the list were to become effective from June 28, 1995. In the Banana case, the USTR published a notice on the Federal Register concerning the proposed retaliation with an attached retaliation list on November 10, 1998, and published a revised list on December 21, 1998, in accordance with section 304(b) of the Trade Act. The DSB did not authorise the proposed retaliation until April 19, 1999.

Suspension of Customs Liquidation

There is no Section 301 provision that requires the USTR to suspend the liquidation of customs entries for merchandise on the retaliation list. Nonetheless, more often than not, the USTR has directed the Customs Service to withhold the liquidation of entries for targeted merchandise in cases where the USTR has published a retaliation list. "Liquidation" means a final computation of duties on imported merchandise accruing on its customs entry. If liquidation is withheld, the final duties that importers must pay remain open.

As a result, their legal liability to importers remains uncertain. In addition, importers in most cases are required to post a bond to secure the payment of additional duties when the retaliation list goes into effect at a later date. This invariably results in additional financial cost for the importers. In the Japan—Auto case, the United States decided to withhold customs liquidation for Japanese luxury-type automobiles as of May 20, 1995, several weeks before the effective date of the proposed retaliation, June 28, 1995. In the EC—Banana case, the United States withheld the liquidation of customs entries for selected EC goods on the USTR's retaliation list, as of March 3, 1999, again several weeks before the DSB's authorisation of the proposed retaliation.

Threats of Retaliation—A Violation of MFN Obligations under GATT 1994—An Assessment

Article I:1 of GATT 1994 provides:

> *With respect to customs duties and charges of any kind imposed on or in connection with importation ... and with respect to the method of levying such duties and charges, and with respect to all rules and formalities in connection with importation ... and with respect to all matters referred to in paragraphs 2 and 4 of Article III, any advantage, favour, privilege or immunity granted by any contracting party to any product originating in or destined for any other country shall be accorded immediately and unconditionally to the like product originating in or destined for the territories of all other contracting parties.*

Article I is obviously an anti-discrimination provision. Before examining whether there is any discrimination between like products from different exporting countries, one needs to look at what kinds of discriminatory conduct are covered by Article I, and then assess whether the U.S. publication of retaliation lists or suspension of liquidation in the Auto and Banana disputes falls within the ambit of that Article. Article I provides for four relevant matters in connection with importation: (1) customs duties and charges of any kind in connection with importation, (2) the method of levying such duties and charges, (3) all rules and formalities in connection with importation, and (4) all matters referred to in Article III:2 and 4. According to Section 301(c)(1)(B), the content of a retaliation list may involve the "imposition of duties or other restrictions on the goods of ... a targeted foreign country."

The forms of retaliation in the Auto and Banana disputes were the imposition of 100% ad valorem duties on the goods from Japan and selected European countries. Clearly, the publication of retaliation lists in these disputes was made with regard to customs duties in connection with importation. Of course, the publication of a retaliation list is not a customs duty itself but is concerned with the method of levying customs duties. This is because the retaliation lists published in these disputes specified the scope and content of the proposed retaliatory duties, as well as when and how such duties will be collected. Obviously, the U.S. with holdings of liquidation of customs entry in these disputes were "with regard to the method of levying customs duties." Article I also provides that any advantage, favour, privilege or immunity granted to a foreign product shall be accorded to all like products from another Member country. Although the meaning of like products was at issue in many other cases involving MFN obligations, this is not an issue that is highly relevant here.

Instead, the important issue is whether there is any relevant discrimination against the targeted products compared with like products from other countries. It should be noted that one of the most important objectives of the GATT/WTO disciplines is to protect the legitimate expectations of Member countries with regard to the competitive conditions for their products in other Member countries. The India—Patent Protection panel confirmed that "the protection of legitimate expectations of Members regarding conditions of competition is a well-established GATT principle," and the MFN principle in particular has been construed to prohibit discriminatory measures that might affect competitive conditions between like products imported from different contracting parties. The Banana III panel adopted this test in determining whether the contested tariff quota system was inconsistent with the MFN obligations under GATT 1994, and found that:- the possibility does exist to pass on tariff quota rent to BFA banana products in such a way, whereas there is no such possibility in respect of non-BFA third-country banana producers, thus the EC's requirement affects the competitive relationship between banana of non-BFA third-country origin and bananas of BFA origin.

The Appellate Body affirmed this finding. Several panels under the GATT system also adopted this test for other GATT principles, such as National Treatment under Article III and the prohibition of quantitative restrictions under Article XI, which was again confirmed by the Appellate Body in Banana III. The publication of a retaliation list affects competitive conditions between the targeted foreign products and like third-country products. Once a retaliation list is published, importers of targeted products may respond in a number of ways. First, importers or distributors shift their purchases from sources in the target country to sources in other countries in order to avoid the imposition of 100% ad valorem duties. There is some evidence that Japanese car importers and dealers in the United States actually responded in this way when the USTR published a retaliation list targeting luxury-type Japanese cars in the Auto dispute. One can easily imagine the same impact on importers and distributors of targeted EC goods in the Banana dispute. The second possibility is that importers will immediately raise prices for the targeted goods in anticipation of future cost increases resulting from the eventual imposition of the retaliatory duties. Under either of these scenarios, there obviously will be an adverse impact on the targeted products' competitive relationship with like products from other countries.

An even stronger case can be made for the suspension of the liquidation of customs entries. Suspension of the liquidation of customs entries for targeted merchandise clearly and visibly affects the competitive conditions between the targeted products and like products from other countries. In the Auto and Banana disputes, the U.S. withholding of customs liquidation exposed importers of the targeted products to a contingent liability of a 100% ad valorem duty, whereas like products from other origins were subject to the normal customs tariff only. The importers of Japanese luxury-type cars and selected EC goods were also required to submit bonds corresponding to the higher contingent liability, thus raising the effective price of the targeted products and imposing an additional financial burden on the importers. Again, it can be reasonably expected that importers facing such a financial burden are likely to switch to like products from other countries or to raise the prices of the targeted goods in anticipation of the proposed retaliation. It follows that both the suspension of customs liquidation and the requirement to submit a bond constitute discriminatory measures that are prohibited by Article I of the GATT 1994. If the publication of a retaliation list is accompanied by the withholding of the liquidation of entries for the targeted merchandise, the adverse impact on competitive conditions is likely to be much more severe. This actually took place in the Auto and the Banana disputes.

To assess whether a measure is illegally discriminatory under Article I, it is not necessary to confirm with statistical data that there has been a decrease in export volume of targeted goods. As confirmed by the Appellate Body in Banana III, "a change in the competitive relationship contrary to basic obligations under the GATT 1994 must consequently be regarded ipso facto as a nullification or impairment of benefits accruing under the GATT 1994." The above two types of retaliatory threats in the Auto and Banana disputes caused a change in the competitive relationship between the targeted goods and like products imported from third countries. For these reasons, the publication of retaliation lists and the suspensions of customs liquidation in both the Auto and Banana cases constitute "discrimination" inconsistent with Article I of the GATT 1994.

U.S. Arguments—Too Early to Challenge

The United States may argue that the proposed retaliatory measures included in a retaliation list are by nature temporary and provisional, and therefore cannot be challenged by other Member countries before the WTO unless the measures become final and conclusive. The content of a retaliation list published pursuant to Section 304(c) may be changed after the USTR receives public comments. It is also possible that the threats of retaliation under Section 301—whether the publication of a retaliation list or the suspension of customs liquidation—are never implemented if the parties to the dispute resolve their disputes through bilateral negotiations. Alternatively, if the United States actually implements the proposed retaliation, the threat of retaliation no longer exists, and the only action that can be challenged in the WTO is the retaliatory measures.

However, this argument has no legal basis. Under Article I of the GATT 1994, there is no requirement that the contested discriminatory measures be final and conclusive. A government grant of any advantage, privilege or immunity to import products in a discriminatory manner constitutes a violation of Article I. Even if temporary or provisional by nature, a threat of retaliation that adversely affects competitive conditions between the targeted products and like products from third countries is illegal discrimination under Article I. Parties to the dispute may reach a mutually agreeable solution at a later stage, but the threat may have already adversely affected competitive conditions between targeted products and other like products. The Panel in its final report also took a similar view in assessing the threats of unilateral determinations under Section 304. The panel eloquently stated:

> *Article 23 of the DSU does apply to legislation that threatens unilateral determinations but does not actually mandate them ... if one interprets it in the light of the*

indirect effect such legislation has on individuals and the market-place, the protection of which is one of the principal objects and purpose of the WTO.... From the perspective of the individual economic operator, ... whether the risk materialises makes little difference....It may affect economic operators competitive economic relationship and deny certain commercial advantages that foreign competitors would otherwise have. The threats of unilateral action can be as damaging on the marketplace as the action itself.

In addition, the Panel confirmed that the risk or threat of discrimination was found in GATT jurisprudence to constitute a violation of Article III of GATT—because of the "chilling effect" it has on economic operators. There is no reason why this test cannot apply to assessing the inconsistency with Article I of GATT. In sum, the Panel confirms that a threat of discrimination can itself constitute a MFN violation and therefore can be challenged by another WTO Member even before the threat materializes.

Measures under Article 4.4 of the DSU

A related and more fundamental U.S. argument is that, due to its temporary and provisional nature, the publication of a retaliation list or the suspension of customs liquidation does not constitute a measure for purposes of Article 4.4 of the DSU (Article 4.4), and therefore cannot be challenged under the DSU procedures. The meaning and scope of the word "measures" under Article 4.4 are not explicitly defined under the DSU or any other relevant WTO Agreement. The ordinary meaning of "measure" in this context is "a plan or course of action intended to attain some object, a suitable action." The announcement of a retaliation list and the withholding of customs liquidation are government actions published in the official Federal Register and therefore fell under the above definition according to its ordinary meaning. In particular, the withholding of customs liquidation by the U.S. Customs Service is taken at the border of a customs territory, which is one of the traditional measures that GATT 1994 was designed to regulate. There is no contextual element for a different interpretation of the meaning of the term "measures" under Article 4.4. Nor has its meaning been restricted under the GATT and WTO jurisprudence. Rather, the panel in the Japan—Film case comprehensively reviewed the past panel decisions on the scope of "measures" and adopted a broad interpretation of "measures." For these reasons, the U.S. "measure" argument is unpersuasive.

Preparing to Follow DSU Procedure

The United States argued that the publication of a retaliation list and the suspension of customs liquidation were done in preparation for complying with DSU procedure and that it was therefore not guilty of any wrongdoing. Since the United States did not follow DSU procedure in the Japan—Auto dispute, however, this argument only applies to the EC—Banana case. In order to assess the validity of this argument, two questions need to be answered: (1) whether the publication of a retaliation list and the suspension of customs liquidation were preparatory steps taken by the United States in order to follow the DSU procedure, and (2) whether these measures are legally justified under the WTO.

The Publication of a Retaliation List

In the Banana dispute, the United States published a retaliation list on November 10, 1999, which was revised on December 21, 1999. Under Article 22.6, a complainant is required to request the DSB to authorise its proposed retaliation within thirty days after the expiration of the reasonable period of time for implementation. In order to follow this procedure, the United States needed to make an internal determination in the EC—Banana dispute as to the content of the proposed retaliation, such as a retaliation list. Whether this is a good domestic policy or not, such a publication is not required by Article 22.6, nor is it necessary in order to follow DSU procedure. The fact that the publication is required by Section 306(c) or 304(c) is a different matter. Therefore, the publication of a retaliation list in the EC—Banana dispute was not a preparatory step taken to follow the DSU procedures.

In addition, the publication of a retaliation list in the EC—Banana dispute cannot be legally justified under the GATT 1994. In order to be legal, the publication list would have to fall under at least one of the exceptions listed in Article XX of GATT 1994. Article XX(d) is the only relevant exception on this issue. It provides that, subject to the preliminary requirement set out under the chapeau of Article XX, a government measure can be justified if it is "necessary to secure compliance with laws or regulations which are not inconsistent with the provisions of the GATT 1994...." In addition to the preliminary requirements under the chapeau, two elements need to be met in order to justify a measure in question: (1) a measure is "necessary to secure compliance with laws or regulations;" and (2) such laws or regulations are "not inconsistent with the GATT 1994."

The United States may argue that the publication of a retaliation list was necessary to secure compliance with Sections 301-310, particularly Sections 306(c) and 304(c), and that this law is not inconsistent with GATT 1994. As for the second element, Sections 306(c) and 304(c) were not questioned in the United States—Section 301 panel proceedings, and therefore, their WTO consistency is still debatable. However, even if the publication of a retaliation list meets this second element, it cannot satisfy the first element: the "necessary to secure compliance" test. The meanings of "necessary" and "secure compliance" need to be discussed separately.

First, the well-established GATT jurisprudence on the necessity test is that the party invoking this exception under Article XX(d) must prove that a measure in question is the least-trade-restrictive measure available and less trade restrictive measures are not sufficient to secure compliance with laws or regulations. In addition, the qualification to "secure compliance with laws or regulations" has been interpreted to mean "to enforce obligations under laws or regulations," rather than to more broadly "ensure the attainment of the objectives of the laws or regulations." As discussed, Sections 304(c) and 306(c) require the USTR to publish a retaliation list once the USTR has made a determination under Sections 304(a)(1)(B) or 306(b). In contrast, the United States argued that the publication of a retaliation list is not required by any provision of Sections 301-310.

Alternative assumptions illustrate the fact that the publication of a retaliation list in the EC—Banana dispute cannot be justified under Article XX(d) of the GATT. If the United States is correct, the USTR did not have to publish a retaliation list in the Banana dispute to "secure compliance" with Sections 304(c) and 306(c) since the USTR was not under the obligation to publish a retaliation list. Alternatively, even if the publication is required by Sections 304(c) or 306(c), the actual publication of a retaliation list in the Banana dispute cannot satisfy the "necessity" test under Article XX(d). This is because the USTR in the Banana dispute published a proposed retaliation list not once, but at least two or three times, all several weeks before the deadline for the U.S. request under Article 22.6. These publications were also accompanied by official and unofficial announcements made by the USTR and other high-ranking officials of the U.S. Administration. These U.S. actions, in combination with the early publication of a retaliation list itself, surely constitute threats of a retaliation that brought a chilling effect on the marketplace for targeted

EC goods and economic operators in it. In addition, publication of a retaliation list already constituted a threat because it distorted the free flow of EC-targeted goods in international trade long before the DSB authorised retaliation.

Clearly the United States could have taken a less-trade-restrictive means in complying with the publication requirement under Sections 304(c) or 306(c). For instance, the United States did not have to repeatedly threaten to retaliate long before the DSB gave its authorisation. The United States could have published its proposed retaliation list just once for the purpose of seeking public comments. This action may take place approximately thirty days before the deadline for the U.S. request for the DSB's authorisation, thereby satisfying the thirty-day prior notice requirement. Other accompanying threats of retaliation made by senior officials of the U.S. Administration were simply unnecessary. In this sense, the publication of a retaliation list accompanied by its announcement made by the U.S. Administration was not the least-trade-restrictive measure to secure compliance with relevant provisions of Sections 301-310. Therefore, the publication of a retaliation list in the Banana dispute cannot be justified under Article XX(d) of the GATT.

The Suspension of Customs Liquidation

The same two questions can be examined with respect to the suspension of customs liquidation. The U.S. Customs Service withheld customs liquidation as of March 3, 1999, the middle of the arbitration proceedings under Article 22.6. This cannot be regarded as a preparatory step taken in order to follow the procedures under Article 22.6, as argued by the United States. First of all, unlike the publication of a retaliation list, no U.S. domestic law requires the USTR or the Customs Service to take this measure in implementing the proposed retaliatory action. Most importantly, Article 22.6 explicitly provides that "concessions or other obligations shall not be suspended during the course of the arbitration." As noted, the withholding of customs liquidation nullifies benefits accruing to the target country under Article I of the GATT 1994 as a result of its effect on the competitive relationship between targeted goods and like products from third Member countries. In other words, the withholding of customs liquidation is a form of retaliation itself. It essentially suspends the U.S. MFN "obligations" under the GATT/WTO against the targeted country. Thus, the withholding of customs liquidation by the United States "during the course of the arbitration" in the EC—Banana dispute violated Article 22.6 of the DSU. Therefore, it cannot be described as a preparatory step for compliance with Article 22.6.

The United States could argue that it withheld customs liquidation on March 3, 1999, to secure U.S. rights under Article 22.6 since this provision mandates the arbitration proceedings to be completed within sixty days of expiration of the reasonable period of time for implementation. However, this argument is unwarranted for two reasons: first, as correctly confirmed by the Panel, most of the time limits in the DSU are indicative rather than mandatory. For instance, even the Appellate Body treated a seemingly compulsory deadline, the ninety-day length of the appellate process under Article 17.5 of the DSU, as merely indicative. The sixty-day time limit under Article 22.6 does not need to be construed to fall under the exception. This view should be endorsed in consideration of the fact that the arbitrator under Article 22.6 cannot always meet the sixty-day time limit, because the arbitrator is not always in a position of influence at the point in time when the DSB refers a matter to arbitration. The arbitrators under Article 22.6 in the Banana dispute correctly pointed this out.

Second, in the context of a Section 306(b) determination, a failure to make a determination under Section 306(b) within thirty-day time limit would result in losing a U.S. right obtainable by reverse-consensus rule under Article 22.6. In that sense, a specific determination under Section 306(b) within the thirty-day time limit prior to the completion of Article 21.5 proceedings was seemingly defensible. This type of defence cannot be applicable here since there would be no risk of losing U.S. rights in that manner, even if there were some delay in the implementation of retaliation.

Regarding the second question—whether the U.S. withholding of customs clearance is legally justifiable under GATT XX(d)—the United States may argue that the suspension of customs liquidation as of March 3, 1999, was "necessary to secure compliance with laws or regulations which are not inconsistent with the provisions of the GATT 1994." The relevant law is Section 305, which requires the USTR to implement retaliatory actions within sixty days of expiration of the reasonable period of time under Article 21.3, subject to exception. For the sake of analysis, alternative assumptions are made here. If Section 305 were inconsistent with Article 23, contrary to the Panel's finding, Article XX(d) could not be used to justify a measure to allegedly secure compliance with a law which is inconsistent with the WTO Agreements. For this reason, the other element—necessary to secure compliance—would not need to be examined any further. Alternatively, assume that the Panel's finding as to the WTO consistency of Section 305 is correct. The Panel considered that Section 305 allows the USTR to exercise discretion to wait until it obtains DSB authorisation to retaliate. In this sense, an early retaliation by way of the withholding of customs liquidation in the middle of the Article 22 arbitration was not necessary to secure compliance with Section 305, since the U.S. Administration was under no statutory obligation to do so. Even if the United States had not withheld customs liquidation as of March 3, 1999, it would still be able to comply with Section 305. In this sense, the withholding of customs liquidation cannot be the least trade restrictive measure necessary to comply with Section 305. Therefore, this type of early retaliation cannot be justified under Article XX(d).

In light of the foregoing analysis, the U.S. publication of a retaliation list and suspension of customs liquidation in the Banana dispute are inconsistent with the U.S. MFN obligation under Article I of the GATT 1994. As anticipated from both parties' responses to the panel report, neither party appealed the Panel's ruling. As the Panel's report was adopted by the DSB, Sections 301-310 will remain intact under the United States Code, as long as the U.S. enforcement of that law does not deviate from the rules and procedures of the DSU, in particular Article 23. This ruling is politically superb.

If the Panel had found that Sections 301-310 as such were inconsistent with WTO obligations and recommended the United States to bring relevant provisions of Section 301 into conformity with the U.S. obligations under the DSU, it would have faced strong political resistance from the United States, particularly from Congress. With the Panel's confirmation that the U.S. Administration, rather than Congress, is given full authority to enforce Sections 301-310 in a manner consistent with U.S. obligations under Article 23, the U.S. Administration, particularly the USTR, will be able to interpret and administer Sections 301-310 in conformity with DSU rules and procedures. In this sense, the Panel has given the USTR room to maneuver politically around Congressional pressure.

On the other hand, the EC achieved a major goal in this panel proceeding by acquiring a U.S. commitment not to exercise the USTR's discretionary power contrary to U.S. obligations under Article 23. The Panel's ruling is, therefore, a political victory for the EC and other U.S. trading partners as well as for the United States. For these reasons, the ruling deserves applause from the entire WTO Membership for its political brilliance. Nevertheless, the Panel's ruling stands on shaky legal ground. First, the Panel did not sufficiently focus on the ambivalent position of the United States expressed in the SAA as well as in other congressional records for the passage of the URAA in 1994. Although the Panel did not make a formal ruling on the WTO consistency of specific actions of the United States in individual cases, it indirectly supports the U.S. claim that the United States has never once enforced Section 301 contrary to WTO obligations since 1995. Strict scrutiny of Japan—Auto and EG—Banana, however, leads to a conclusion that certain actions of the United States in both cases constitute violations of WTO obligations. This may make the Panel's ruling very questionable, because the Panel's ruling is implicitly based on an assumption that the United States had not exercised its discretionary power contrary to WTO obligations by the time of the Panel's ruling. Finally, the Panel's heavy reliance on the assurances made by the United States before it would appear to create a risk for the WTO dispute settlement system, since it will probably create incentives for WTO Members to craft their domestic legislation in an ambiguous manner in terms of the WTO consistency.

When the United States—Section 301 panel proceedings were pending, many other WTO Members expected that the case would resolve all of the controversial disputes concerning the WTO inconsistencies of Sections 301-310. This was not the case. There remain many important unresolved issues. Therefore, trade disputes involving U.S. Section 301's WTO consistency will probably continue to arise. On the basis of the foregoing analysis, the following actions are recommended for the United States: first, the United States should accept that its decision as to whether to refer to DSU rules and procedures after initiating a Section 301 investigation shall not be unilateral, and instead be subject to the panel and/or Appellate Body's review. Accordingly, it is recommended that the United States not repeat its practice in this regard as it did in the Japan—Auto dispute. In addition, the United States should be restrained from invoking a Section 301(b)—unreasonable/discriminatory determination—rather than Section 301(a), with an intent to avoid the WTO dispute settlement procedures, as it did in the Japan—Auto case. Section 301(b) determinations and subsequent actions by the USTR may also constitute a violation of Article 23.

Finally and most importantly, the United States is recommended not to employ the threat of retaliation in order to achieve its goals prior to the completion of relevant DSU procedures. As correctly pointed out by the Panel, "Members faced with a threat of unilateral action, especially when it emanates from an economically powerful

Member, may in effect be forced to succumb to the demands imposed by the Member exerting the threat, even before DSU procedures have been activated." The United States should be restrained from taking advantage of this fact. Exercising a threat of unilateral action is not only contrary to the objects and purpose of the WTO but may also constitute a violation of several provisions of the WTO Agreements. For instance, the U.S. early and repeated publication of a retaliation list accompanied by a series of official announcements of the U.S. intention to retaliate would be inconsistent with WTO obligations, such as the MFN obligation under Article I of GATT 1994. The U.S. withholding of customs liquidation prior to the DSB's authorisation to retaliate is also a MFN violation.

Therefore, it is recommended that the United States make judicious use of the publication of a retaliation list in order to avoid a violation of WTO obligations while preparing for the DSU procedures. In addition, the United States should be refrained from effectively implementing an early retaliation by way of its withholding of customs liquidation for the targeted goods prior to the DSB authorisation. The goal of this chapter was not to unilaterally blame Section 301 on behalf of U.S. trading partners. Rather, the goal was to provide an objective legal and policy analysis of whether and under what circumstances specific U.S. actions under Sections 301-310 may constitute violations of WTO obligations. With the adoption of the Panel's ruling by the DSB, the U.S. Sections 301-310 can now coexist with the multilateral trading system. It is true that Section 301 serves legitimate objectives and performs valuable functions as a domestic trade policy tool. It allows private parties to participate, although indirectly, in the WTO dispute settlement process. It also requires the USTR to participate in the WTO dispute settlement proceedings in a transparent manner. Should it be misused or overused, however, specific actions and determinations under Section 301 procedures might constitute a violation of WTO obligations. This Chapter showed how specific actions and determinations taken under Section 301 procedures in the Auto and Banana cases violated WTO obligations, and sought to advise the United States on how to avoid further violations of WTO obligations in the future. The failure of last year's Seattle Ministerial Conference strongly indicates that the lack of U.S. leadership in the WTO poses a serious problem for the future of the multilateral trading system. Now more than ever, the WTO needs the United States to be a leader in creating and maintaining "an integrated, more viable and durable multilateral trading system."

Bibliography

Aaron V.: *The Social Organisation of Juvenile Delinquency,* New York: John Wiley, 1968.

Abel, Richard L.: *The Politics of Informal Justice,* New York: Academic Press, 1982.

Abu-Rabi, Ibrahim M : *Intellectual Origins of Islamic Resurgence in the Modern Arab World,* Albany: State University of New York Press, 1996.

Adam, R.: *Elements of Government,* New York, Random House, 1960.

Aharon Layish : *Women and Islamic Law in a Non-muslim State,* New York, Wiley, 1975.

Akers, R.: *Criminological Theories: Introduction, Evaluation, and Application,* Roxbury, Los Angeles, 2000.

Ali, Shaheen Sardar : *Gender and Human Rights in Islam and International Law,* The Hague/London/Boston: Kluwer Law International, 2002.

Allen, H.: *Justice Unbalanced Gender, Psychiatry and Judicial Decisions,* Open University Press, Milton Keynes, 1987.

Allen, Tim: *Trial Justice: the International Criminal Court and the Lords Resistance Army.* London: Zed Books, 2006.

Allison, G. Burgess and Roberta Ramo. *The Lawyer's Guide to the Internet.* Chicago, IL.: American Bar Association, 1995.

Ambedkar, B. R.: *Annihilation of Caste: An Undelivered Speech,* Arnold Publishers, New Delhi, 1990.

Aquinas, Thomas: *On Law, Morality and Politics,* Hackett Publishing Co., Indianapolis, 1988.

Arlow, Brenner: *Psychoanalytic Concepts and the Structural Theory,* International Universities Press, NY, 1964.

Atherton, M.K.: *International Organizations: A Guide to Information Sources,* Gale Research, Detroit, 1976.

Austin, Granville: *The Indian Constitution: Cornerstone of a Nation,* Oxford, Clarendon Press, 1966.

Baderin, Mashood A : *International Law and Islamic Law,* Ashgate, 2008.

Barber, James David: *The Pulse of Politics, Electing Presidents in the Media Age,* Norton, New York, 1980.

Beyerly, J.: *Public International Law. A Guide to Information Sources,* Mansell, London/New York, 1991.

Blau, M.: *Bureaucracy in Modern Society,* New York, Random House, 1956.

Blythe, James M.: *Ideal Government and the Mixed Constitution in the Middle Ages,* Princeton University Press, Princeton, 1992.

Braithwaite, John: *Crime, Shame, and Reintegration.* New York: Cambridge University Press, 1989.

Brinson, Dianne J. *Internet Law & Business Handbook: A Practical Guide.* Menlo Park, CA.: Ladera Press,1998.

Bromley, R. and Gerry, C.: *Casual Work and Poverty in Third World Cities,* John Wiley and Sons, New York, 1979.

Brownlie, M.K.: *Principles of Public International Law,* Clarendon, Oxford, 1990.

Carlen, P. and Worrall, A.: *Gender, Crime and Justice,* Open University Press, Milton Keynes, 1987.

Cavazos, Edward A. and Gavino Morin. *Cyberspace and the Law: Your Rights and Duties in the On-Line World.* Cambridge, MA.: MIT Press, 1994.

Chandra, R.: *Judicial System in the World,* Lucknow, Print House (India), 1992.

Charles Howard McIlwain: *Constitutionalism: Ancient and Modern,* N.Y., Cornell University Press, 1958.

Clarke, R.V. & Eck, J.: *Becoming a Problem-Solving Crime Analyst,* University College London, London, 2003.

Cobban, Helena: *Amnesty After Atrocity: Healing Nations After Genocide and War Crimes.* Boulder, CO: Paradigm, 2007.

Coleman, S.: *The Promise of Representative Bureaucracy: Diversity and Responsiveness in a Government Agency,* New York, M. E. Sharpe, 1997.

Crowe, Tim.: *Crime Prevention Through Environmental Design,* Butterworth - Heinman, Boston, 2000.

Daube, David: *Roman Law: Linguistic, Social and Philosophical Aspects,* Edinburgh University Press, Edinburgh, 1969.

David R. Johnson & David Post : *The Rise of Law in Cyberspace,* 48 Stan, L. Rev. 1367, 1996.

Deulkar, Sita : *Caste and Communities in Conflict of Modernisation,* Dominant, Delhi, 2005.

Dixit, A. K. : *Politics and Policies of International Relations,* Cyber Tech Pub, Delhi, 2009.

Dwight Waldo: *Study of Public Administration,* New York, Random House, 1955.

Eaton, M.: *Justice for Women,* Open University Press, Milton Keynes, 1986.

Enderlein and Maskow: *International Sales Law,* Oceana, Dobbs Ferry, NY, 1992.

Ezra, N.: *Bureaucrats and Policy Making*, New York, Holmes & Meier, 1984.

Francis, E.: *Bureaucratic Power in National Politics*, Boston, Little Brown and Company, 1978.

Friedrich, J.: *Constitutional Government and Democracy,* Boston, Ginn, 1950.

Gagarin, Michael: *Early Greek Law,* Univesity of California Press, Berkeley, 1989.

Gans, Herbert J. : *Democracy and the News*, Oxford University Press, New York, 2003.

Goldziher, Ignaz : *Introduction to Islamic Theology and Law*. Princeton, NJ: Princeton University Press, 1981.

Goswami, B : *Constitutional Safeguards for Scheduled Castes and Scheduled Tribes*, Rawat, Delhi, 2003.

Hans J. : *Politics Among Nations: The Struggle for Power and Peace,* New York, Knopf, 1960.

Harris, M.S.: *Cases and Materials on International Law*, Sweet & Maxwell, 1991.

Hoebel. E. Adamson: *The Law of Primitive Man*. New York: Atheneum, 1968.

Hoog and Steinmetz: *International Conventions on Protection of Humanity and the Environment* , W de Gruyter, Berlin/New York, 1993.

Johansen, Baber : *Contingency in a Sacred Law: Legal and Ethical Norms in the Muslim Fiqh*. Boston: Brill, 1999.

John, J.: *Handbook of Local Government Administration*, New York, Marcel Dekker, 1997.

Kumar, D.: *Administration Report of the Political Agency*, Agartala, Tripura State Cultural Research Institute & Museum, 1995.

Kunig, Lau, and Meng: *International Economic Law: Basic Documents*. Gruyter, Berlin/NewYork, 1993.

Lander, Bernard : *Towards an Understanding of Juvenile Delinquency*, New York, Columbia University Press, 1954.

Langbein, John H.: *Torture and the Law of Proof, Europe and England in the Ancien Regime*, Chicago, University of Chicago Press, 1977.

Lingat, R.: *The Classical Law of India*, Berkeley, University of California Press, 1973.

Makdisi, George : *The Rise of Colleges: Institutions of Learning in Islam and the West*. Edinburgh: Edinburgh University Press, 1981.

Mamdani, Mahmood: *Citizen and Subject: Contemporary Africa and the Legacy of Late Colonialism*. Princeton, NJ: Princeton University Press, 1996.

Merton, Robert K.: *On Social Structure and Science*, Robert K. Merton, Piotr Sztompka, Chicago, University of Chicago Press, 1996.

Mishra, J.: *Equality vs Justice. The Problem of Reservations for Backward Classes,* New Delhi, Deep & Deep, 1996.

Nygh, J.: *Conflict of Laws in Australia,* Butterworths, Sydney, 1991.

Oomen, Barbara: *Chiefs in South Africa: Law, Power and Culture in the Post-Apartheid Era.* New York: Palgrave, 2005.

Parry, Grant, and Watts: *Encyclopaedic Dictionary of International Law,* Oceana, New York, 1988.

Pouligny, Beatrice, Simon Chesterman, and Albrecht Schnabel: *After Mass Crime: Rebuilding States and Communities.* Tokyo: United Nations University Press, 2007.

Prahlad K.: *Governance and Public Administration for Poverty Reduction,* Salvador, Brazil, 1997.

Robert, W.: *Public Bureaucracy and the Incentive Problem,* Washington, D.C., World Bank, 1994.

Rosenne, K.: *Practice and Methods of International Law,* Oceana, Dobbs Ferry, NY, 1984.

Schudson, Michael : *Watergate in American Memory, How We Remember, Forget and Reconstruct the Past,* Basic Books, New York, 1992.

Schwarzenberger, A.: *International Law as Applied by International Courts and Tribunals,* Stevens, London, 1986.

Srivastava, R.C.: *Judicial System in India,* Lucknow, Print House (India), 1992.

Sugata, J.: *Nationalism, Democracy, and Development: State and Politics in India,* Delhi; New York: Oxford University Press, 1997.

Surya Dandekar: *Asian Government and Politics : Studies in People, Power and Political Development,* Kanishka, Delhi, 1998.

Tierney, Brian: *Church Law and Constitutional Thought in the Middle Ages,* Variorum Reprints, London, 1979.

Tobin and Green: *Guide to Human Rights Research,* Harvard Law School Human Rights Program, Cambridge, MA, 1994.

Turk, Austin: *Criminality and Legal Order,* Rand McNally, Chicago, 1969.

Weiss, Bernard : *The Search for God's Law: Islamic Jurisprudence in the Writings of Sayf al-Din al-Amidi.* Salt Lake City: University of Utah Press, 1992.

Whicker, L.: *Handbook of Research Methods in Public Administration,* New York, Marcel Dekker, 1999.

Zartmann, William I.: *Traditional Cures of Modern Conflicts: African Conflict Medicine."* Boulder, CO: Lynne Rienner, 2000.

Index

J

K

L

M

N

P

R

S

T

U

W